The Ethics of Theory

Also available from Bloomsbury

Philosophy of History After Hayden White, edited by Robert Doran
René Girard and Political Philosophy, Kent U. Enns
René Girard and Raymund Schwager: Correspondence 1974–1991, edited by Scott Cowdell, Chris Fleming, Joel Hodge, and Mathias Moosbrugger
Foucault and Nietzsche, edited by Joseph Westfall and Alan Rosenberg
Foucault's Ethics, Mark Olssen
Richard Rorty, Ronald A. Kuipers
Deconstruction without Derrida, Martin McQuillan
Literature and Moral Theory, Nora Hämäläinen
Crimes of the Future: Theory and its Global Reproduction, Jean-Michel Rabaté

The Ethics of Theory

Philosophy, History, Literature

ROBERT DORAN

Bloomsbury Academic
An imprint of Bloomsbury Publishing Plc

B L O O M S B U R Y
LONDON • OXFORD • NEW YORK • NEW DELHI • SYDNEY

Bloomsbury Academic
An imprint of Bloomsbury Publishing Plc

50 Bedford Square
London
WC1B 3DP
UK

1385 Broadway
New York
NY 10018
USA

www.bloomsbury.com

BLOOMSBURY and the Diana logo are trademarks of
Bloomsbury Publishing Plc

First published 2017

© Robert Doran, 2017

Robert Doran has asserted his right under the Copyright, Designs and
Patents Act, 1988, to be identified as Author of this work.

All rights reserved. No part of this publication may be reproduced or transmitted
in any form or by any means, electronic or mechanical, including photocopying,
recording, or any information storage or retrieval system, without prior permission
in writing from the publishers.

Chapter 6 is adapted from a previously essay entitled "Metahistory and the
Ethics of Historiography," *Storia della Storiografia* 65.1 (2014): 153–162.

No responsibility for loss caused to any individual or organization acting on
or refraining from action as a result of the material in this publication can be
accepted by Bloomsbury or the author.

British Library Cataloguing-in-Publication Data
A catalogue record for this book is available from the British Library.

ISBN: HB: 978-1-4742-2592-2
PB: 978-1-4742-2593-9
ePDF: 978-1-4742-2591-5
ePub: 978-1-4742-2594-6

Library of Congress Cataloging-in-Publication Data
Names: Doran, Robert, 1968- author.
Title: The ethics of theory : philosophy, history, and literature / by Robert Doran.
Description: New York : Bloomsbury, 2016. | Includes index.
Identifiers: LCCN 2016016468 (print) | LCCN 2016021536 (ebook) | ISBN
9781474225922 (hardback) | ISBN 9781474225939 (pbk.) | ISBN 9781474225915
(epdf) | ISBN 9781474225946 (epub)
Subjects: LCSH: Critical theory. | Ethics.
Classification: LCC B809.3 .D67 2016 (print) | LCC B809.3 (ebook) | DDC
170–dc23
LC record available at https://lccn.loc.gov/2016016468

Typeset by Deanta Global Publishing Services, Chennai, India

In memory of René Girard (1923–2015):
teacher, mentor, and friend

CONTENTS

Acknowledgments ix

Introduction 1

PART ONE Philosophy 17

1 Ethics beyond existentialism and structuralism: Sartre's *Critique of Dialectical Reason* and the debate with Lévi-Strauss 19
2 Foucault's "ethics of the self" 35
3 Derrida in Heidelberg: The specter of Heidegger's Nazism and the question of ethics 60
4 Richard Rorty's "cultural politics": Ironist philosophy and the ethics of reading 79

PART TWO History 97

5 From *Metahistory* to *The Practical Past*: Hayden White's existentialist philosophy of history 99
6 Hayden White and the ethics of historiography 114

PART THREE Literature 125

7 The ethics of conversion: Metaphysical desire in René Girard and Jean-Paul Sartre 127
8 The ethics of realism: Literary history and the sublime in Erich Auerbach's *Mimesis* 136

9 The ethics of philology: Erich Auerbach and the fate of humanism 149

10 Edward Said, *Orientalism*, and the "political turn" in literary and cultural studies 159

Notes 169
Index 221

ACKNOWLEDGMENTS

Chapters 2, 3, 4, 10, and the Introduction were newly written specifically for this volume and are not based on any previously published material or public lectures. The remaining six chapters are revisions or adaptations of previously published essays. Chapter 1 is a slightly revised version of an article that appeared in *Yale French Studies* 123 (2013): 41–62, under the title "Sartre's *Critique of Dialectical Reason* and the Debate with Lévi-Strauss." Chapter 5 has been adapted from my editor's introduction ("Choosing the Past: Hayden White and the Philosophy of History") to *Philosophy of History After Hayden White*, ed. Robert Doran (London: Bloomsbury, 2013), 1–33. Chapter 6 is a slightly revised version of an essay published under the title "*Metahistory* and the Ethics of Historiography," in *Storia della Storiografia* 65, no. 1 (2014): 153–62. (The article was first given as a talk at a conference entitled "40 Years of Metahistory: From the Historiographical Past to the Practical Past," held at the University of Espirito Santo in Vitoria, Brazil, October 8–11, 2013.) Chapter 7 is a completely reworked and rewritten version of an article published in *Journal of Religion and Literature* 43, no. 3 (2012): 36–45, under the title "René Girard's Concept of Conversion and the *Via Negativa*: Revisiting *Deceit, Desire, and the Novel* with Jean-Paul Sartre." (It was first presented at a conference entitled "*Deceit, Desire, and the Novel* 50 Years Later," held at Yale University on October 14, 2011.) Chapter 8 is a slightly revised version of an article published in *New Literary History* 38, no. 2 (2007): 353–69, under the title "Literary History and the Sublime in Erich Auerbach's *Mimesis*." Chapter 9 is a somewhat revised version of an essay published in the journal *Moderna* 11, no. 1/2 (2009): 99–108, entitled "Erich Auerbach's Humanism and the Criticism of the Future." (It was originally given as a talk at a conference entitled "Erich Auerbach and the Future of Criticism," held at the University of Illinois, Urbana-Champagne on April 19, 2008.) I would like to thank the organizers of all the abovementioned events for their generous invitations and hospitality.

My introduction to this volume was helped immeasurably by a conference I participated in at the University of California, Irvine, on May 22–23, 2015, titled "Is Theory Critical?" I would like to thank Georges Van Den Abbeele for his kind invitation to and organization of this very stimulating event.

I would also like to note that I was fortunate enough to have had the opportunity to study with and/or attend the seminars of many of the figures discussed in this book. This volume thus has an autobiographical flavor for me (and I have occasionally taken the liberty of quoting from some personal conversations, emails, and seminars in the notes, as well as from manuscript versions of texts when they differed from the printed version). Hayden White was my dissertation advisor and René Girard one of my dissertation readers at Stanford University. (I was also Girard's teaching assistant in 2003 for a course on "Literature and Modernity.") I took or audited four of Richard Rorty's seminars on philosophy at Stanford University in the late 1990s and early 2000s (including one, "Heidegger and Derrida," in winter 1999, for which I was his teaching assistant). I attended Jacques Derrida's seminars at the École des hautes études en sciences sociales in Paris in 1996–97 and 1999–2000. (I presented a paper, "L'esthétique de la peine de mort: Burke et Schiller," in the latter course in March 2000; it was later integrated into my book *The Theory of the Sublime from Longinus to Kant* [Cambridge: Cambridge University Press, 2015.])

Finally, I would like to thank those who provided critical comments and suggestions on various chapters: Razvan Amironesei, Alain Billault, Marcel Hénaff, Kalle Pihlainen, Samuel Weber, and especially Hayden White, who commented on most of the book. I am also grateful to my editor at Bloomsbury, Liza Thompson, and her assistant Frankie Mace, for their interest in this project and for their patience, diligence, and attention to detail.

Introduction

This book explores the ethical dimension and implications of what goes under the general category of Theory or Critical Theory, that is to say, the thought that emerged mostly in France in the 1960s and 1970s in the wake of phenomenology and existentialism, appearing in successive waves labeled *structuralism*, *La Nouvelle Critique*, *poststructuralism*, and *postmodernism*. These critical currents had a broad and lasting impact on the humanities (and, to a lesser extent, on the social sciences), in particular on literary studies, but also on philosophy, art history, visual studies, history, gender studies (feminist theory and queer theory), postcolonial studies, cultural studies, cultural anthropology, sociology, political theory, media studies, film studies, religious studies, ethnic studies, critical legal theory, critical race theory, musicology, and education. More specifically, this book endeavors to examine the seeming contradiction of how the same Theory that, in its formative phase, was denounced as amoral, nihilistic, and quietist, due to its "relativist," "textualist," and "anti-subjectivist" bent, could also be the source of the "political turn" in the humanities as well as a wellspring for liberal activists. Was it a matter of an illegitimate appropriation? Was Theory hijacked by well-meaning but naïve academics and do-gooders? Or was the development of an activist-political dimension of Theory simply the logical or inevitable consequence of this discourse itself?

It should be noted that, even if we are now in an era of globalization,[1] this paradoxical evolution and situation of Theory is largely a North American phenomenon, tied, on the one hand, to the peculiar arrangement of the American university system—namely the wide gulf that separated, and still separates to a large extent, literature departments from philosophy departments, and the humanities from the social sciences—and, on the other, to the increasingly diverse and multiethnic population of the United States. This said, I still believe that it is possible to address the question of the ethics of Theory without necessarily resorting to an empirical sociology (an approach pursued, most notably, by François Cusset in his well-researched monograph *French Theory: How Foucault, Derrida, Deleuze, & Co. Transformed the Intellectual Life of the United States*).[2]

This volume does not, however, strive for a comprehensive or even a systematic treatment of the question of the ethics of Theory—certainly a quixotic pursuit for a single volume; nor is its aim to provide a kind of history, a narrative account of how Theory was shaped by ethics, even if it does seek to *historicize* Theory.³ Rather this volume endeavors, in a series of discrete interventions, to bring out what is at stake in this problematic across a wide range of well-known theorists: in philosophy (Jean-Paul Sartre, Michel Foucault, Jacques Derrida, Richard Rorty), anthropology (Claude Lévi-Strauss), historiography/historical theory (Hayden White), literary studies (Erich Auerbach, René Girard), and postcolonial studies (Edward Said). The multidisciplinary and international nature of this group is intended to emphasize the interdisciplinary and international nature of Theory itself, the idea that Theory does not "belong" to or "reside" in any particular discipline or cultural context but rather exists in tension with disciplinary, linguistic, and geographical boundaries. I thus also seek to broaden the concept of Theory by including a progenitor who is often overlooked (Sartre), a critic not normally considered to be "theoretical" (Auerbach), as well as some thinkers who are in some ways antagonistic to Theory, while nevertheless contributing to its discourse (Girard, Said). The omission of certain theorists is not at all meant as a signal of a lack of importance or pertinence.⁴ As I note in the acknowledgments, the selection is in large part a function of my own interests, competencies, and training (since, as noted, I studied with or attended the seminars of four of the nine thinkers examined in this volume). Although my choices will no doubt be seen as eclectic, perhaps even arbitrary, I think that the reader will find that a coherence of common themes emerges in the course of the work, emphasized by cross-references between the chapters.

As a counterpoint to the unsystematic and protean character of this volume, I offer in this introduction a brief overview of the evolution and situation of Theory as it relates to ethics, which will hopefully provide a framework and context for the chapters that follow.

From Theory to ethics

Although it would be difficult to define Theory in a way satisfying to its practitioners or its detractors—and, of course, resisting precise definition is part and parcel of what it means to "theorize" in this tradition—it is probably safe to say that, while remaining resolutely interdisciplinary, Theory is largely rooted in the French philosophy that emerged in the 1960s, in particular that of Michel Foucault and Jacques Derrida, two figures who have reconfigured the intellectual landscape in ways that are still being felt, more than fifty years after their first groundbreaking contributions. These two figures played a decisive role in bringing the Continental tradition of thought into a broad dialogue with the humanities and the social sciences, making in particular the iconoclastic works of Friedrich Nietzsche and

Martin Heidegger relevant and productive in a way that would otherwise be difficult to imagine.

As philosophical insurgents, what Nietzsche and Heidegger endeavored to accomplish was the dethroning of *theoretical knowledge* as the dominant understanding of Western philosophy, claiming that the best philosophy or science could achieve is an *interpretation* of the world, which, *qua* interpretation, is necessarily perspectival, contingent, historical, and non-definitive. Thus, one of the most striking paradoxes of the use of the term "Theory" to denote the type of critical engagements cited above is that much of what goes under the name of "Theory" is actually *antitheoretical*. That is, the figures associated with Theory are adamant that they not be seen as offering a "theory of" something, in the sense of a transcendental, ahistorical, or universal account (e.g., a theory of the subject, of language, of signification, etc.). Theory's *raison d'être* is to contest theoretical knowledge, showing it to be derivative and lacking in authority—and hence as possessing an irreducible ethico-political significance underlying its supposedly neutral objectivity.

As tempting it might seem, it would, however, be a mistake to simply conflate Theory with Continental philosophy or with philosophy *tout court*.[5] For Theory also possesses an essential relation to literature and the literary, deriving inspiration from a variety of avant-garde authors such as Baudelaire, Mallarmé, Joyce, and Genet.[6] This "aestheticist" strain of contemporary Theory is certainly one of the principal reasons for its quick assimilation, in the United States, into departments of literature,[7] as well as for the aversion of the more logically and scientifically minded Anglo-American departments of philosophy. But it is also one of the sources of its reputation for ludic irresponsibility—as if ethics and aesthetics were necessarily opposed forces. The philosophical attention to literature also characterizes the current of "Critical Theory" associated with the Frankfurt school (Theodor Adorno, Max Horkheimer, Walter Benjamin), an early-twentieth-century German tradition we must be careful to distinguish from French-based Theory, even if Benjamin is very often treated as if he were a French poststructuralist thinker *avant la lettre* (many of his texts were, in fact, originally written in French).

The origins of Theory, in particular of its penchant for cultural critique, are often located in the writings of Marx and Freud. However, while Marxism and psychoanalysis have certainly made important contributions to Theory, these currents developed for the most part independently, following their own trajectory, having been institutionalized in ways that Theory has always resisted: in political parties such as the Parti Communiste Français or professional organizations such as the Paris Psychoanalytical Society and the International Psychoanalytical Association. In fact, one could argue that Theory actually represents a *liberation* from Marxism and Freudian psychoanalysis, two theoretical traditions that, by the 1940s and 1950s, had achieved in France a widespread, even hegemonic influence.[8] As

Foucault noted in an interview: "We should not forget that throughout the period from 1945 to 1955 in France, the entire French university . . . was very preoccupied with the task of building . . . the phenomenology-Marxist relation."[9] Foucault also spoke of what he called the "inhibiting effect" of "global, *totalitarian theories*" such as "Marxism and psychoanalysis."[10] Indeed, after the Soviet invasion and repression of Hungary in 1956, enthusiasm for communism began to wane among Parisian intellectuals. Even the last gasp in the effort to fuse phenomenology and Marxism, Sartre's *Critique de la raison dialectique* (*Critique of Dialectical Reason*, Vol. 1), published in 1960, was nevertheless written "against the communists."[11] In 1966, Foucault created a sensation with his pseudo-structuralist "archeology of the human sciences," *Les mots et les choses* (translated as *The Order of Things*), of which Sartre remarked, "Behind history, of course, it is Marxism which is attacked."[12] While Marxism still thrived in the 1960s at the elite École Normale Supérieure, under the influence of Louis Althusser and his progeny (Étienne Balibar, Alain Badiou, Jacques Rancière), French thinkers writing after 1968 either gave up the cause (Jean Baudrillard, Jean-François Lyotard) or generally avoided Marx, in particular the phenomenologists (Emmanuel Levinas, Derrida). Teaching at the École Normale in the mid-1960s, Derrida was "condemned to silence" on the subject of Marx by the "intellectual terrorism" of the Althusserians.[13] It is perhaps no accident that the political failure of the student protests and strikes in France in May 1968 mark at once the failure of political Marxism and the ascendancy of Theory,[14] as if the success of the second were somehow predicated on the demise of the first, as if Theory offered a more appropriate intellectual response to the social upheaval of the 1960s.[15] Nevertheless, this did not stop many from seeing in the intellectual retreat from Marxism a sign of social and political *disengagement*. Thus, while Derrida remarked intriguingly at a conference in October 1968 that "every philosophical colloquium necessarily has a political significance,"[16] he also admitted that he was never really a *soixante-huitard*: "I did not say no to '68,' I took part in the demonstrations, I organized the first assembly at the École Normale. Still, rightly or wrongly, my heart was not really 'on the barricades.'"[17]

The picture is more complicated for psychoanalysis, given the singular figure of Lacan, who almost singlehandedly brought psychoanalysis into dialogue with Theory by integrating it with structural linguistics and with a deep awareness of the philosophies of Sartre, Husserl, and Heidegger (Heidegger in fact visited Lacan at his home in 1955, when he came to France to deliver his "What is Philosophy?" lecture at Cerisy-la-Salle). Lacan has also been important for the interpretation of Hegel in such figures as Judith Butler.[18] However, I would argue that Lacanian psychoanalysis, like Marxism, forms a kind of subspecialty of its own; indeed, many of Lacan's works are notoriously difficult, even for those well versed in Theory. Most important, unlike other areas of Theory during its formative period (with the notable exception of Levinas), the question of ethics was dealt with in an explicit and elaborate manner by Lacan in his celebrated Seventh Seminar, "The Ethics of Psychoanalysis" (1959–60).[19]

I therefore exclude Marxism, an intrinsically ethico-political discourse, and psychoanalysis from my discussions of the ethics of Theory, even if figures such as the Marxist critics Fredric Jameson and Terry Eagleton and the Lacan scholar and theorist Jean-Michel Rabaté have obviously contributed a great deal to current debates on Theory.[20]

Much more important for twentieth-century French philosophy than either Marxism or psychoanalysis was German phenomenology, in particular the works of Husserl and Heidegger, which had their first great impact through Sartre, especially his philosophical masterpiece *Being and Nothingness: A Phenomenological Essay on Ontology* (1943),[21] and to a somewhat lesser degree through Maurice Merleau-Ponty, whose magnum opus *Phenomenology of Perception* was published in 1945.[22] Sartre was a towering figure for the generation educated in the postwar era.[23] Derrida recounts:

> I recognize my debt, the filiation, the huge influence, the huge presence of Sartre in my formative years. I have never striven to evade it. ...When I was in the philosophy class in *hypokhâgne* or *khâgne*, not only the thought of Sartre, but the figure of Sartre, the character Sartre who allied philosophical desire with literary desire, were for me what is vacuously called a model, a reference point.[24]

Indeed, the alliance between literature and philosophy would become an important rallying cry, not only for Derrida, but also, as mentioned above, for Theory in general. Even if Derrida and others (including, most notably, Foucault)[25] would later seek to distance themselves from Sartre, preferring a much different approach to philosophy—as Gary Gutting notes, "the early existentialism that had made Sartre famous was the perfect whipping boy for the attack on subjectivity"[26]—Sartre nevertheless exercised a constant, if often unacknowledged, influence, as several scholars have shown and as I endeavor to elucidate in several chapters of this book.[27]

While phenomenology and existentialism were formative for French philosophers of the 1960s, and while Marxism and psychoanalysis competed for philosophical allegiance, by far the most important intellectual force during this period was *structuralism*, a movement that originated in linguistics,[28] gaining prominence in the 1950s in the "structural anthropology" of Claude Lévi-Strauss.[29] Based on Ferdinand de Saussure's structural linguistics—Saussure advances the idea of language as a *differential system of signs*, privileging synchronic (*langue*) over diachronic (*parole*) elements and *semiology* over historical approaches to language (etymology, philology)—this theoretical model proved to be an especially powerful analytical tool, one that had the advantage of eliminating the subject as the nodal point of analysis in favor of structure and system. Unlike Marxism or even psychoanalysis, however, there was no clear moral content to structuralism; it appeared as a neutral, quasi-scientific, detached, even dry method of analysis (which, while it might be able to find a structure in ethical discourse and practices, was not itself ethically inclined.) Structuralism thus offered a stark contrast not only to the transcendental ego of phenomenology (Husserl), but also to the existentialist individual who strives for "authenticity" (Heidegger, Sartre).[30] Nevertheless, there were important continuities with Heidegger's effort, in *Being and Time*, to distinguish an "ontological" (structural) from an "ontic" (factical) level of analysis (*Existentiale* vs. *Existentiell*), thereby dissolving the subject-object epistemology that had dominated much of modern philosophy (Descartes, Kant, Husserl). In addition to anthropology, structuralism also became an important force in literary theory (via Roland Barthes, Gérard Genette, Tzvetan Todorov, and Jonathan Culler), helping to dislodge the dominant paradigm of literary history (often focused on authorial biography) in France. Indeed, one could, as Culler does, locate the birth of Theory in the impulses that came out of structural linguistics: "*Theory* [originally] meant a particular body of structuralist theory that would elucidate diverse sorts of material and be the key to understanding language, popular culture, societies with and without writing, and structures of the human psyche."[31] While Culler is right to stress the interdisciplinary and protean nature of structuralism as foundational to Theory, it is also the case that Theory comes into its own only at the moment when it attempts to *transcend* structuralism, all while co-opting its language and categories.[32]

This is most strikingly apparent when one considers the event that commentators regularly cite as the birth of Theory: the famous conference held at Johns Hopkins University on October 18–21, 1966, titled "The Languages of Criticism and the Sciences of Man: The Structuralist Controversy" (later published in book form).[33] This conference marked both the highpoint of structuralism and the beginning of what would soon be called "poststructuralism" and "deconstruction."[34] Organized by three literature professors, Eugene Donato, Richard Macksey, and René Girard, this conference brought together several figures who would soon be seen as avatars of Theory, namely Derrida, Barthes, Lacan, and Todorov.[35] But it was the unknown Jacques Derrida who caused the most stir with his critique of structuralism in his now classic essay "Structure, Sign, and Play in the Discourse of the Human Sciences."[36] In its climatic peroration, Derrida takes the reigning master of structuralism, Lévi-Strauss, to task for "a sort of ethic of presence, an ethic of nostalgia for origins, an ethic of archaic and natural innocence, of a purity of presence and self-presence in speech"[37]—themes that would soon reverberate throughout American academic writing as the major preoccupations of Derridian thought.[38] Interestingly, this defining moment of Theory—and of Derrida's emergence as a major thinker—involves an invocation of "ethics," as if ethics were somehow at the "center" of what Theory was about, even if no one yet suspected it.[39]

Thus, Theory in fact grows out of the *confrontation* between philosophy and structuralism, a confrontation already prefigured in Sartre's *Critique of Dialectical Reason* (as I show in Chapter 1). It was indeed the "structuralist *controversy*" that launched a thousand theoretical ships. A Johns Hopkins student who attended the 1966 conference and who later became an academic recalled that "we were just discovering what structuralism was, and he [Derrida] came and started to call into question what we were starting to learn."[40] Indeed, as the popularity of "French Theory" grew in the United States, the first contact with structuralism most often came via its "poststructuralist" critique. Derrida later reminisced that "what is now called 'theory' in this country [the United States] may even have an essential link with what is said to have happened there in 1966," even if it "only came to light afterwards."[41] That is, the event was not programmatic but rather took on the meaning of a beginning retrospectively.

Prima facie, it might seem highly improbable or even odd that a philosopher who throughout much of the 1960s was known principally for his abstruse and highly technical readings of Husserl (an obscure figure to American literature professors, who barely knew his name, much less read his work) could become the de facto leader of a critical movement that would soon sweep literature departments like wildfire. In fact, Derrida's first book to appear in English, *Speech and Phenomena, and Other Essays on Husserl's Theory of Signs* (it was originally published in 1967, the same year as the French edition *Of Grammatology*, and translated into English in 1973),[42] was greeted with virtual silence by US academics. Theory, it is safe to say, would never have taken off had it simply been about innovative interpretations of German phenomenology. It was rather Derrida's engagement with structuralism, particularly in *Of Grammatology* (English translation, 1976)—still his best-known work—that allowed him to reach a broad audience in the United States. Prepared by Jonathan Culler's seminal *Structuralist Poetics* (1975), Derrida's treatment of structuralist semiology, his rhetoric of "the text," and his dazzling (and playful) writing style brought philosophy into dialogue with literary criticism, creating the conditions under which Theory could capture the imagination of literature professors who were more than ready to fill the void left by the indifference of American philosophy departments to Continental thought. Derrida appeared to demonstrate how philosophy could be practiced as kind of literary theory, thereby subordinating the former to the latter, and, as Jürgen Habermas lamented, "upgrading" literary criticism to the level of "the critique of metaphysics."[43] Ignoring arcane philosophical debates like those around Heidegger's *Dasein* and Husserl's "phenomenology of internal time consciousness,"[44] literary critics seized on what was for them the more relevant and comprehensible topics of meaning and interpretation. Thus Culler, in his influential *On Deconstruction: Theory and Criticism after Structuralism* (1982), the self-described "sequel" to *Structuralist Poetics*, proclaims categorically: "I will not attempt to discuss the relation of Derridian deconstruction to the work of Hegel, Nietzsche, Husserl, and Heidegger."[45] One could thus speak of a "literary-critical" version of Derrida,[46] informed mostly by structuralist semiology (Cusset speaks of a "lack of philosophical culture" in the American reception of Derrida),[47] as opposed to the more properly philosophical understanding that one finds, for example, in Rodolphe Gasché's *The Tain of the Mirror: Derrida and the Philosophy of Reflection* (1986), or, more recently, in Leonard Lawlor's *Derrida and Husserl: The Basic Problem of Phenomenology* (2002).[48] In the first instance, Derrida was read alongside the later Roland Barthes and the European transplant Paul de Man as pursuing a common "poststructuralist" project, one that saw meaning as inherently problematic, unstable, and equivocal. What would be called "deconstruction" was also generally seen as "formalist," as a radicalized version of New Criticism that proclaimed that one could dispense with anything "outside of the text," according to the widely circulated mistranslation of Derrida's dictum *il n'y a pas de hors-texte* (the text has no outside, or nothing controls meaning from the outside).[49]

Let us return to the French context for a moment, lest we get ahead of ourselves. When what we are calling Theory emerged in the 1960s in the first writings of Foucault and Derrida—namely in Foucault's *Madness and Civilization* and *The Order of Things* and in Derrida's *Of Grammatology* and his essay collections *Dissemination* and *Writing and Difference*—May 1968 had not yet happened,[50] even if there existed a certain cultural energy around the liberalization of many aspects of society (in particular, sexual liberation). Philosophically speaking, the important events in the run-up to May 1968 were the founding of the avant-garde journal *Tel Quel* in 1960 (in fact, the publication dates of this periodical, 1960–82, correspond fairly exactly to the formative era of Theory), which became a crucial forum for structuralist and poststructuralist thought, and the publication, in 1962, of Gilles Deleuze's *Nietzsche et la philosophie*, a turning point in the French reception of the late-nineteenth-century thinker, who had not received much serious academic consideration prior to that time. The interest generated by Deleuze's book resulted in two legendary conferences on Nietzsche: in 1964 at Royaumont (featuring Deleuze, Foucault, Gabriel Marcel, Jean Wahl, Gianni Vattimo, Jean Beaufret, and Karl Löwith)[51]; and in 1972 at Cerisy-la-Salle (which included Deleuze, Derrida, Jean-François Lyotard, Pierre Klossowski, Jean-Luc Nancy, and Philippe Lacoue-Labarthe). The impact on French philosophy was enormous. In his *Nietzsche's French Legacy: A Genealogy of Poststructuralism*, Alan Shrift notes that "Nietzsche's emergence as a philosophical voice played an unparalleled role in the development of poststructuralism as a historical corrective to the excesses of both its predecessor movements [existentialism and structuralism]."[52] However, it is probably fairer to say that it was Nietzsche *together with* Heidegger who paved the way for a philosophical renewal in the face of structuralism. For it was in large part Heidegger's four-volume *Nietzsche* (based on a series of lectures given from 1936 to 1940) that brought the former professor of classical philology at the University of Basel to philosophical prominence.⁵³ In a late interview, Foucault remarks that "I had tried to read Nietzsche in the 1950s, but Nietzsche by himself didn't hold much interest for me [*Nietzsche tout seul ne me disait rien*]! But Nietzsche and Heidegger, that was a philosophical shock!"⁵⁴

The anti-subjectivist bent of Theory inherited from Heidegger and structuralism, with the concomitant privileging of a nonempirical (transcendental) *structure*—Derrida's *différance*, Foucault's *power*—made it increasingly difficult to locate the ethical self: the site of responsibility, decision, freedom, and the will. Indeed, during the formative years of Theory, the self/subject is seen (following Nietzsche) rather as a *fiction* or *fable*: an *effect* of the play of language (Derrida), the *result* of acculturation and institutional control (Foucault). Although resolutely antiauthoritarian and anti-naturalist, Theory nevertheless flirted with a form of determinism: that in which the self, overwhelmed by extrinsic forces, is seemingly drained of its spontaneity, of its potential for effective action and creative originality (or, in another context, of the possibility of a revolutionary politics—this is essentially Sartre's critique of structuralism in his *Critique of Dialectical Reason*, as I show in Chapter 1). Under the influence of Nietzsche and Levinas, respectively, the later work of Foucault and Derrida will seek to restore a sense of balance by creating some space for individual agency (as in Foucault's turn in the 1980s toward the "ethics of the self," the subject of Chapter 2, and in Derrida's increasing use of the language of alterity and responsibility after 1987, discussed in Chapter 3). Richard Rorty and Hayden White go a step further, exalting a Nietzschean and quasi-existentialist concept of self-creation (in Rorty's concepts of "irony" and "literary culture" and in White's notions of "choosing the past" and "the practical past"; see Chapters 4 and 5).

This move was somewhat foreshowed in the poststructuralist privilege granted to the reader-interpreter over the author-creator, as in such canonical texts as Roland Barthes's "The Death of the Author" (1967), Foucault's "What is an Author?" (1969), and Derrida's "Signature, Event, Context" (1972). It became an article of faith that the author-subject had no "authority" over his or her text, no capacity to decide or fix its meaning; for the meaning of the text, the infinite range of possible interpretations, always exceeds the author's intentional grasp or horizon (though this did not thereby imply that there were no qualitative differences between interpretations, as many critics of poststructuralism charged). The "freedom" of interpretation—and, by extension, of the interpreter, himself or herself—is thus prized over the "dead" author/letter and seeming "fixity" of his or her text. "Literal interpretation" thus became an oxymoron; to interpret is ipso facto to assert a plurality of possible meanings. Of course, this antiauthoritarianism is necessarily *relational*, since any assertion of interpretive freedom is unidirectional; that is, it will be immediately usurped in turn by *being interpreted* (reminiscent of Sartre's conflictual doctrine of "the look"—each freedom curtails all the other freedoms precisely by defining/interpreting them). To more conservative critics, however, this interpretive Bacchanal reeked of anarchy and chaos.

The assault on the subject and on the figure of the author in particular will in fact be one of the main points of contention when Theory is appropriated by the "political turn." Edward Said, for example, asserts that "unlike Michel Foucault, to whose work I am greatly indebted, I do believe in the determining imprint of *individual writers* upon the otherwise anonymous collective body of texts constituting a discursive formation like Orientalism."[55] Postcolonial theory, feminism, queer theory, identity politics, and other ethico-political discourses thus take what is in effect a more *conservative* position, seeing the figure of the author as a crucial aspect of their critical practice, insofar as the author is a privileged locus of power, ethnic identity, gender/sexual identity, and ethical responsibility.[56] Hence the difficulty, after the "political turn," of speaking *for the other*: queer theorists are generally homosexual, feminist theorists are generally women, and so on. While a male author could obviously engage in feminist criticism, he would have difficulty in achieving any recognized *authority* in such a discourse, due to his inability to speak *as a woman*, to adopt her subject-position, even if male philosophers such as Sartre and Derrida have, of course, inspired and influenced feminism tremendously (in the work of Simone de Beauvoir and Gayatri Spivak, respectively).

Theory and the ethico-political turn

As noted above, Nietzsche was a major new influence in the French philosophy of the 1960s, and this is no less true in the realm of ethics. Nietzsche's extreme antipathy toward moral prescriptivism, normativity, reason-based ethics (Kant), and above all, Christian morality (which Nietzsche castigated as "slave morality"), coupled with his exaltation of the "transvaluation of all values," were widely shared and seemed to cohere with the 1960s as an era of sexual permissiveness, self-fulfillment, and live-and-let-live abandon.[57] At the other extreme was the ethical philosophy of the Jewish thinker Emmanuel Levinas,[58] whose critique of phenomenology and of Heidegger, in particular in his magnum opus *Totality and Infinity* (1961), was especially noteworthy for its elevation of ethics to first philosophy: our infinite responsibility to the Other as the primordial condition for any philosophizing. The antipodes of Levinas and Nietzsche, the mutual exclusivity of ethics and aesthetics, of responsibility to the Other and self-creation, polarized the discussion of ethics in French philosophy to a great extent. Thus, while Derrida devotes a substantial and well-known essay to Levinas in 1964, "Violence and Metaphysics," he is quite critical, taking issue with Levinas's reading of Heidegger in *Totality and Infinity* and noting that Levinas's "ethics" is not an ethics per se but rather an "ethics of ethics."[59]

Derrida would not devote another essay to Levinas until 1980.[60] Even if, as many commentators allege, Derrida ultimately becomes more "Levinasian" in his later work, this evolution takes place only after the "political turn" (see Chapter 3). As for Foucault, it is well known that Nietzsche's *On the Genealogy of Morals* provides the model for *Discipline and Punish* (1975), both in terms of methodology (genealogy) and thought (will to power),[61] and it is only in his last years that he treats ethics in an explicit and positive way.

The political and ethical situation of Theory would dramatically change in 1987, following the sensational publication in France of Victor Farias's *Heidegger et le nazisme*, which claimed that Heidegger's association with National Socialism in the 1930s was much more profound than previously reported,[62] and the discovery of Paul de Man's early writings for a Belgian journal, a few of which express anti-Semitic views. Although the Heidegger controversy was largely French and the de Man controversy largely American, both fed off each other to some degree, prompting a reconsideration of the ethical and political situation of Theory. In France, philosophers seen as devotees of Heidegger were taken to task for their seemingly obliviousness to Heidegger's ethical failings and political leanings, prompting a storm of publications in response (by Lyotard, Pierre Bourdieu, et al.).[63] The controversy also inspired the 1988 Heidelberg encounter between Gadamer and Derrida, the proceedings of which were published (in French) only in 2014 (this publication forms the basis of my discussion of Derrida and ethics in Chapter 3).[64]

It is thus no accident that 1987 marks a turning point in the ethical-political understanding of Theory. (As I note in Chapter 3, the number of publications devoted to the idea of ethics or politics in Derrida, to cite a prominent example, starts to spike immediately after 1987.) Just a year later, Gayatri Spivak—who had studied under Paul de Man at Cornell University and who had introduced Derrida's thought to an American audience in her translation of and formidable commentary on *Of Grammatology*—publishes a seminal essay, "Can the Subaltern Speak" (1988),[65] effectively inaugurating the "political turn" in Theory.[66] With this essay, Spivak helps define a new field, "postcolonial studies," thereby bringing Edward Said—retroactively considered the progenitor of this field on the basis of his 1978 *Orientalism*—into the mainstream of Theory. After seeing his political critique of Theory languish for almost a decade, Said attracts renewed interest: A new edition of *Orientalism* with an afterword was published in 1995, followed by a twenty-fifth anniversary edition in 2003; panels and publications on "postcolonialism" and "Orientalism" proliferate; politics is suddenly everywhere in literary studies.

In some general sense, of course, Theory had always been "political." It was associated with the transformation of literary studies in the United States from a very conservative discipline (in every sense of the term *conservative*) to one that was increasingly avant-garde and aligned with the political left, even if, apart from the Marxist critics, there was initially little or no overt political posturing in the scholarship itself. From the right, Theory was derided first for its supposed nihilism and relativism, for declaring the death of the author-subject, for its seeming ahistoricism and obliviousness to reality, and then, after the "political turn," for precisely the opposite reason: for being *too* engaged, for exalting identity, for destroying scholarship by turning it into simple activism. From the left, on the other hand, Theory was attacked from within, as it were, by critics, such as Said, who delivered sharp broadsides against Theory's lack of political consciousness.[67] In his 1982 collection *The World, the Text, and the Critic*, for example, Said decried "a philosophy of pure textuality and critical noninterference,"[68] even though his own theoretical model was based on Foucault's analysis of discourse and power.

On the left, we can discern two basic processes: (1) activists who had not previously evinced an interest in French philosophy suddenly realized the power of Theory for their purposes, even if it entailed a reevaluation of their own shibboleths (such as essentialism)[69]; (2) Theory undergoes an internal transformation: Those who had closely followed the work of Foucault and Derrida felt the pull of their activist brethren, transitioning into a more politically driven stance. It should be recalled that both Said and Spivak began their careers by engaging in rather traditional literary scholarship—Said's first book was *Joseph Conrad and the Fiction of Autobiography* (1966) and Spivak's was *Myself, I Must Remake: The Life and Poetry of W.B. Yeats* (1974)—before embracing an activist-scholar role. Many followed a similar path. Not everyone on the left made this transition, however.[70] Some cleaved to a de Man-like textualist model.[71] But it was clear that the general tide had shifted (one need only compare the titles of Modern Language Association [MLA] panels in the deconstruction-dominated 1980s with those of the postcolonial 1990s).

The transformation of Theory into an ethico-political discourse was so sudden, successful, and complete that it now appears to many as if Theory had *always* been conceived or understood as a socially committed or activist discourse. Even as astute an observer as the late philosopher Arthur Danto could write, in his final book (2013), that "deconstruction, after all, is taken to be a method for demonstrating the way in which society has advanced and reinforced interests of special groups—white, for example, and male; and along a different coordinate, western or North American."[72] (Although originally associated with Derrida's thought, "deconstruction" is here used as a metonym for Theory in general.) Notwithstanding Danto's conflation of two divergent moments of Theory—literary-textualist-formalist and social-political-activist—he (perhaps unwittingly) reveals the seamlessness with which the new political orientation was assimilated by Theory (or the other way around, depending on one's perspective).

As a symbol of this new fusion, consider Judith Butler's 1990 blockbuster *Gender Trouble: Feminism and the Subversion of Identity*, which sold more than 100,000 copies—unheard of for an academic monograph.[73] In her book, Butler weaves together Continental philosophy (she was trained as a philosopher at Yale, with a dissertation on Hegel), recent French thought (Lacan, Foucault, Kristeva), feminist theory, queer theory, and an activist appeal that made it a must-read both inside and outside academia (although many of the old-guard feminists derided her work as overly abstruse).[74] As a lesbian, Butler embodies existentially the perspective she pursues in her academic work. This becomes a recurrent pattern after the political turn: Spivak speaks about feminist and postcolonial issues as they relate to her native India; Said writes about the image of the Arab world and the Israeli-Palestinian conflict (in *The Question of Palestine*, for example) from the perspective of one who was born in Jerusalem to Palestinian parents and raised in Egypt; and so on. Personal experience and group identity become an index of theoretical authenticity. The death of the author gives way to a new kind of "authority." The fact that Derrida was a Jew born in (French) Algeria and the fact that Foucault was a homosexual, facts that were considered philosophically irrelevant in the 1960s and 1970s, suddenly become salient after the political turn.[75]

The politicization of literary studies did not, of course, occur without controversy. Many lamented its effect on the MLA, including the increasing polarization over certain issues (e.g., the vitriolic standoff between academics sympathetic to Israel and those sympathetic to the Palestinian cause).[76] In her presidential address to the MLA convention in 2006, entitled "It Must Change," Marjorie Perloff wondered if the field of literary studies was in danger of losing its specificity and thus its value within the academy:

> Is our expertise, then, in literary theory? For a brief moment in the sixties and seventies, this seemed to be the case: "everyone" had to know Marx and Freud, Benjamin and Adorno, Foucault and Derrida, Lacan and Kristeva. But increasingly this Eurocentric theory has come to seem less than adequate for dealing with the growing body of minority, transnational, and postcolonial literature, and so poststructuralist theory is being replaced by critical race studies and related models, but so eclectic have the categories become that in most colleges and universities there is now no theory requirement at all.[77]

In other words, Eurocentric (more precisely, Euro-American) literary theory increasingly becomes synonymous with politically oriented approaches and ceases to be an autonomous discourse. To counter the "political turn," Perloff thus appeals to a kind of *literary desire*, a reclaiming of a specifically literary space, which she feels has been abandoned: "I have heard graduate students discussing the vagaries of Romantic self-consciousness in Shelley's 'Ode to the West Wind' who cannot tell you what an ode is, what apostrophe is, or why (much less how) this one is written in *terza rima*."[78] While this might be interpreted as a call for "purity," in effect Perloff is asking: Why do we need literary studies if the same critical work can be done in other departments and programs? In other words, if "content" is all that interests us, what is to distinguish literary criticism from history, sociology, anthropology, women's studies, ethnic studies, and so on? Thus: "It is time to trust the literary instinct that brought us to this field in the first place and to recognize that, rather than lusting after those other disciplines that seem so exotic primarily because we don't really practice them, what we need is more theoretical, historical, and critical training in our own discipline."[79]

Of course, one might construe Perloff's "conservative" lament as part of a more general backlash against "the academic left," a desire to return to bourgeois aestheticism, to an era when the Romantic lyric was the paradigm of "literature"[80] and when New Criticism taught us to ignore everything outside the text.[81] However, while views such as Perloff's might appear to make common cause with reactionary academics who shun the MLA for ideological reasons, it also coheres with attempts by first-wave Theory warriors to nudge literary studies back toward the "literary." Hence Jonathan Culler's 2007 book *The Literary in Theory*, which advocates for a revival of the "theory of literature" (recalling the eponymous work by René Wellek and Austin Warren that became a classic of New Criticism), namely poetics and literary semiotics, approaches that attend to the literary text in its specificity. Practicing what he preaches, Culler publishes, in 2015, *Theory of the Lyric*.[82] Although ostensibly an exercise in genre criticism, this magisterial effort nevertheless features a chapter on "Lyric and Society" and numerous references to politics and social critique.

The debate over Theory is still with us. In some sense, little has changed, with some commentators advocating a return to good old-fashioned literary study, construed as a kind of literary "natural attitude."[83] Thus, Kathryn Lynch, an English professor at Wellesley College, writes in a recent op-ed article published in the *Washington Post* ("Cutting the Liberal Arts Undermines Our Cultural Traditions," June 6, 2015):

> It is commonplace to think of the modern academy (or the liberal arts) as "liberal." But most teachers and scholars working in the humanities are not driven by a "liberal" agenda, leveraging the tools of post-structuralists to undermine truth claims, as some mockers like to imply. . . . For every literature professor who is pressing forward to put a literary tradition into the service of an identity claim, there are 10 who are patiently bearing witness to the great works of history and tenaciously grading their students' freshman papers on Dante, Shakespeare or Wordsworth.

This passage is symptomatic of a certain attitude that forty years of Theory have yet to change and have perhaps even reinforced: that there is a "common sense" way of studying literature that contains no theoretical presuppositions.[84] On the other hand, even a theorist as staunchly political as Said would agree—and agree wholeheartedly—that we should continue to read "the classics," as he himself did. Indeed, the literary canon has not been so much displaced as it has been expanded and enriched by the inclusion of works that present a more varied set of ideas and perspectives. It is thus not clear if Lynch is advocating the purging of literary studies, the elimination of any work susceptible of advancing an "identity claim," or (as I suspect) if her complaint involves rather the *use* of the canonical authors for nonliterary ends—in which case her view might be aligned with that of Perloff, even if Perloff would never agree with the idea of a "bearing witness to the great works," as if idolatrous appreciation were the only legitimate mode of literary criticism.

It bears remembering that Lynch is a professor at a liberal arts college, not a research university—a crucial distinction. This is not to say that professors in such four-year colleges are naïve in comparison to their research university brethren; simply, it is that they are subject to very different expectations, particularly in regard to tenure. It cannot be denied that much of the enthusiasm for Theory, for both the textualist and the political currents, was due in no small part to the "publish or perish" fervor that gripped the American academy starting in the 1980s, when tenure requirements were tightened and when even many non-research institutions expected a robust research agenda (including a number of elite liberal arts colleges, which had previously been guided by the student-oriented mantra "cherish or perish"—many college professors from the earlier generation could receive tenure at these institutions without publishing at all). The pressure to publish something that could be considered original and "cutting edge"—an idea modeled on the sciences—led academics in the humanities to embrace Theory as the most expeditious way of fulfilling this requirement. Theory provided two major benefits to beleaguered humanists: (1) it offered a coherent *critical perspective* that was ipso facto "cutting edge" and "original," thus effortlessly solving the problem of how to say something new about even the most written-about authors—one need not worry about the originality of a queer theory approach to a Shakespeare play, since no one had ever looked at Shakespeare in such a manner before the advent of queer theory (and this applies to deconstruction, feminist interpretations, etc.); (2) it offered a quick (although not easy) way of creating a research program that involved little actual "research" in the traditional sense, like toiling in the library or the archive, consulting early editions, reading all the secondary material (since this material was largely irrelevant if it did not conform to the theoretical perspective adopted), and so on; one need only be an expert in Derrida, Lacan, or Butler, to generate, respectively, deconstructive, psychoanalytic, or queer-feminist readings of a chosen text (although attaining competence in Theory was often a challenge for literary scholars unfamiliar with philosophy—hence the hostility of an older generation of literary critics ill-equipped to understand the newfangled approaches).[85]

This said, it should nevertheless be recognized that, since the Renaissance, literary studies has always been torn between a philosophical culture (for a long time dominated by Plato and Aristotle) and the historical impulse (classicism, scholarship, philology). Just as Renaissance critics framed their approaches by appealing to the theory of *enthousiasmos* (divine inspiration) attributed to Plato (the *furor poeticus*) and to Aristotle's *Poetics* (the *ars poetica*), twentieth- and twenty-first-century critics invoke Foucault and Derrida.[86] Conversely, it is difficult to deny the implicit role that context plays, even in the most formalist or theoretical of literary approaches, especially when, as a professional practice, the field of literary studies is defined by divisions into *historical periods* (Renaissance, nineteenth century, etc.) rather than by problems or genres (as in philosophy: philosophy of mind, philosophy of language, etc.).[87] It is also the case that literature and philosophy have always been mutually enriching, as evidenced by the literary philosophers (Plato, Rousseau, Kierkegaard, Nietzsche, Sartre) and the philosophical poets, essayists, and novelists (Montaigne, Voltaire, Schiller, Hölderlin, Emerson, Proust, Mann, Camus).[88]

As a corollary to this, the fraught relation between history and theory—a major preoccupation of the present volume—also needs to be rethought. As Hayden White has shown, the idea of history as an objective or commonsensical ground, putatively "free of the kind of epistemological and methodological disputes"[89] that affect other areas of inquiry, is deeply misguided. In his seminal *Metahistory: The Historical Imagination in Nineteenth-Century Europe*, White argues against the view of history as an ideologically neutral, quasi-scientific endeavor. For White, there is no essential difference between "proper" history and philosophy of history, for any historical account presupposes a concept of history-in-general and as such involves ethical *choices* that condition the treatment of the historical particulars (see Chapters 5 and 6). The other thinker to have brought history to the fore of theoretical debates is, of course, Foucault, whose "archeological" and "genealogical" approaches defined a new way of philosophizing. Although Foucault does not theorize history per se, he is highly conscious of its ability to introduce contingency: to strip discourses and institutions of their appearance of necessity or naturalness. Thus, to the extent that Foucault uses history as a privileged means of highlighting the plight of the socially marginal and the dangers that institutions pose to modern societies, his is an *ethical* historiography. History is also an ethical force in Sartre's *Critique of Dialectical Reason* (as shown the debate between Sartre and Lévi-Strauss, which I analyze in Chapter 1), in Auerbach's Literary History (as I show in Chapter 8), and in Said's Postcolonial Theory (Chapter 10).

* * *

In sum, this book deals with the question of ethics at the intersection of philosophy, history, and literature. Despite the Theory-is-dead mantra, "theory," as Culler notes, "is everywhere"[90]; it has become synonymous with the ethical and political questions that agitate our times. The essays in this volume endeavor to understand how this happened.

PART ONE
Philosophy

CHAPTER ONE

Ethics beyond existentialism and structuralism

Sartre's *Critique of Dialectical Reason* and the debate with Lévi-Strauss

It is almost an article of faith that the existentialism of Jean-Paul Sartre and the structuralism of Claude Lévi-Strauss are antipodes and that the displacement of the former by the latter represented the triumph of unconscious structures over a philosophy of consciousness and freedom. And yet, in works published at the beginning of the 1960s, there was an attempt on the part of both thinkers to synthesize aspects of their respective systems. In 1960, Sartre published his massive *Critique of Dialectical Reason* (*Critique de la raison dialectique*), which extends his existential phenomenology into the domains of social ontology and the philosophy of history. But Sartre also situates his work in the context of the contemporary debate over structuralism: "It could be said that the aim of the critical investigation is to establish a structural and historical anthropology."[1] This claim, coupled with Sartre's substantial discussion of Lévi-Strauss's *The Elementary Structures of Kinship* (*Les structures élémentaires de la parenté*, 1949) in the *Critique*, inspired Lévi-Strauss to devote the final chapter of *The Savage Mind* (*La pensée sauvage*, 1962), titled "History and Dialectic," to an examination of Sartre's tome. Although Lévi-Strauss therein expresses his "disagreement with Sartre regarding the points which bear on the philosophical fundaments of anthropology,"[2] he also considers *The Savage Mind* (and not merely the final chapter) as a kind of tribute to Sartre, "an homage of admiration and respect,"[3] as he writes in his preface to this work.

Sartre's engagement with Lévi-Strauss and structuralism in his *Critique* can certainly be seen as opportunistic. Elected to the Collège de France in 1959, Lévi-Strauss was on the verge of becoming an international sensation, much like Sartre himself had been a little more than a decade earlier. The publication of Lévi-Strauss's *The Elementary Structures of Kinship* in 1949 had generated a great deal of attention; it was reviewed favorably by Simone de Beauvoir, and was considered by many to be a seminal work.[4] The essays written in the 1940s and 1950s and collected in *Structural Anthropology* (1958) had laid out a bold intellectual agenda that was quickly growing into a movement. It was, however, the highly literary travelogue *Tristes tropiques* (1955, English translation 1961) that made Lévi-Strauss famous outside his discipline, in some sense replicating Sartre's success in generating popular interest in his thought through his early novel *Nausea* (*La nauseé*, 1938) and his plays *The Flies* (*Les mouches*, 1943) and *No Exit* (*Huis clos*, 1944). Thus Sartre, in his most important philosophical work since *Being and Nothingness* (*L'être et le néant*, 1943), no doubt wished to demonstrate the pertinence of his philosophy by co-opting an ascendant current of French thought. It should also be noted that, although Sartre's intellectual career had climaxed in France in the late 1930s and 1940s, while Lévi-Strauss was living abroad, Lévi-Strauss was only three years younger than Sartre, and thus Sartre could still view him (like Emmanuel Levinas) as a contemporary—in contrast to the general indifference that would later characterize Sartre's attitude toward the next generation of philosophers, such as Michel Foucault and Jacques Derrida.

For his part, Lévi-Strauss immediately recognized the importance of Sartre's *Critique*, assigning it in his seminar at the École pratique des hautes études during the 1960–61 academic year and recommending it to colleagues. As a Sartre biographer recounts:

> In the spring of 1960, Claude Lévi-Strauss asks Jean Pouillon to talk about [the *Critique of Dialectical Reason*] in his [Pouillon's] seminar at the École Pratique des Hautes Etudes. This happened three months after its publication. Pouillon remembers, "at first I refused, thinking that nobody as yet had the time to read the entire text. But then I changed my mind and proposed to divide my reading of the *Critique* into three two-hour seminars. Generally, my courses in anthropology drew about thirty people . . . but this one drew a real crowd. I recognized a few faces, such as, for instance Lucien Goldmann's."[5]

Although it is little read or studied today,[6] Sartre's *Critique*, as this passage suggests, made a rather large splash among the Parisian intelligentsia at the time of its publication, particularly among those interested in structuralism. The neglect of Sartre's *Critique* is unfortunate, and it has more to do with the ascent of Lévi-Strauss, but also of Foucault, than with the *Critique* itself (i.e., the *Critique* would have no doubt been more successful if it had been published in 1950 as opposed to 1960.)

In this chapter, I propose to examine debate that broke out in the early 1960s between Sartre and Lévi-Strauss over the question of history and of how it relates to anthropology and philosophy. What is especially revealing in this debate is how both thinkers see the question of history as a specifically *ethical* question, for it revolves around an idea of human dignity—thus demonstrating their common commitment to a certain humanism.[7]

Sartre's *Critique* and Lévi-Strauss's *The Elementary Structures*

If, as Thomas Flynn suggests, "Sartre's interest has always been primarily ethical,"[8] the *Critique of Dialectical Reason* is certainly no exception. In fact, it can be said to address the issue of ethics in a much more forceful and direct way than the earlier writings that made him famous. The *Critique* was the first of a projected multivolume work laying out Sartre's philosophy of history (Volume 2 appeared posthumously and will not be discussed in this chapter).[9] The *Critique* is not, however, philosophy of history in the traditional sense, that is, in the speculative sense of Hegel and Marx. It does not seek to determine the meaning and direction of history-in-general but aims rather to elucidate the tools of analysis from which any meaning or directionality of history might be discerned. The *Critique* is often seen as a "Marxist turn" in Sartre's thought, even though Sartre himself insists that it was written "against the communists."[10] With respect to its place in his own oeuvre, the *Critique* cannot be said to break with the existentialism of *Being and Nothingness*; it represents rather a reformulation, an extension of its major concepts into the analysis of social being. The fundamental dichotomy of Sartre's *Being and Nothingness*—that between bad faith and authenticity—is thus revived in the central dialectic of the *Critique*: that between an inauthentic "seriality" and an authentic "group praxis." But Sartre's vocabulary also shows signs of being influenced by Lévi-Strauss, with concepts such as "structure" and "reciprocity" playing major roles.

Sartre believes that the great error of social science, including Marxist social science, lies in its inability to distinguish between two types of social structure, which he calls "groups" and "collectives." According to Sartre, groups are the true motor of history, whereas collectives, which resemble groups only superficially, possess no intrinsic historical force. Groups are defined by a common *purpose*, collectives by a common *interest*. Groups *actively* seek to achieve consciously conceived goals through concerted, committed action; in a group, my goal is the other's goal, and the other's goal is my goal. This is what Sartre calls *praxis* (praxis thus corresponds to Sartre's existentialist concept of the "project"). But Sartre rejects the idea of collective consciousness (à la Durkheim) or "group mind" (à la Hegel's *Geist*). The group is rather a special coincidence of individual and group praxis, which Sartre terms "mediated reciprocity" or reciprocity mediated by a "third party" (*le tiers*). The third party can also be the group itself: "This newcomer joins a group of 100 *through me* insofar as the group which I join will have 100 *through him*. . . . Each of us is the 100th of the other."[11] Collectives, on the other hand, are composed of atomistic individuals incapable of acting in concert; even in a panic or riot, it is "every man for himself." This is because the interest that unites members of a collective is purely extrinsic: It does not emanate from the gathering itself but arises contingently from an amalgam of discrete, uncoordinated actions. Collectives are thus what Sartre calls a *series*: neither purely random (like a clustering of individuals at an intersection waiting for the light to change) nor purposeful (a group). Serial gatherings are *passive* social structures; they are figures of social and political impotence.

A close corollary of Sartre's notion of seriality is the concept of the "practico-inert," Sartre's term for the material remains of past praxis, insofar as they persist as inertia and no longer respond to or actually resist the needs of the group. The practico-inert resides in language, institutions, rituals, and norms; it is the functional equivalent of the more familiar Marxist notion of "objectification," except that it retains a more explicit dialectical relation to praxis. Sartre's location of language in the practico-inert recalls the structuralist binary of signifying system versus speech-act (though Lévi-Strauss's version is significantly more complex than the basic Saussurian schema).[12] Thomas Flynn observes that "[Sartre] translates Saussure's *langue/parole* distinction into his own practico-inert/praxis scheme. But unlike the structuralists Sartre places the emphasis on praxis-parole."[13] As we shall shortly see, Sartre effectively defines Lévi-Strauss's structural anthropology as a discipline that seeks to reveal the structures of the practico-inert; because it remains at this level, it is incapable of accounting for human *praxis* (freedom) or the dialectic (history); thus (according to Sartre) it is ethically deficient in that it effectively denies to the human being his or her full dignity.

What Sartre calls the "practico-inert field" is the domain of the *passive activity* of seriality, that is, an activity permeated by impotence, indifference, and unfreedom. To the extent that the practico-inert inhibits or cancels out group praxis, it shows itself to be "anti-praxis" or even "anti-dialectical": the repository of the non-volitional effects (unintended consequences) of human praxis (e.g., the invention of the automobile was designed to increase mobility but often results in the traffic that restricts it). However, the practico-inert field is *not an ethically neutral* inertia; for in this condition individuals are constantly subject to *scarcity* (*rareté*), that is, the impossibility of satisfying the needs of a social ensemble, which Sartre sees as the most basic, untranscended condition of humanity. Only the cooperation of group praxis—the affirmation of freedom on the level of the social ensemble—can transcend the rivalry and competition (social conflict and violence) that inevitably arise among serial, atomized individuals in the practico-inert field.

Sartre's famous everyday examples of seriality—waiting in line for the bus and listening to the radio—are vivid descriptions of the "alterity" (a degraded form of sociality) that Sartre sees as the essence of serial existence. In the bus queue, no organic relations subsist among the bus riders; I am as indifferent to my fellow bus rider as he is to me. The common interest in transportation is extrinsic to the gathering itself; it has no unifying potential, even if it unites individuals in a *shared* (but not a *common*) activity: "The acts of waiting are not a communal fact, but are lived separately as identical instances of the same act."[14] Though this being-together is a relation of sorts, it is nevertheless based on a fundamental alterity, a kind of pseudo- or counter-reciprocity that is diametrically opposed to the reciprocity of true groups. Moreover, the seriality of the bus queue is conditioned by the practico-inert field of the bus transportation system itself: the insufficient number of seats (scarcity), the density and interchangeability of people (massification),[15] the rigidity of the time schedule (standardization), and so on, all of which augment the alienation and isolation of the individual.[16] The other bus riders are seen as either superfluous (their addition is unimportant) or an obstacle (they are taking my seat). Serial individuals relate to one another as others: "The Other is me in every Other and every Other in me and everyone as Other in all the Others."[17] The self-alienation I experience in situations such as the bus queue is the result of an "interiorization" of alterity: "Everyone's interiorization of his common-being-outside-himself in the unifying object can be conceived as the unity of all in the form of common-being-outside-oneself-in-the-other."[18] In other words, the "unity" of a serial gathering does nothing to diminish my social alienation, for I can, in fact, only be "isolated" with others.[19] Seriality thus defines a whole mode of social being: "There are serial behavior, serial feelings and serial thoughts" (i.e., received or unexamined opinion, social imitation).[20]

According to Sartre, there are different levels of serial alterity, as evidenced in the more extreme example of "indirect gatherings," such as the radio broadcast, which is also defined by *absence*: I am united through the disembodied voice to listeners who lie outside my perceptual field; however, there is nothing that I as an individual can do to effectively respond to the Voice; the very form of the radio audience—the lack of two-way communication— inhibits group formation and engenders feelings of extreme impotence and passivity (much more so than in the example of the queue, in which at least a riot could erupt in response to some sudden scarcity). Particularly in this example, Sartre's *Critique* can be seen as a contribution to the study of mass media culture, an emerging field in the 1960s. Fredric Jameson avers that Sartre's account of seriality is "the only genuine philosophy of the media that anyone has proposed to date" and that its power derives from its avoidance of the "conceptual traps of collective consciousness on the one hand, and of behaviorism or manipulation on the other."[21] Sartre's analysis of seriality has also been important to feminist thought, most notably in Iris Marion Young's essay "Gender as Seriality: Thinking about Women as a Social

Collective."²² Both Jameson and Young see Sartre's notion of seriality as a superior way of conceiving of social ensembles that have been traditionally thought of as groups.

Indeed, the ultimate aim of Sartre's discussion of seriality is to criticize the Marxist tendency to treat classes as if they were true groups, as organic forces that motivate historical change.²³ According to Sartre, socioeconomic classes are, in fact, collectives; they are characterized by seriality and impotence. The class system is simply the differentiated effect of the practico-inert field as modified by scarcity: Membership in a class is not freely chosen; it is an external determination based on the unequal allocation of resources. Responsible group praxis thus involves transcending the entire practico-inert structure of serial class being (the negation of scarcity), toward the creation of a classless society of *abundance*: "*It is seriality* which must be overcome in order to achieve the smallest common result."²⁴

Sartre's characterization of groups and collectives should not, however, be seen as static or essentializing; groups ceaselessly arise out of and devolve back into collectives, in the "totalizing" movement of history.²⁵ "Totalization" (in contradistinction to Georg Lukács's static notion of "totality") is Sartre's term for the constantly developing, dynamic relations between part and whole—for example, agent and environment, past and present—insofar as these make up *synthetic* entities (e.g., the farmer and his or her field, the historian and the history he or she writes). Sartre contrasts the dynamic structures revealed in the dialectic of totalization with the fixed structures studied by the analytical rationality of the sciences (including anthropology)—a contrast Lévi-Strauss will reject, as we shall shortly see.

It is important to note that seriality recalls what Martin Heidegger outlined in *Being in Time* under the concept of "the they" (*das Man*), which, though ostensibly a neutral, onto-existential (structural) concept, is also an ethico-historical one, insofar as it describes the negative effects of the mass urbanized society that arose in the West in the late nineteenth and early twentieth centuries. Heidegger similarly uses the examples of mass transportation and mass media in his evocation of "the they":

> In utilizing public transportation, in the use of information services such as the newspaper, every other is like the next. This being-with-one-another dissolves one's own Dasein completely into the kind of being of 'the others' in such a way that the others, as distinguishable and explicit, disappear more and more.²⁶

Sartre shares Heidegger's antipathy toward mass culture, which both see as the apogee of inauthentic social relations. However, Heidegger's *das Man*, the inauthentic crowd from which the authentic individual must distinguish him- or herself, lacks the sense of conflict or violence that permeates Sartre's (Marxist) conception of serial scarcity.²⁷

The fact that seriality is designed to describe modern or at least urbanized social forms would appear to exclude from the dialectic, and thus from history, the types of societies that anthropologists such as Lévi-Strauss typically study. Lévi-Strauss thus objects that

> indeed what can one make of peoples "without history" when one has defined man in terms of dialectic and dialectic in terms of history? Sometimes Sartre seems tempted to distinguish two dialectics: the "true" one which is supposed to be that of historical societies, and a repetitive, short-term dialectic, which he grants to so-called primitive societies whilst at the same time placing it very near biology.[28]

Given anthropology's own roots in colonialism, Lévi-Strauss necessarily approaches the question of history as an ethical as well as a theoretical problem. Indeed, Lévi-Strauss's entire career is predicated on erasing the hierarchical difference between the "savage mind" and the modern (Western) mind, so as to declare them equal in their humanity. Thus, for Lévi-Strauss, Sartre's "dialectical reason" is simply another example of Western ethnocentrism masquerading as "philosophy of history." From Sartre's perspective, however, it is Lévi-Strauss who is denying archaic societies their full humanity by refusing to consider them dialectically, that is, in terms of free praxis.[29]

I will return to Lévi-Strauss's perspective later in this chapter. But let us first examine how Sartre proposes to "save" Lévi-Strauss's analyses of kinship by integrating them into the dialectical framework of the *Critique*. Sartre discusses Lévi-Strauss in the part of the *Critique* devoted to groups, thus placing "primitive" societies on the side of authentic praxis, which, given what was said above, may seem counterintuitive. Indeed, Sartre introduces the section on Lévi-Strauss by asking if there is not a paradox in the fact that organized praxis can be analyzed as an objective structure by social science (such as structural anthropology) and yet at the same time be an expression of group freedom:

> If it really is possible to devise a theory of reciprocal multiplicities in organized groups, independently of all concrete, historical ends and of any particular circumstances, do we not immediately collapse in the face of an inert ossature of the organization? And do we not abandon the terrain of liberating *praxis* and the dialectic and revert to some kind of inorganic necessity?[30]

Prima facie, it would appear that the kind of unconscious necessity Lévi-Strauss seemingly posits in his concept of *structure* (which, for Sartre, is simply the intelligibility of a group's organization) would inhibit the possibility of authentic praxis (the spontaneous, conscious construction of social forms) on the part of organized groups. Indeed, highly structured groups appear to be ossified in their very organization, namely in the resistance of this organization to change (its seeming permanence). Sartre remarks that "function as lived *praxis* appears in the study of the group *as objectivity* in the *objectified* form of structure."[31] But if this were the whole story, then organized groups, and, in particular, "primitive" groups, would simply be reducible to the practico-inert and would therefore lose their status as "groups" in Sartre's terminology. The dialectical analysis of such organized groups thus presents more hurdles than the other group types that Sartre sketches, which are spontaneous and evanescent: namely the "group-in-fusion" (*groupe en fusion*) (e.g., the group of citizens that stormed the Bastille in 1789) and the "pledged group" (e.g., the Tennis Court Oath by members of the Third Estate).

Sartre endeavors to resolve the dilemma by arguing—contra Lévi-Strauss—that it is not structure that conditions praxis but rather praxis that conditions structure. Though the rules of kinship that Lévi-Strauss observes in *The Elementary Structures* appear, on the structural-analytical level, to restrict possibilities and choice, on the structural-dialectical level they reveal themselves as a transcendence; for the "rules" are a mode of group praxis, which, precisely because of its inertia, the inertia of praxis-structure, enables it to resist the inertia of the practico-inert (anti-praxis, scarcity) that the group would otherwise fall into. Sartre thus sees the relation between structure and the practico-inert as the relation between two inertias: "active passivity" and "passive activity," respectively.[32] The passivity of structure reveals itself as a kind of activity insofar as it resists the ruinous passivity of the practico-inert, namely the threat of scarcity: "The exchange of women [is] organized in such a way as to combat, *as far as possible*, scarcity and its consequences for the human ensemble."[33] Far from being inimical to freedom, the structure actually realizes it (albeit in a way that Lévi-Strauss finds unconvincing when compared to Sartre's "higher" dialectic of seriality-group praxis). Joseph Catalano observes that "freedom is the act by which we interiorize exterior structure, actualizing and transcending it to accomplish our purpose. The organized group . . . protects the individual from the unconscious structure of the practico-inert and provides consciously chosen structures."[34] Lawrence Rosen similarly remarks that, in Sartre's analysis, structure is not a "supra-individual constraint" but rather "a construction of human intelligence."[35] Needless to say, Lévi-Strauss would find the idea of being "protected" from the "constraints" of unconscious structures anathema to his theory (as if one needed to be "protected" from grammar). In Sartre's view, however, to the extent that Lévi-Strauss refuses to recognize the praxis of structure, its conscious and creative aspect (active passivity), he, in effect, reduces structure to the practico-inert.

Lévi-Strauss clearly felt the sting of Sartre's critique, as when he laments (in *The Savage Mind*):

> I must now confess to having myself unintentionally and unwittingly lent support to these erroneous ideas, by having seemed all too often

in *Les structures élémentaires de la parenté* as if I were seeking out an unconscious genesis of matrimonial exchange. I should have made more distinction between exchange as it is expressed spontaneously and forcefully in the *praxis* of groups and the conscious and deliberate rules by which these same groups ... spend their time in codifying and controlling it.... Thus we must, as Sartre advocates, apply dialectical reason to the knowledge of our own and other societies. But we must not lose sight of the fact that analytical reason occupies a considerable place in all of them.[36]

Lévi-Strauss sounds much more Sartrean in this passage than he perhaps intends, but we should not be led to think that Lévi-Strauss has thereby embraced a philosophy of consciousness and freedom. For the supposedly "conscious and deliberate rules" are still expressions of the universal structures of the mind. Even if the mere assertion of universality does not ipso facto make human beings into automatons, Lévi-Strauss is nonetheless resistant to determining the scope of freedom according to observable praxis; most often, in fact, he describes such "freedom" as an illusion. For example, Lévi-Strauss notes that the goal of "ethnographic research" is to reach "a level where necessity reveals itself as immanent in the illusions of freedom."[37] For his part, Sartre, in an essay from 1969, sums up his differences with Lévi-Strauss thus: "I am in complete agreement that social facts have their own structure and laws that dominate individuals, but I see in this the reply of worked matter [i.e., the practico-inert] to the agents who work it.... Structures are created by activity which has no structure, but suffers its results as structure."[38]

We will return to Lévi-Strauss's response to Sartre in the second part of this chapter. But let us briefly consider how Sartre himself might have benefited from Lévi-Strauss's analyses. In a footnote to the section we have just been discussing, Sartre offers a very personal example of the dynamic he observes in Lévi-Strauss's analyses of kinship. Whereas Sartre had previously held that atheism, since it is supposedly unstructured, is more conducive to individual freedom than indoctrination into a specific belief system, he now acknowledges that baptism may, in fact, lead to greater freedom, because it opens the possibility of a richer structure, *in the context of the group to which the individual belongs*:

> As someone who had been baptized, but who had no real links with the Catholic group, it seemed to me that baptism was a mortgage of future freedom.... I thought that total indeterminacy was the true basis of choice. But from the point of view of the group ... the opposite is true: baptism is a way of creating freedom in the common individual at the same time as qualifying him by his function and his reciprocal relation to everyone; he interiorizes common freedom as the true power of his individual freedom.[39]

The idea of individual freedom being conditioned by "common freedom" (i.e., reciprocal relations in the group), particularly in this very personal example, shows just how far Sartre has evolved since *Being and Nothingness*. While it is impossible to precisely locate the inspiration for Sartre's change of position, one could speculate that, whatever his differences with Lévi-Strauss, it was *The Elementary Structures* that taught Sartre to see that an understanding of human groups was essential to any conception of human reality and that the "scandal of the existence of others"[40] in *Being and Nothingness* (or "hell is other people," from *No Exit*) was perhaps overblown, leading him to neglect the positive meaning of reciprocity. Sartre surely took note of the famous last paragraph of *The Elementary Structures*, in which Lévi-Strauss writes (perhaps thinking of Sartre), "To this very day, mankind has always dreamed of seizing and fixing that fleeting moment when it was permissible to believe that the law of exchange could be evaded, that one could gain without losing, enjoy without sharing."[41] One could perhaps read Sartre's entire *Critique* as a response to this passage: the elucidation of the "law of exchange"—reciprocity—as freedom.

Lévi-Strauss's *The Savage Mind* and Sartre's *Critique*

Lévi-Strauss's professional concern with the question of history certainly predates the debate with Sartre in *The Savage Mind*. In 1949, the same year *The Elementary Structures* appeared, Lévi-Strauss published an article entitled "Histoire et Ethnologie"[42]; nine years later the essay (translated as "History and Anthropology") would serve as the "Introduction" to his *Structural Anthropology* (1958).

What is most striking in this essay is its rhetoric of complementarity. Lévi-Strauss chastises those (like Franz Boas and Bronisław Malinowski) who tend to regard the discipline of history with suspicion and seek to distance themselves from it. Though each discipline has certain advantages over the other—the anthropologist speaks about a society he or she has "experienced as a living reality,"[43] whereas the historian has extensive written records to work with, documents that seemingly provide a higher level of objectivity—Lévi-Strauss does not see this distinction as crucial. He argues first (*pace* Malinowski) that "the best ethnographic study will never make the reader a native,"[44] for the perspective of the ethnographer is no closer to "objective reality" than that of the historian[45]; and second, that the idea that "the critical study of documents by numerous observers" (history) is methodologically superior to "the observations of a single individual" (anthropology) is not an indictment of anthropology; it simply highlights the need "to increase the number of ethnographers."[46] Moreover, the cherished documents that the historian cites as evidence are, after all, simply "the testimony of amateur ethnographers."[47] Thus, history and anthropology share a method. But this method differs in one crucial respect: "History organizes its data in relation to conscious expressions of social life, while anthropology proceeds by examining its unconscious foundations."[48] In this distinction, Lévi-Strauss introduces his structural theory of anthropology as the making explicit of patterns or invariants that underlie conscious actions and thoughts. The anthropologist's task is to uncover these implicit structures, whereas the historian is interested in motivations and desires—that is, the self-understanding—of historical actors as they manifest themselves in the evidence adduced. The dichotomy in this early essay between conscious expression (praxis, history) and unconscious structures (the practico-inert) already sets the stage for Sartre's dialectical critique of Lévi-Strauss.

It must be stressed, however, that Lévi-Strauss is speaking in this essay about the *discipline* of history, not history as a philosophical concept. As Michael Harkin notes, one of this essay's principal motivations was to establish "the institutional identity of anthropology, which in France lagged far behind its status in the United States and Great Britain."[49] Boas and Malinowski had founded national traditions of ethnological study in the United States and Great Britain, respectively, but France had no comparable figure. While Émile Durkheim and Marcel Mauss had established the French tradition of sociology (even if Mauss is more remembered today for his contributions to anthropology), Lévi-Strauss felt that sociology could not be used as a model, given its tendency to study its own society instead of that of the Other. Lévi-Strauss instead saw history as the more complementary discipline to anthropology, due to the above-described similarity in method. Although, as Harkin argues, this alignment with history was perhaps more immediately motivated by a desire to associate anthropology with the prestige of an established discipline,[50] Lévi-Strauss appears to have continued to believe in a natural affinity between the disciplines of history and anthropology throughout his career. In a 2001 interview with Marcello Massenzio, Lévi-Strauss affirmed that "now I would say that history and ethnology are the same thing, with the slight difference that we study societies spread out in space whereas history studies societies spread out in time."[51] Lévi-Strauss had written the almost identical phrase in *The Savage Mind*—"[the anthropologist] conceives [of history] as a study complementary to his own: one of them unfurls the range of human societies in time, the other in space"[52]—except that in this work, Lévi-Strauss is quite critical of history, both as a discipline and as a philosophical concept. Nevertheless, the proximity Lévi-Strauss posits between the disciplines of history and anthropology appears to support Sartre's attempt in his *Critique* to bring the two disciplines together as a "structural and historical anthropology."

In 1967, a year after the appearance of the English translation of *The Savage Mind*, Lévi-Strauss published a reedition of *The Elementary*

Structures. Though this reedition contains no substantive changes,[53] Lévi-Strauss nevertheless adds a footnote in which he briefly responds to Sartre:

> In *Critique de la raison dialectique* (p. 744), Sartre has called attention to this formula, in which he sees a confusion between dialectical and analytical reasoning. But we do not conceive of dialectical reasoning in the same way as Sartre. As we see it, the dichotomous approach is in no way incompatible with dialectical thought, but clearly the contrary. See on this subject, Lévi-Strauss, 1966, ch IX.[54]

Indeed, in the chapter of *The Savage Mind* to which Lévi-Strauss refers, he will take great pains to reject Sartre's dichotomy between analytical and dialectical reason. Lévi-Strauss's objections are threefold: (1) inconsistency: Sartre both opposes dialectical and analytical reason and sees them as complementary; therefore, the distinction is either "contradictory" or "superfluous"[55]; (2) ethnocentrism: dialectical reason is used to establish the superiority and singularity of Western historical humanity over peoples who "refuse history" ("Sartre resigns himself to putting 'a stunted and deformed' humanity on man's side, but not without implying that its place in humanity does not belong to it in its own right")[56]; (3) lack of foundation or legitimacy ("dialectical reason can account neither for itself nor for analytical reason").[57] I shall address these objections in turn.

With regard to the first, Lévi-Strauss is keen to extricate himself from Sartre's prison-house of analytical reason and the limiting concept of scientific rationality it denotes. In effect, Sartre, like Heidegger before him, is reasserting through this dichotomy the primacy and encompassing nature of philosophy in the face of the ever-increasing prestige accorded to techno-scientific inquiry (hence the bifurcation—still prevalent today—between a Continental approach that defines itself in contradistinction to scientific rationality and an Anglo-analytic approach that embraces it). Sartre's distinction between dialectical and analytical reason thus recalls Heidegger's famous "ontological difference" between *being* (phenomenological ontology, hermeneutics) and *beings* (objective science, metaphysics, epistemology). By reinterpreting philosophy as the search for being and thus as the more encompassing form of inquiry, Heidegger carves out an autonomous and imperious space for philosophy, thereby reasserting its preeminence vis-à-vis science.

For his part, Lévi-Strauss seeks to turn the tables on philosophy: In his view, structural anthropology, as the *human* science *par excellence*, should be considered the more encompassing discipline, for it alone reveals the fundamental structures that condition philosophical thought itself (including dialectical thought). Philosophical works such as Sartre's should thus be treated like ethnographic documents:

> It is precisely because all these aspects of the savage mind can be found in Sartre's philosophy, that the latter is in my view unqualified

to pass judgment on it: he is prevented from doing so by the very fact of furnishing its equivalent. To the anthropologist, on the contrary, this philosophy (like all others) affords a first-class ethnographic document, the study of which is essential to an understanding of the mythology of our own time.[58]

This intellectual jujitsu thus allows Lévi-Strauss to disarm Sartrean concepts by noting their proximity to "savage thought": "[Sartre's] analysis of the practico-inert quite simply revives the language of animism"[59]; "it is possible that the requirement of 'totalization' is a great novelty to some historians, sociologists, and psychologists. It has been taken for granted by anthropologists ever since they learned it from Malinowski."[60] Given its encompassing nature, structural anthropology cannot, in Lévi-Strauss's view, be reducible to Sartre's analytical reason, nor can it be opposed to it without relinquishing the mantle of science. Lévi-Strauss thus concludes that there is one type of rationality with two aspects: "I do not regard dialectical reason as *something other than* analytical reason . . . but as something *additional in* analytical reason."[61]

In making this move, Lévi-Strauss neglects two points. One concerns Lévi-Strauss's (ethically charged) complaint that "sometimes [Sartre] opposes dialectical and analytical reason as truth and error, if not as God and the devil, while at other times these two kinds of reason are apparently complementary,"[62] which fails to recognize the fact that, for Sartre, *analytical reason is not ethically neutral.* Catalano notes that "Lévi-Strauss has . . . missed this important distinction in methodology. . . . As a 'tool' the analytic reason of science can be a source of benefit or harm."[63] The other point is that Sartre sees the dialectical unity of human praxis as irreducible. Thus, Lawrence Rosen points out that "if for Lévi-Strauss the constituent elements of man's existence and works are to be reintegrated through the dialectic, Sartre denies the possibility of their original analytic dissolution and argues that man is at base a unity of dialectical forces."[64] In other words, there is no bridge between the ahistorical (the universal, the totality) and the historical (the dialectic, totalization) that would preserve their difference; hence, Sartre's separation between the two types of reason. Since this separation is, moreover, the basis for the divide between Continental and Analytic philosophy, one better understands why "poststructuralism," which reaffirms the Heideggarian position, could so easily displace structuralism. Thus, Lévi-Strauss's attempted appropriation of Sartrean terms is ultimately much less effective than Sartre's appropriation of terms such as *structure* and *reciprocity*.

With regard to the second point, the charge of ethnocentrism, Lévi-Strauss appears to be on firmer ground. As was discussed above, the idea that the dialectic applies most fully to modern, capitalistic societies and only in a more limited way to nonhistorical, archaic societies does suggest that

Sartre sees the latter as embryonic. As Marcel Hénaff puts it in his book on Lévi-Strauss:

> They ["primitive" societies] would thus be waiting for their true temporality: that in which we are already immersed. In short, they are in the "not yet." The historical dimension is supposed to provide them with the meaning they are lacking. Such is the general—implicit or explicit—conception of historical thought respecting traditional societies.[65]

In other words, all historical thought contains an inherent bias against unhistorical societies, and thus it is not on the basis of historical thought that any ethically legitimate understanding of the latter can be sought. Hénaff summarizes Lévi-Strauss's structural approach as the elucidation of an alternative form of meaning to the historical—an alternative temporal meaning—which is no less rich or less human and that manifests itself as a *necessary refusal* of historical temporality, in favor of a mythical temporality of continuity and permanence.

Thus, on one level, structural anthropology itself must also "refuse history"—not history as a discipline but as a concept conditioned by a specific philosophical conception, such as the dialectic—to maintain its encompassing ambition and to show that the same mental structures inhere in historical and nonhistorical humanity. Lévi-Strauss thus seeks to delegitimize the notion that "some special prestige seems to attach to the temporal dimension, as if diachrony were to establish a kind of intelligibility not merely superior to that provided by synchrony, but above all more specifically human."[66] But Lévi-Strauss has perhaps obscured his own point in this passage by making it appear as if the diachrony/synchrony dyad can simply be grafted onto the temporal/nontemporal opposition.[67] In fact, this dyad is a matter of two temporalities—succession and simultaneity—rather than a simple equation of diachrony with history. Although chronology and succession are most often associated with history, if one takes a sufficiently long period of time—the *longue durée*, as the *Annalistes* historians demonstrated—it is possible to see how history might also be subjected to synchronic analysis.[68]

Lévi-Strauss addresses the relation between time and history with greater clarity (and more powerfully, in my view), in an essay published around the same time as *The Savage Mind* entitled "Cultural Discontinuity and Economic and Social Development" (1963):

> The question is not knowing whether societies called "primitive" have or do not have a history in the sense that we give this term. These societies exist in time like all others, and with the same title to it, but unlike us, they refuse to belong to history and they try very hard to inhibit, within themselves, whatever would constitute the faint promise of a historical

development. . . . Our Western societies are made for change; it is the principle of their structure and their organization.[69]

Here, Lévi-Strauss separates the question of time from the question of history. One cannot assume that just because a society does not see itself or show itself as historical that it is static or incapable of history. The idea that such societies *actively refuse* history, that they "try very hard to inhibit" historical change, is another way of saying that they essentially *choose* to be nonhistorical and affirm their freedom thereby. This quasi-existentialist manner of putting the matter may have been unintended, but the Sartrean resonances are clear. In Sartrean terms, this is their *praxis-structure*: "Primitive" societies transcend history by consciously and actively *refusing the dialectic*. Western societies, on the other hand, are "made for change," that is, *for the dialectic*; thus, any refusal on their part necessarily appears as stagnation (the fall into the practico-inert). Lévi-Strauss might therefore be seen as more Sartrean than Sartre in this instance, since he appears to have unwittingly uncovered a new layer of the dialectic (a dialectical anti-dialectic).

With regard to the final point, concerning the foundation, or lack thereof, of dialectical reason, Lévi-Strauss is no doubt reacting to passages such as the following: "Volume I of the *Critique of Dialectical Reason* stops as soon as we reach the 'locus of history'; it is solely concerned with finding the intelligible foundations of a structural anthropology."[70] Although Sartre here employs the language of foundationalism, he is in fact staking out a more nuanced position, which Catalano helpfully summarizes as follows:

> The dialectic must accept the idealist goal that reason founds itself, but it must reject the foundationalism of this view. There is no wider, nondialectical perspective from which the dialectic can be justified. Nevertheless, the dialectic does not validate itself in one stroke as an abstract schema that is then imposed on the facts. If the dialectic is true, it is so because material conditions are such that it must be true. From this perspective, the dialectic is a nominalism; that is, what exists are individuals and totalities produced by individuals.[71]

Catalano's methodological description of Sartre's dialectic resonates with many aspects of Lévi-Strauss's approach. For Lévi-Strauss has also been accused of imposing an "abstract schema" on the facts. But Lévi-Strauss's schemas, like Sartre's, are constructed from the empirical data and thus have no *a priori* or transcendental basis. Hénaff observes that "as Lévi-Strauss demonstrates in all his work, a structure is precisely a constant relation between contents (a relation that can thus be formalized). There is therefore no question of *its being applied* to them."[72] And Lévi-Strauss's approach can also be described as nominalist, as when he asserts that "'social structure' has nothing to do with empirical reality but with models which are built up after it."[73]

Clearly, some of the intellectual methods and positions of Sartre and Lévi-Strauss, particularly with regard to the question of history, have more in common than either would care to admit and more than the gulf that is typically assumed between existentialism and structuralism would lead us to believe. At the very least, Sartre's careful attention to *The Elementary Structures* in his *Critique* and the fact that Lévi-Strauss allowed himself "to borrow a certain amount of Sartre's vocabulary"[74] in *The Savage Mind* reveal a good-faith effort to find common ground. If on some questions, in particular the question of freedom, Sartre and Lévi-Strauss are irreconcilable, their ethical intuitions regarding the idea of history and its relation to human dignity nevertheless bring them together.

CHAPTER TWO

Foucault's "ethics of the self"

*My point is not that everything is
bad, but that everything is dangerous.*
—MICHEL FOUCAULT[1]

In an interview conducted in 1983, just one year before his untimely death from AIDS, Michel Foucault characterized his published oeuvre as containing three distinct phases: (1) "an historical ontology of ourselves in relation to truth through which we constitute ourselves as subjects of knowledge," as developed in the 1960s (*The Birth of the Clinic* and *The Order of Things*); (2) "an historical ontology of ourselves in relation to a field of power through which we constitute ourselves as acting on others," as elaborated in the mid-1970s (*Discipline and Punish*); and (3) "an historical ontology in relation to ethics through which we constitute ourselves as moral agents," as pursued in *The History of Sexuality*, in particular in volumes 2 and 3, which were forthcoming at the moment Foucault was speaking.[2] Although Foucault offered many versions of this tripartite view of his work in the last years of his life, all of them suggest that Foucault underwent an ethical and subjective turn that intensified around 1980.

For a long time, however, our knowledge of this turn has been somewhat sketchy. Although several books and numerous articles endeavored to give an account of the "final Foucault," as one such book is titled,[3] these efforts were severely hampered by the fact that comparatively little of the relevant material—the course summaries, the last interviews—appeared during Foucault's lifetime.[4] It is only with the long-delayed publication of the annual lectures given at the Collège de France between 1970 and 1984 that a more complete picture of Foucault's thought, in particular his later thought, has emerged, rendering many of the studies published prior to 2000 fairly obsolete.[5] The final four lecture courses form a group, for they all deal in some essential way with the subject or self: the 1980–81 course, *Subjectivity and Truth*, appeared in French in 2014 and is due to appear in English in 2017; the 1981–82 course, *The Hermeneutics of the Subject*, was published in 2001 (English translation in 2005); this was followed by the publication in 2008 (English translation in 2011) of the courses of 1982–83, *The Government of Self and Others*, and 1983–84, *The Courage of Truth: The Government of Self and Others II*.[6] Foucault's final publications—the last two volumes of *The History of Sexuality*, published in 1984, the year of his death, and a few interviews and essays—capture only a small part of the content of these lectures.[7] Had Foucault lived a few more years, these courses would have certainly yielded a major new book[8]; indeed, as the editor, Frédéric Gros, has observed, Foucault's final seminars are "like the substitute of a projected book that never appeared."[9] It is therefore impossible to understand the nature and significance of Foucault's "ethical turn" without an examination of the lecture courses, in particular the pivotal 1981–82 course (*The Hermeneutics of the Subject*).

It should be noted at the outset that the course lectures are based on audio recordings. Although Foucault did use notes (which were consulted in the editing of the course lectures for publication), he never wrote his lectures out. One might therefore be tempted to question the legitimacy of treating such material as truly representative of Foucault's thought. It is thus instructive to see what Foucault himself thought of their value. At the beginning of the lecture of March 10, 1982, Foucault remarks:

> I understand that there are some people here recording the lectures. Very well, you are absolutely within your rights. The lectures here are public. It's just maybe you have the impression that all my lectures are written. But they are less so than they seem to be, and I do not have any transcripts or any recordings. Now it happens that I need them. So, if by chance there is anyone who has (or who knows someone who has) either recordings . . . or obviously transcripts, would you be kind enough to tell me, it could help me. It is especially for the last four or five years.[10]

Foucault evidently felt that what he said during the lectures to be important enough to want to use them himself. I thus think that, like his many interviews, these lectures were intended for a wide public dissemination and that they are comparable in significance to the publications he authorized during his lifetime.[11]

The roads to ethics

Although the topic of ethics is addressed in the final two volumes of *The History of Sexuality*, it is relegated for the most part to the area of sexual morality. In the final courses, however, Foucault seeks to theorize ethics as such—in such notions as the "ethics of the self," the "*rapport à soi*," and "governmentality"[12]—and with little reference to sexual practices. The 1980–81 course, *Subjectivity and Truth*, lays much of the groundwork for Foucault's "ethical turn" by refocusing his thought on the self or subject.[13] But it is only with the 1981–82 course (*The Hermeneutics of the Subject*) that the ethical import of this "turn" toward the subject becomes apparent. Frédéric Gros goes so far as to say that *The Hermeneutics of the Subject* is "the living heart of a change of problematic, of a conceptual revolution,"[14] and that it is "the conceptual crowning achievement of [Foucault's] work, something like the principle of its completion."[15] This "revolution" involves not only a turn "toward" ethics but also a reconceptualization of ethics itself, namely a move away from normativity (Kant) or the primacy of the relation to the other (Levinas)[16] and toward an idea of ethics as based on the relation of the self to the self (*le rapport de soi à soi*). As we will see, this "ethics of the self" does not at all represent an abandonment of Foucault's inveterate Nietzscheanism; on the contrary, it can be seen as an intensification of it.

The exact impetus for this change in orientation is not easy to discern. Of the many contributing factors, perhaps the most immediate is the appearance of Pierre Hadot's 1981 book *Exercices spirituels et philosophie antique* (although Hadot had published an article on the topic as early as 1974).[17] Hadot's contention that the ancient Greeks conceived of philosophy primarily as a way of life or "art of living" (*technê tou biou*), which included "spiritual exercises" that prepared the aspirant for the rigors of theoretical inquiry, deeply impressed Foucault and is clearly the source of his idea of the "care of the self" (*le souci de soi*), developed in the 1981–82 lecture course as well as in the eponymous volume of *The History of Sexuality* (volume 3).[18] The close association between Foucault's late work and Hadot is reflected in Arnold Davidson's 1995 collection of Hadot's writings: *Philosophy as a Way of Life: Spiritual Exercises from Socrates to Foucault* (this edition also collects essays written after the 1981 text, including Hadot's essays on Foucault's interpretation of his work).[19] On Foucault's initiative, Hadot was elected to the Collège de France in 1982, becoming the Chair of History of Greek and Roman Thought (Foucault had been elected in 1969).

While Hadot may have been the catalyst for the form that Foucault's change in direction eventually took, the roots of the shift itself go back to a "period of prolonged intellectual and personal crisis" that followed the publication of *Discipline and Punish* (1975).[20] Gilles Deleuze describes Foucault during this period as "very different, more inward, perhaps more depressive, more secret."[21] A lecture given in 1976 reveals the depth of Foucault's dissatisfaction with his intellectual trajectory:

> I have sketched a genealogical history of the origins of a theory and a knowledge of an anomaly and of the various techniques that relate to it [in the *History of Sexuality*, volume 1]. None of it does more than mark

time. Repetitive and disconnected, it advances nowhere. Since it never ceases to say the same thing, it perhaps says nothing. It is tangled up into an indecipherable, disorganized muddle. In a nutshell, it is inconclusive.[22]

Rarely has a thinker been so honest about his own perceived shortcomings. One of the reasons for Foucault's despondency, according to his biographer, James Miller, was his inability "to elaborate a 'new form of right' through a positive *political* philosophy."[23] Indications of such an effort can be discerned in the lecture courses that follow Foucault's 1976–77 sabbatical from the Collège de France: *Security, Territory, Population* (1977–78) and *The Birth of Biopolitics* (1978–79), lectures that yielded no book publication, despite the development of the concept of "biopower" (discussed in the last chapter of volume one of *The History of Sexuality*).[24]

This personal and intellectual crisis was no doubt a prime factor in Foucault's abandonment of the original plan for the multivolume *The History of Sexuality*.[25] As Foucault notes in the introduction to volume two, *The Use of Pleasure* (1984), "This series of studies is being published later than I had anticipated, and in a form that is altogether different."[26] Indeed, whereas Foucault focuses in the first volume on the seventeenth and eighteenth centuries, a period he had dealt with extensively in his earlier writings, the later volumes reach back to Greek antiquity (from the fifth century BC to the advent of Christianity), a period Foucault had not previously focused on. Thus, the publishing hiatus between 1976 and 1984 reflects in part the time Foucault needed to expand his knowledge of ancient Greek culture.

But perhaps the most compelling reason for Foucault's turn toward subjectivity and ethics lay in the paradoxical nature of Foucault's philosophy itself, in the irresolvable tension or contradiction between its two main impulses: on the one hand, Foucault's dark social vision, the idea that every apparent sign of enlightened social progress is invariably a new form of oppression, and, on the other, Foucault's seeming (though unarticulated) desire to have some beneficial effect through his writings; for what otherwise would be the point of writing all of these books highlighting the plight of the marginal groups in society (the mentally ill, the deviant)—which can only be interpreted as an effort to argue for a better (less cruel) treatment by society as a whole—if there is no hope of ameliorating their condition? Certainly Foucault could not help noticing that while some derided what they saw as his "amoralism" or defeatism,[27] others were discerning ethical or political messages in his texts (often markedly different to those to which he subscribed to himself or thought were plausibly suggested by his work). Thus, in my view, Foucault's "ethical turn," as fragmentary and incomplete as it was, can be seen as an effort to address this conundrum at the heart of his own philosophy and of his activity as a philosopher,[28] one whose homosexuality becomes salient in an era of gay rights and AIDS.[29] That Foucault saw his role as a coming to terms with his place in contemporary society is clearly evident in the first lecture of his 1982–83 course ("The Government of

Self and Others"), which begins by positing the idea of a philosophy of the present or, as he calls it, an "ontology of the present," a countertradition in philosophy that Foucault locates in Kant. Combining a consideration of Kant's 1784 essay "Answering the Question: What is Enlightenment?" ("Beantwortung der Frage: Was ist Aufklärung?") with Kant's late work *The Conflict of the Faculties* (1798), which Foucault considers a "sequel" to the earlier essay,[30] Foucault sketches a bifurcation between, on the one hand, the search for theoretical truth, as exemplified in Kant's *Critique of Pure Reason* (the conditions of possibility of knowledge, which are universal and necessary, and thus nonhistorical), and, on the other, the attention to the present, as manifested in these occasional works, namely the concept of modernity (in the Enlightenment essay) and the philosophical significance of current events, such as the French Revolution (in *The Conflict of the Faculties*). Foucault sees in this bifurcation the source of the rupture between Analytic and Continental philosophy, with the former oriented toward the Kantian "analytic of truth" (nonempirical truth) and the latter toward

> another type of question, of critical questioning whose birth we see precisely in the question of *Aufklärung* or in Kant's text on the Revolution. This other critical tradition does not pose the question of the possibility of a true knowledge; it asks the question: What is present reality? What is the present field of our experiences? What is the present field of possible experiences? Here it is not a question of the analytic of truth but involves an ontology of the present, of present reality, an ontology of modernity, an ontology of ourselves.[31]

Foucault makes a similar point in his well-known essay "What is Enlightenment?"[32] published in English in 1984 (the lecture from which the above-quoted passage was taken was made publically available only in 2008), without, however, making the crucial contrast with theoretical rationality: "It ['Answering the Question: What is Enlightenment?'] is a reflection by Kant on the contemporary status of his own enterprise. . . . It is in the reflection on 'today' as difference in history and as motive for a particular philosophical task that the novelty of this text appears to me."[33] Foucault further qualifies this "relating to contemporary reality" as an "attitude": "A *voluntary choice* made by certain people . . . a way, too, of acting and behaving that at one and the same time marks a relation of belonging and presents itself as a task. A bit, no doubt, like what the Greeks called an *êthos*."[34] I underline "voluntary choice" because of its existentialist-voluntarist overtones, a theme to which we will return. Most immediately important, however, is Foucault's linkage of a philosophy of the present to the Greek conception of *êthos*, a term Foucault uses to define the Greek conception of ethics in his 1981–82 course: "The moral attitude or the *êthos*"; "the subject's way of doing things . . . his *êthos*."[35] It is thus also connected with *style*: "A person's *êthos* was evident in his clothing, appearance, gait, in the calm with which he responded to every event, and so on."[36] This confluence of ethics and aesthetics is what Foucault calls in his last interview "styles of existence."[37] As we shall see in more detail below, the contrast Foucault draws with theoretical rationality in the 1982–83 lecture course allows him to bring together the ideas of philosophy as a way of life/self-transformation (Hadot) and a philosophy of the present (Kant) under the aegis of the ethics of the self.

Foucault's ideas about the "other Kant" have a long history, going back to his "minor thesis" (*Thèse complémentaire pour le Doctorat ès Lettres*—the major thesis was *Madness and Civilization*), which consisted in a translation and commentary on Kant's *Anthropology from a Pragmatic Point of View* (1798, a compendium of Kant's lecture courses from 1772 to 1796, a period that coincides with Kant's Critical Philosophy). (Although written and submitted in 1961, Foucault's *Introduction à l'anthropologie* was published in its entirety only in 2008.)[38] In this text, Foucault interrogates the relation between the empirical and the transcendental sides of Kant, asking if the *Anthropology* can be seen as undermining Kant's theoretical-transcendental focus in the first *Critique*. Foucault thus proposes "to read the *Anthropology* as if the *Critique* [*of Pure Reason*] did not exist—which is what the text itself invites us to do."[39] Foucault notes suggestively that the *Anthropology* is "a book of daily exercise" and "not a theoretical book or a school textbook,"[40] an especially pertinent observation given Foucault's discussion of "spiritual exercises" in the last lecture courses. Foucault also aligns Kant's *Anthropology* with the *Conflict of the Faculties* (1798) and thereby with the countertradition described above: "Written at the same time, the two texts [the *Anthropology* and the *Conflict of the Faculties*] issue from the same vein of thought."[41] Just a year and a half before his death, Foucault thus comes full circle, as it were, returning to his philosophical point of departure: the conflict between history and system, empirical research and conditions of possibility, and contingency and necessity.

This brings us to the third idea on which Foucault's "ethical turn" is based: the self or subject. Although the new attention accorded to subjectivity was no doubt partly due to Foucault's encounter with Hadot's work on ancient spiritual exercises, this in itself cannot explain the magnitude of such a shift, for in embracing the concept of the subject, Foucault appeared to be swimming against the tide of twentieth-century Continental thought, including his own work, which, in the words of one critic, "proclaimed 'the disappearance of man' and explicitly repudiated the very concept of the individual as a 'subject.'"[42] Myriad phrases from Foucault's writings can be adduced in support of such a statement.

In the introduction to *The Use of Pleasure*, Foucault divides his oeuvre into the familiar three phases, corresponding to three "theoretical *shifts*," the last of which can be described as a "subjective turn":

> A theoretical shift . . . led me to examine the forms of discursive practices that articulated the human sciences. A theoretical shift had also been

required in order to analyze what is often described as the manifestations of "power"; it led me to examine, rather, manifold relations, the open strategies, and the rational techniques that articulate the exercise of powers. It appeared that I now had to undertake a third shift, in order to analyze what is termed "the subject."[43]

According to this passage, "the subject" is not only a new topic in Foucault's work, it requires a new philosophical approach, a *"theoretical* shift."[44] Although Foucault might be taken as saying that he had achieved a *new understanding* of the subject, thereby allowing him to reinterpret his earlier work as in fact being concerned with different ways of addressing the problem of the subject, this still begs the question of how Foucault can so easily assimilate a notion of which he had previously seemed highly suspicious (per the anti-subjective legacy of Nietzsche and Heidegger).

Responding in a 1984 interview to a question that implies a kind of apostasy in Foucault's sudden interest in the subject, Foucault avers:

No, I haven't forbidden it [people to talk to him about the subject in general]. Perhaps I did not explain myself adequately. What I rejected was the idea of starting out with a theory of the subject—as is done, for example, in phenomenology or existentialism—and, on the basis of this theory, asking for how a given form of knowledge/cognition [*connaissance*] was possible. What I wanted to try to do was try to show how the subject *constituted itself*, in one specific form or another, as a mad or healthy subject, as a delinquent or nondelinquent subject, through certain practices that were also games of truth, practices of power, and so on.[45]

Foucault makes three important points in this passage. First, he recasts his philosophy as *from the first* having been concerned in some sense with the subject, no doubt an effort to blunt the suggestion of a volte-face. Elsewhere in the same interview, Foucault similarly notes, "In actual fact, I have always been interested in this problem [the hermeneutics of the subject], even if I framed it somewhat differently."[46] This is certainly debatable, but the fact that Foucault *wants* to reinterpret his own work in this way is nevertheless revealing. Second, Foucault insists that his "subjective turn" not be construed as a return to *subjectivism*, to "the theory of the subject," that is, the transcendental ego and the subject-centered philosophies of Descartes, Kant, and Husserl; his implicit reference to Sartre in this context is somewhat dubious, given Sartre's insistence on "ontology" as opposed to "subjectivity" per se.[47] Moreover, Foucault asserts that in his estimation only Lacan and Heidegger have posed the question "What is the relation of the subject to the truth?" He thus declares that "I have tried to reflect on all this from the side of Heidegger and starting from Heidegger [*du côté de Heidegger et à partir de Heidegger*]."[48] Nevertheless, even if Foucault endeavors to systematize certain aspects along the lines of Heidegger's distinction between the ontological and ontic levels of analysis, Foucault's conception of the self is thoroughly historical (or genealogical, to use Foucault's preferred term). The third point—and in my view the most problematic, since it is belied by Foucault's own analyses—is the idea that Foucault's earlier work (*Madness and Civilization, Discipline and Punish*) showed how the subject "constituted itself," understood as some form of self-mastery. We might nevertheless clarify Foucault's intellectual evolution thus: as a shift from the subject being considered *as object*, as determined to a great degree by extrinsic forces—by institutions, discourses, or practices of power, or simply by historical forces—to the subject being considered *as subject*, as *self*-constituting (self-forming) in a more original or creative way, namely as an "ethical" relation with oneself[49]: "The kind of relationship you ought to have with yourself, *rapport à soi*, which I call ethics and which determines how the individual is supposed to *constitute himself* as a moral subject of his own actions."[50] It would, then, appear to be a matter of two different *kinds* of subject: (1) the marginal, oppressed subject that had been the focus of Foucault's earlier work, and (2) the subject that has social freedom—even if in certain situations, for example, the homosexual subject, these can be viewed as two poles of the same subject.[51] Indeed, one of Foucault's last interviews is titled "The Ethics of the Concern [Care, *souci*] of the Self as a Practice of Freedom."

The fact that many commentators describe this shift in Foucault's late work as that from *subjection* (being constituted by some power) to *subjectivation* (having the power to self-constitute) would appear to confirm my interpretation. According to Foucault, "Subjectivation [is] the process by which one obtains the constitution of a subject, more precisely, of a subjectivity, which is obviously but one of the possibilities of the organization of a self-consciousness."[52] Nevertheless, the seeming tension and radical shift between passive subjection (in Foucault's work between 1961 and 1975) and an active self-constitution (1980–84) remains one of the more intractable points of contention in Foucault scholarship.[53] For how to transform an oppressed subject—a *passive* entity (constituted), a slave to history, institutions, discourse, and power—into a "practice of freedom," an *active* entity (self-constituting) that creates itself, like an artwork, marking a new beginning and distinguishing itself from all other subjects. As we will shortly see, Foucault is especially concerned with how to treat the various "liberation" movements that sprang up in the late 1960s and 1970s (e.g., decolonization, the women's movement, the gay rights movement, sexual liberation in general), the idea of which Foucault found to be philosophically problematic, even if he personally supported such movements. Given his own homosexuality and the burgeoning gay culture in San Francisco, with which Foucault became intimately familiar during his time as a visiting professor at the University of California, Berkeley, starting in 1980, Foucault could not have been unmoved by the quandary of the homosexual subject: the desire to have one's sexuality accepted by society while at the same time maintaining a distinctive subculture that defined itself in opposition to mainstream social norms.⁵⁴ But by infusing the notion of the subject with a heightened sense of agency and freedom, Foucault risked falling into the existentialist trap he spent his life trying to avoid: "When I was a young man, [Sartre] was the one—along with everything he represented . . . from whom I wanted to free myself."⁵⁵ Before delving into Foucault's existentialist tendencies, let us first explore what Foucault means by an "ethics of the self."

The "Ethics of the Self": The 1981–82 lecture course

I begin this discussion by noting the controversial nature of Foucault's work on ancient Greek culture, which has been criticized by some specialists as philologically inadequate or overly schematic.⁵⁶ Foucault himself invites such critiques by adding the following note to *The Use of Pleasure* (*The History of Sexuality*, volume two):

> I am neither a Hellenist nor a Latinist. But it seemed to me that if I gave enough care, patience, modesty, and attention to the task, it would be possible to gain sufficient familiarity with the ancient Greek and Roman texts; that is, a familiarity that would allow me—in keeping with a practice that is doubtless fundamental to Western philosophy—to examine both the difference that keeps us at a remove from a way of thinking in which we recognize the origin of our own, and the proximity that remains in spite of that distance which we never cease to explore.⁵⁷

Foucault is perhaps being overly modest. Gros contends that Foucault was actually quite knowledgeable about Greek language and culture, noting that Foucault had discussed archaic Greek law in his first course at the Collège de France in 1971.⁵⁸ It should also be said that most of the critiques of Foucault's philology are based solely on the published material, before the lecture courses became widely available. Thus, Alexander Nehamas, who had access to a few of the unpublished lectures, is much more positive in his assessment of the late Foucault in his 1998 book *The Art of Living: Socratic Reflections from Plato to Foucault*.⁵⁹ This controversy has little bearing on the present chapter, however, since what interests me is not how well Foucault knows or manipulates his Greek sources but what kind of philosophy he tried to extract from them.

One may nevertheless ask: Why the Greeks? Why did Foucault require a new *Ansatzpunkt*?⁶⁰ For one thing, by going back to the Greeks, to the birth of philosophy, like Nietzsche and Heidegger before him, Foucault can bypass both Christian subjectivity as well as and the subjectivisms that grew up after and around it (Augustinian introspection, Cartesian self-evidence,

Kantian conditions of possibility, Husserlian intentionality) and examine the historical conditions under which they could emerge. Moreover, since Greek philosophy is metaphysical-objectivist in nature (the search for the immutable reality behind changing appearances), Foucault is able to claim that if, for the Greeks, only an ethical subject can constitute itself as a philosophical subject, then philosophy, no matter its theoretical ambitions, is at bottom an ethical-practical endeavor: "As he is, the subject is not capable of truth . . . there can be no truth without a conversion or a transformation of the subject."[61] This is what is lost in the "subjective turn" of modern philosophy, according to Foucault: "Before Descartes, one could not be impure, immoral, and know the truth. With Descartes, direct evidence is enough. After Descartes, we have a non-ascetic subject of knowledge. This change makes possible the institution of modern science."[62] Moreover, Foucault speaks of Descartes's "intellectual method," as exemplified in the *Meditationes de prima philosophia* (1641), which is developed in contradistinction to the spiritual exercise: "I do not think we can understand the meticulousness with which [Descartes] defines his intellectual method unless we have clearly in mind his negative target . . . which is precisely these methods of spiritual exercise that were frequently practiced within Christianity and which derived from the spiritual exercises of Antiquity, especially from Stoicism."[63] Objective, scientific knowledge becomes possible once it is detached from the ethical inclinations of the scientist; the search for scientific truth thus becomes an amoral enterprise. To the extent that modern (analytical) philosophy models itself on science and mathematics, it separates the search for truth from the ethical subject.

But there is another reason to return to the Greeks: In resurrecting the Greek conception of the self, Foucault refutes the assumption that our modern (Christian) liberal-democratic subject is necessarily superior to all others that came before, an assumption that all of Foucault's work seeks in some way to debunk. Richard Rorty observes that

> like Habermas and Sellars, [Foucault] accepts Mead's view that the self is a creation of society. Unlike them, he is not prepared to admit that the selves shaped by modern liberal societies are better than the selves earlier societies created. A large part of Foucault's work—the most valuable part, in my view—consists in showing how the patterns of acculturation characteristic of liberal societies have imposed on their members kinds of constraints of which older, premodern societies had not dreamed. He is not, however, willing to see these constraints as compensated for by a decrease in pain.[64]

In other words, the social constraints placed on the modern individual do not outweigh, in Foucault's mind, the progress that has been made in reducing social injustice and physical cruelty; or, put another way, the "progress" has been anything but. Thus, to the extent that, as Hadot observes, Foucault's focus on ancient Greek culture "was meant to offer contemporary man a model of life,"[65] the concept of "the care of the self" (*le souci de soi*), based on the primacy of the relation to oneself (*le rapport à soi*), appears to offer Foucault an alternate path, as it were, beyond the conundrum of "modern individualism"—namely, how the self can be a true individual if it is entirely a social creation, a problem whose importance had climaxed in existentialism and its concept of authenticity, before it was abruptly abandoned (by structuralism) along with the discourse of the subject.[66] This is not to say that the Greek concept of the "self" provided the *solution* to this problem: "I am not looking for an alternative [in the Greek context]; you can't find the solution of a problem in the solution of a problem raised at another moment by other people."[67] Foucault is in fact not interested in "solutions" *tout court* (because they are definitive and narrowly prescriptive) but rather in new ways of thinking about things, what he calls "problematizations" (*les problématiques*).[68] Thus, Foucault is not suggesting that the Greek conception of the self can simply be superimposed on the contemporary situation; rather, it offers a model of how it might be possible to rethink the subject in the wake of the critique of modern subjectivity in Nietzsche and Heidegger.[69]

Foucault begins his 1981–82 lecture course (*The Hermeneutics of the Subject*) by making a fundamental distinction between the Delphic maxim *gnôthi seauton* (know thyself) and the *epimeleia heautou* ("the care of the self"), which Socrates highlights in the *Apology*: "For I do nothing but go about persuading you all, old and young alike, not to take thought for your persons or your properties, but first and chiefly to care about the greatest improvement of the soul."[70] Foucault's basic contention is that "the *epimeleia heautou* is . . . the justificatory framework, ground, and foundation for the imperative 'know yourself,'"[71] thereby reversing the priority traditionally ascribed to the latter. Foucault asks, "Why did Western thought and philosophy neglect the notion of *epimeleia heautou* (care of the self) in its reconstruction of its own history? How did it come about that we accorded so much privilege, value, and intensity to the 'know yourself?'"[72] As is his custom, Foucault aims to articulate a *counter-history* that subverts and overturns the dominant understanding: "I have therefore tried to explore the possibilities of a genealogy of the subject while knowing that historians prefer the history of objects and philosophers prefer the subject who has no history."[73] Foucault's attitude thus represents a "philosophical and ethical position on history," as one critic remarks.[74]

Given the paucity of references to the "care of the self" in the Platonic corpus, much of Foucault's case regarding the *epimeleia heautou* is based on *Alcibiades I*, whose authenticity as a Platonic dialogue has been the subject of much debate.[75] This dialogue is crucial for Foucault's effort to root the tradition of the "care of the self" in Plato, thereby highlighting what is, for Foucault, an unheralded countertradition of ancient philosophy. For Foucault insists that the idea of caring for oneself, like the idea of philosophy as a way of life, with which it is "coextensive,"[76] was "a truly general phenomenon" in Greek and Roman antiquity,[77] and not just in philosophy; it was rather a "precept of life."[78] Nevertheless, it is its specifically philosophical meaning that interests Foucault.

In addition to Plato, Foucault proposes to treat what he calls the "golden age of the culture of the self,"[79] that is, "from the period of Roman Stoicism in its prime, with Musonius Rufus, up to Marcus Aurelius," a period that ends "just before the spread of Christianity and the appearance of the first great Christian thinkers."[80] The broad historical scope of Foucault's analyses—almost 600 years, covering a diversity of philosophical traditions—raises the question of how Foucault can make seemingly general statements about the *epimeleia heautou* while also providing a "*history* of the practices of subjectivity."[81] This is, of course, the same tension that pervades all of Foucault's "histories" and leads many to wonder if Foucault is more of an intellectual historian than a philosopher, properly speaking (as Foucault's choice of the title for his chair at the Collège de France would lead us to believe: History of Systems of Thought). However, throughout Foucault's oeuvre—including his methodological shift from "archeology" to "genealogy," from showing the *effects* of power to showing the *operation* of power—one can see that Foucault was always interested in the *systematic* or *structural* aspect of history,[82] that is, in how an historical investigation can reveal contingent patterns that show themselves as analytical necessities, or what Foucault calls (paradoxically) the "historical a priori" (recalling the methodology of Fernand Braudel and the *Annales* historians).[83]

On the most general level, Foucault sees the whole tradition of the *epimeleia heautou* as divisible into three aspects: (1) "an *attitude* towards the self, others, and the world"; (2) "a certain *form of attention*" directed toward "what we think and what takes place in our thought"; (3) "*actions on the self by the self* . . . by which one changes, purifies, transforms, and transfigures oneself*,*" actions such as "techniques of meditation, of memorization of the past, of examination of conscience, of checking representations which appear in the mind."[84] It is from the third aspect—from the idea of a *practical relation* of the self to itself, a self-transformation or *conversion* (a term that Foucault will regularly employ)—that Foucault derives the idea of an "ethics of the self."

But how can there be an "ethics" of the self? Seemingly, by definition, "ethics" involves our relations with others; it is a matter of rules or norms of conduct. According to Foucault, it is the Christian tradition that has predisposed us to see ethics as primarily other-directed (altruism): "Christianity and the modern world has based all these themes and codes of moral strictness on a morality of non-egotism, whereas in actual fact they were born within an environment strongly marked by the obligation to take care of oneself."[85] On the other hand, the care of the self is not to be confused with simple egotism or narcissism. As we saw above, Foucault seizes on the Greek concept of *êthos*—character, disposition, guiding beliefs, or values—as the etymological basis for thinking this ethics of the self.

(*Êthos* is the root of *ethikos*: ethics, the study of morals.) Through the contrast between the "ethics of the self," the relation of the self to the self, and the other-directed ethics of Christianity, Foucault aims to provide a pre-Christian "genealogy of morals."

As befits his structural or systematic intuitions, Foucault deems the *epimeleia heautou* to be "ontologically" prior, in addition to being historically prior, to the idea of altruism: "I don't think we can say that the Greek who cares for himself must first care for others. To my mind that view came later. Care for others should not be put before the care of oneself. The care of the self is ethically prior in that the relationship with oneself is ontologically prior."[86] Although this comes close to articulating a "theory of the subject," Foucault would insist that his analysis is historically ("the Greek who . . .") rather than transcendentally grounded. Nevertheless, there is still a debate about whether "Socrates' project was more private than Foucault allows," as Nehamas asserts. According to Nehamas, "Socrates' primary object of care is his own self, his own soul, not the soul of others."[87] I do not think that Foucault would necessarily disagree on this point,[88] unless "primary" also means "sole" (Nehamas appears to be somewhat equivocal on this). As I read Foucault, care for oneself (in Plato) is not opposed to care for others as egotism is opposed to altruism; rather the "care of the self" is "ethically prior" in the sense that one must first *master oneself* to be able to treat the other ethically. Thus, to be generous with the other, I must first surmount my stinginess; to not be easily provoked and harm the other, I must first be able to overcome or control my anger, and so on. In other words, the ethical relation to the other is contingent on my own ability to act ethically, on my *êthos*, which I modify through various "techniques of the self" (meditation, examination of conscience, *askesis*, etc.). Nevertheless, Foucault does see Plato's understanding of the *epimeleia heautou* as a notion that "quite clearly opened out onto the question of the city-state, of others, of the *politeia* of *dikaiosunê*,"[89] without thereby negating the idea that the care of the self is "ontologically prior." He contrasts this (Platonic) orientation with the way in which, in the first and second centuries AD, this notion develops into a "self-sufficient end, without the care of others being the ultimate aim and indicator by which the care of the self is valued."[90] However, even if, as in this later development, "the self is the definitive and sole aim of the care of the self,"[91] one could still not properly speak of "egotism" or "selfishness"; for it in fact marks a turn to an ascetic form of life, the precursor to Christian monasticism (even if, in Christianity, the aspirant absconds in order to devote himself or herself entirely to God).

Although in *principle* the injunction to "take care of yourself" is universal in the sense that it is addressed to all, in *practice*, however, only "a very small number of individuals" will actually heed this call.[92] The care of the self can thus be described as an "elite privilege"[93]:

> In reality, care of the self in ancient Greek and Roman culture was never really seen, laid down, or affirmed as a universal law valid for every

individual regardless of his mode of life. The care of the self always entails a choice of mode of one's life, that is to say, a division between those who have chosen this mode of life and the rest.[94]

Foucault notes that the division between the *oi prôtoi* and the *oi pôlloi*, the elite and the many, the privileged and the masses, is fundamental to ancient culture. But as the (existentialist-sounding) word "choice" indicates, it is not a matter of a preexisting elite (the aristocracy) whose ranks form the natural constituency of the care of the self; the "elite" is self-chosen. Foucault's interest in the idea of the care of the self cannot therefore be taken as evidence of an "elitist," anti-egalitarian attitude. On the contrary, the separation between the *oi prôtoi* and the *oi pôlloi* is not "hierarchical" (socially determined) but "practical": "It is a practical division by which those who are capable [of tending to the self] are distinguished from those who are not. It is no longer the individual's status that, in advance and by birth, defines the difference that sets him apart from the mass and the others."[95] It is rather "the individual's relation to the self" that determines his or her membership in the *oi prôtoi* or the *oi pôlloi*[96]; membership in the former amounts to an affirmation of autonomy (self-overcoming and self-mastery) and uniqueness:

> The effect, meaning, and aim of taking care of oneself is to distinguish oneself from the crowd, from the majority, from the *oi polloi* [the many] who are, precisely, the people absorbed in daily life. There will be an ethical divide then . . . the principle "take care of yourself" can only be carried out by a moral elite and those with the ability to save themselves.[97]

This willful separation from the many places Foucault's ethics of the self in close proximity to the existentialist dichotomy between the *authentic* individual and the masses, between *choosing* one's own mode of being and the socially determined "they-self" (*das Man*). Indeed, Foucault suggests that in the modern world, individuality is an end to be *achieved*, an object of *constant striving*,[98] as opposed to simply being a function of the rights conferred by a liberal political order. It further suggests that, in an egalitarian context, the distinction between the few and the many should not be based on an extrinsic conception of "merit"—that is, wealth, power, success, fame—but rather on the intrinsic self-to-self relation, which is at once a moral and aesthetic ideal. Indeed, as noted above, there is an intimate association between the ethics of the self and what Foucault calls "styles of existence."[99]

In keeping with what one can only characterize as a voluntarist-existentialist conception of the care of the self, in which the movement from being part of "the many" to being one of "the few" involves a deliberate *choice* to change the orientation of one's life, Foucault carefully distinguishes the Greek-philosophical from the Christian concept of conversion. Unlike the religious variety, the Greek concept of conversion is about a process rather than a moment; it is a kind of initiation that occurs at the beginning of philosophy, not the end result of a philosophical program. Although he does not reference conversion specifically in this passage, Pierre Hadot remarks—with heavy existentialist overtones—that

> at least since the time of Socrates, the choice of a way of life . . . stands at the beginning, in a complex interrelation with critical reaction to other existential attitudes, with a global vision of a certain way of living and of seeing the world, and with voluntary decision itself. . . . Philosophical discourse, then, originates in a choice of life and an existential option—not vice versa.[100]

The Greek-philosophical notion of conversion thus shows itself as an ethic of existentialism *avant la lettre*.[101]

Foucault calls conversion "one of the most important technologies of the self the West has known."[102] It is roughly synonymous with the idea of self-transformation ("there can be no truth without a conversion or a transformation of the subject"),[103] and it is at the heart of the "ethics of the self" ("the notion of conversion is also critically important in connection with morality").[104] Despite its obvious importance for Christianity, Foucault insists that its role should not be restricted to religion: "The notion of conversion is also an important philosophical notion that played a decisive role in philosophy, in practical philosophy . . . [and] in connection with morality."[105] In Plato, the idea of conversion is expressed in the term *epistrophê*, which means at once a "turning away" from the world of appearances, the "soul's release from the body," and emancipation through self-knowledge.[106] Foucault follows Hadot in asserting that the Platonic *epistrophê* and the Christian *metanoia* are the "two great models of conversion in Western culture." The first involves a movement of return and recollection, "the soul's return to its source"; in the second there is a radical change, a shedding of one's former self and the rebirth or resurrection in a new self: "a radical renewal."[107] Foucault notes that *metanoia* had negative connotations in ancient Greek texts; it was associated with repentance and thus was "something to be avoided."[108] Structurally speaking, the largest difference between the two models involves what Foucault terms a "trans-subjectivation" in the Christian version[109]: a "radical" and "sudden" change, a transition from one type of being to another, and renunciation of the self and subsequent rebirth.[110] On the other hand, according to the philosophical concept of conversion, "*self*-subjectivation," there is a gradual process of becoming; it is thus less a "break within the self" than "a break with everything around the self." Speaking of Marcus Aurelius, Foucault notes that "to make the soul great [*megalophrosynê*] means to free it from this framework [the bonds and constraints to which one has had to submit one's opinions], from all this tissue that surrounds, fixes, and delimits it."[111] Thus, Foucault sees the philosophical version of conversion as implying a greater degree of subjective autonomy. Two other differences with Christian conversion involve introspection ("the self must be kept before your eyes") and resoluteness/deliberateness ("you must advance toward the self as you advance toward an end").[112] It is difficult, however, based on Foucault's pronouncements, to discern how the inside is supposed to be distinguished from the outside in the idea of the conversion of the self (or conversion "to" the self, as Foucault sometimes terms it); for all of Foucault's analyses point to a kind of inner transformation regardless of the relation to external forces. He thus appears, at times, to be exaggerating the differences to draw a cleaner contrast with Christian conversion.

More precisely, Foucault aims to situate the ancient practices of conversion *between* Platonic *epistrophê* and the Christian *metanoia*. Switching to the systematic-structural level, Foucault identifies four types of expressions that denote "actions" of the self on the self[113]: (1) the most literal is the idea of "turning round toward the self" (*metanoia/convertere*), which involves "an overall movement of existence"; (2) expressions that refer to withdrawal, "retiring into the self," or "descending to the depths of oneself," thereby connoting the idea of the self as a "fortress" or "citadel"; (3) expressions that refer to a legalistic assertion of "rights one has over oneself," namely emancipation from "debts and obligations" but also honoring and respecting oneself; (4) expressions that "designate a certain kind of constant relationship to the self" such as mastery or sovereignty, or of "experiencing delight with oneself."[114] Conversion is not, however, simply a matter of individual well-being; it is a propaedeutic for philosophy: "In all ancient philosophy there is the idea of conversion ... which alone can give access to the truth."[115] Thus, the concept of the "care of the self" that interests Foucault—namely the philosophical understanding—is the one that entails the question: "How must I transform my own self so as to be able to have access to the truth?"[116] This is the question that is abandoned by Descartes and modern philosophy, with its emphasis on neutral, objective, and value-free knowledge. It is in this movement from the care of the self to self-knowledge, from the ethics of the self to normative ethics, from philosophy as a way of life toward philosophy as theoretical knowledge, that Foucault's cultural critique of modernity can be located.

Ethics, politics, and freedom: Specters of Sartre

For the reader of the late Foucault, the burning question is, what use can all of this have for us, denizens of the twentieth or twenty-first centuries? Foucault's interest in antiquity is obviously not simply antiquarian. Foucault believes in using history for life, as Nietzsche taught in his Untimely Meditation "The Use and Disadvantage of History for Life" (a text Foucault comments on extensively in his pivotal 1971 essay "Nietzsche, Genealogy,

History").[117] In his last interview, conducted just a month before his death, Foucault addresses the question of the pertinence of ancient morality:

> From a strictly philosophical point of view, the morality of Greek Antiquity and contemporary morality have nothing in common. On the other hand, if you take them for what they prescribe, intimate and advise, they are extraordinarily close. It's the proximity and difference that we must bring to light and, through their interplay, we must show how the same advice given by ancient morality can work [*jouer*, play] differently in the style of contemporary morality.[118]

Although in this instance Foucault appears to sound a hopeful note with regard to the example of the ancient ethics, he had also stated (just two years earlier) that "I think that we may have to suspect that we find it impossible today to constitute an ethic of the self."[119] Be that as it may, the question is why Greek morality in particular should be worthy of attention as a practical concern of the present, as opposed to being of merely scholarly interest. In another late interview, Foucault offers a more precise rationale for the importance of Greek morality, stressing the existential commonalties:

> I wonder if our problem nowadays is not, in a way similar to this [ancient] one, since most of us no longer believe that ethics is founded in religion, nor do we want a legal system to intervene in our moral, personal, private life. Recent liberation movements suffer from the fact that they cannot find any principle on which to base the elaboration of a new ethics. They need an ethics, but they cannot find any other ethics than an ethics founded on so-called scientific knowledge of what the self is, what desire is, what the unconscious is, and so on. I am struck by this similarity of problems.[120]

Like the Greeks, who sought to define the self as a *practice* (technologies of the self, care of the self) in the absence of any guiding principle or theory about the self, the modern, liberal-democratic subject finds itself in an analogous *situation*, in which "knowledge" about the self is revealed (as per Foucault's philosophy) to be the product of contingent effects of institutional or disciplinary power. Whether this analogy is actually warranted or legitimate is less important than the fact that Foucault finds in the "ethics of the self" a corollary for the lack of a common ground or reference point in religion, science, or other normative system. One erects one's own "system," which is unique to oneself and that counters all systems. In effect, Foucault seeks to both contest and to reconfigure the meaning of "modern individualism." Against the "familiar expressions that continue to permeate our discourse—like getting back to oneself, being oneself, being authentic, etcetera,"[121] Foucault counterposes a self with no nature and no essence, the other to all others.

The reference to contemporary "liberation movements" in the above-quoted passage raises the question of the relation of the ethics of the self to politics—a highly vexed question I have deferred until this section. Before turning to such a discussion, however, I first want to draw attention to the contrast between what in the preceding passage Foucault calls a "style" of morality and "scientific knowledge of what the self is." Like Sartre, Foucault holds that the self, as a "practice of freedom," cannot be the object of scientific inquiry. Indeed, the idea of the "ethics of the self," as we have explored it in this chapter, is an irreducibly *aesthetic* concept; the *rapport à soi* is nothing but self-creation, self-invention, self-making, in the tradition of Nietzsche and Sartre.[122] However, when asked, in an interview, how his view of the "ethics of the self" differs from Sartrean existentialism, Foucault is evasive:

> I think that from the theoretical point of view, Sartre avoids the idea of the self as something that is given to us, but through the moral notion of authenticity, he turns back to the idea that we have to be ourselves—to be truly our true self. I think that the only acceptable practical consequence of what Sartre has said is to link his theoretical insight to the practice of creativity—and not that of authenticity. From the idea that the self is not given to us, I think that there is only one practical consequence: we have to create ourselves as a work of art. In his analyses of Baudelaire, Flaubert, and so on, it is interesting to see that Sartre refers the work of creation to a certain relation to oneself—the author to himself—which has the form of authenticity or inauthenticity. I would like to say exactly the contrary: we should not have to refer the creative activity of somebody to the kind of relation he has to himself, but should relate the kind of relation one has to oneself to a creative activity.[123]

The interviewer interjects that this "sounds like Nietzsche's observation in *The Gay Science* that one should create one's life by giving style to it though long practice and daily work." To which Foucault replies, "Yes, my view is much closer to Nietzsche's, than to Sartre's."[124]

That Foucault would much prefer to be seen as closer to Nietzsche than to Sartre is certainly understandable.[125] As noted above, Foucault had spent the early part of his career trying to free himself from Sartre's influence. However, in his later years (coincidentally after Sartre's death in 1980), Foucault actually draws closer, in my view, to the author of *Being and Nothingness*. I thus completely agree with Gary Gutting, who sees Foucault's remark as "an obvious distortion of Sartre's conception of authenticity, which involves total acceptance of the fact that any self (essence) we have is our own free creation."[126] Gutting notes that Sartre offers a comparable "aesthetic model of self-making" in his famous 1946 lecture "Existentialism Is a Humanism."[127] It would appear that Gutting is thinking about the following passage from Sartre's lecture:

> No one can tell what the painting of tomorrow will be like; one cannot judge a painting until it is done. What has that to do with morality? We

are in the same creative situation. We never speak of a work of art as irresponsible; when we are discussing a canvas by Picasso, we understand very well that the composition became what it is at the time when he was painting it, and that his works are part and parcel of his entire life. It is the same upon the plane of morality. There is this in common between art and morality, that in both we have to do with creation and invention. We cannot decide a priori what it is that should be done.[128]

In other words, just as the true artwork is not the product of principles but of free creativity in a situation, true (authentic) moral choice presupposes a creative element irreducible to principles; otherwise it is merely a mechanical matter of applying a rule (grounded in reason, tradition, or religion) and as such nullifies the kind of freedom that true morality requires. Indeed, this idea fulfills Foucault's condition that "we have to create ourselves as a work of art" (quoted above).[129]

We now turn to the political implications of the ethics of the self. While the 1981–82 course is concerned mostly with the care of the self, it too, like the contemporaneous interviews, posits an essential relation to politics:

> In the type of analysis I have been trying to advance for some time you can see that power relations, governmentality [*gouvernmentalité*], the government of the self and of others, and the relationship of the self to self constitute a chain, a thread, and I think that it is around these notions that we should be able to connect together the question of politics and the question of ethics.[130]

In effect, Foucault is subsuming his earlier analyses of power under the rubric of "governmentality" (the only mention of this term in the 1981–82 course), by which "power" is *redefined* to include the *rapport à soi*: "It seems to me that the analysis of governmentality—that is, power as a set of reversible relationships—must refer to an ethics of the subject defined by the relationship of self to self."[131] What has changed, then, with the concept of governmentality,[132] is the idea of *reversibility*, the idea that *effective resistance is always possible, even necessary*; for resistance is not outside power but constitutes its very dynamic: "If there were no possibility of resistance [of violent resistance, flight, deception, strategies capable of reversing the situation], there would be no power relations at all."[133] The terminological shift from "power relations" (or "power/discourse"), employed in the mid-1970s, to "governmentality" in the late 1970s and 1980s,[134] allows Foucault to connect conceptually the two realms of ethics and politics: "the government of the self *and* of others." Thus, Gros observes, "Foucault does not abandon politics to dedicate himself to ethics, but complicates the study of governmentalities through the exploration of the care of the self."[135] Hence the titles of Foucault's final two course lectures: *The Government of Self and Others* (1982–83), *The Courage of Truth: The Government of*

Self and Others II 1983–84); these are, in fact, devoted to this redefinition of power.

While this nexus between the ethics of the self and politics helps define the contemporary relevance of ancient morality, it is also the most controversial part of Foucault's late thought. Thus, Richard Rorty, while admiring Foucault's ability to highlight "a new set of dangers to democratic societies," nevertheless sees the extension of private ethics into politics as deeply misguided:

> Much of the time, [Foucault's] only politics was the standard liberal's attempt to alleviate unnecessary suffering. . . . At other times, Foucault ran together his moral and ethical identity—his sense of responsibility to others and his *rapport à soi*. At these times, like Nietzsche, he projected his own search for autonomy out into the public space. In both his and Nietzsche's case, the results were bad.[136]

Although one critic laments that Rorty here "misinterprets Foucault, downplaying the political and radical implications of his work,"[137] in fact Rorty sees Foucault's projection of the private into the public as *too* radical, even dangerous:

> The Romantic intellectual's goal of self-overcoming and self-invention seems to me a good model . . . for an individual human being, but a very bad model for society. We should not try to find a societal counterpart to the desire for autonomy. Trying to do so leads to Hitlerlike and Maolike fantasies about "creating a new kind of human being." Societies are not quasi-persons; they are at their (at their liberal, social democratic best) compromises between persons.[138]

This passage demonstrates why Rorty, in his own work, insists on the strict separation between the public and private realms (see Chapter 4); for our private search for meaning and autonomy from social determination (irony) is incompatible with the requirements of liberal democracy (consensus). Indeed, only fascist or totalitarian societies would appear to be able to realize this aesthetic ideal of individual autonomy on a collective level. But is this "projection" of private autonomy into the public sphere in fact what Foucault is proposing?

It is extremely doubtful that Foucault would hold that the political significance of the care of the self lies in a collective autonomy, the volitional self-fashioning of an entire nation or people, given his categorical assertion that "the search for a form of morality that would be acceptable to everyone—in the sense that everyone would have to submit to it—would be catastrophic."[139] In fact, Foucault conceives of the "urgent, fundamental, and politically indispensable task" of the ethics of the self in terms of *resistance*: "There is no first or final point of resistance to political power other than the relation one has to oneself."[140] And, according to Foucault, "*resistance is the main word, the key word*" in relations of power.[141] This suggests that the ethics of the self is indeed the crucial link that would connect Foucault's analyses of power with some kind of progressive politics (for otherwise, resistance would be futile).

In a late interview, Foucault further specifies that

> my point is not that everything is bad, but that everything is dangerous, which is not exactly the same as bad. If everything is dangerous, then we always have something to do. My position leads not to apathy but to a hyper- and pessimistic activism. I think that the ethico-political choice we have to make every day is to determine which is the main danger.[142]

Foucault makes several interrelated points in this important passage: (1) he dismisses the critique of his philosophy as simply pessimistic and "one-sided,"[143] leading to apathy; (2) he connects his philosophy to "activism," construed as a kind of extreme vigilance toward ever-present threats (i.e., resistance); (3) by using the hyphenated term "ethico-political," Foucault implies *both* that the ethics of the self has a fundamental political dimension and that an authentic politics is rooted in the *rapport à soi*, thereby countering the assumption that his late turn to the care and ethics of the self represented a retreat from politics; (4) Foucault inadvertently emphasizes the existentialist interpretation of his philosophy in the phrase "ethico-political *choice* we have to make every day," which is strongly reminiscent of Sartre's slogan "we are condemned to be free." Although Foucault would no doubt have vigorously contested the last point, it bears noting, as Gutting does, that "Foucault's ethical objection to modern practices seems to have been broadly existentialist: they make people be something they have not *chosen for themselves*."[144] While this might be construed as banal or even vacuous—since *any* social practice is necessarily impositional (e.g., all education can be construed as a kind of indoctrination), the relevant point is that, by making people aware of the contingency of their practices, Foucault (like Nietzsche and Sartre) defines individual freedom "aesthetically" as self-overcoming and self-invention, as opposed to "politically," in terms of liberation, where "liberation" is understood in purely oppositional terms as emancipation and the return to some natural or original state.

This distinction is crucial with regard to Foucault's conception of an authentic politics:

> I have always been somewhat suspicious of the notion of liberation, because if it is not treated with precautions and within certain limits, one runs the risk of falling back on the idea that there exists a human nature or base that, as a consequence of certain historical, economic, and social processes, has been concealed, alienated, or imprisoned in and by mechanisms of repression. According to this hypothesis, all

> that is required is to break these repressive deadlocks and man will be reconciled with himself, rediscover his nature or regain contact with his origin, and reestablish a full and positive relation with himself. . . . But we know very well . . . that this practice of liberation is not in itself sufficient to define the practices of freedom that will still be needed if this people, this society, and these individuals are to be able to define admissible and acceptable forms of existence or political society. This is why I emphasize practices of freedom over processes of liberation. . . . This ethical problem of the definition of practices of freedom, it seems to me, is much more important than [for example] the rather repetitive affirmation that sexuality or desire must be liberated.[145]

Foucault here refers obliquely to his "repressive hypothesis" as outlined in the first volume of *The History of Sexuality*, in which he argued against the idea that simply ending sexual repression would lead to true sexual and political liberation. (Foucault's critique of liberation in this passage also applies to Marxism, as James Marshall points out.)[146] Foucault is thus effectively saying that if his earlier work on the asylum, the prison, and on sexuality is construed merely as efforts to "liberate," such an understanding would only reveal their "insufficiency," for this conception of freedom-as-liberation presupposes an inviolate " true " or " universal " self, and thus an act of self-discovery (as in psychoanalysis, for example), as opposed to one of self-making. Hence "liberation" is illusory: It merely substitutes one oppressive force for another that is even more insidious, insofar as it appears to be "inherent" or "natural." Put another way: One does not liberate oneself from a discourse that defines the self by falling back on another discourse that defines the self ("human nature"). One must develop ever new and contingent self-definitions: "My books don't tell people what to do. . . . People have to build their own ethics."[147] Nevertheless, it can be asked: How can individual practices of freedom function on the interindividual level without falling into the problem of projecting autonomy into the public realm, as Rorty describes it?

Foucault does not, in my estimation, provide a satisfactory answer to this question. On at least one occasion, Foucault (in the 1981–82 course) does make the observation that the care of the self cannot be abstracted from the social milieu and group membership, thereby introducing an element of reciprocity into the ethics of the self:

> The care of the self is expressed and appears in this splitting into, or rather this belonging to a sect or group. If you like, you cannot take care of the self in the realm and the form of the universal. The care of the self cannot appear and, above all, cannot be practiced simply by virtue of being human as such, just by belonging to the human community. . . . It can only be practiced within the group, and within the group in its distinctive character.[148]

For Foucault, the abstract individual necessarily appears in the form of the universal; it is group membership that makes the individual historical and contingent, and makes possible the *rapport à soi*. One does not invent oneself in a vacuum, but only *in* and, to some extent, *for* the group. Thus, individual autonomies are reciprocal within the group they constitute. In effect, this is the same place where Sartre ends up (as we saw in Chapter 1), when he revises his individualist position of *Being and Nothingness* to encompass the authentic mode of "group praxis" in the *Critique of Dialectical Reason*. But Foucault would no doubt disavow any such connection.

Another way of approaching the conundrum of integrating individual ethics with the collective is illustrated in this passage (from an interview conducted in 1980):

> In a sense, I am a moralist, insofar as I believe that one of the tasks, one of the meanings of human existence—the source of human freedom—is never to accept anything as definitive, untouchable, obvious, or immobile. No aspect of reality should be allowed to become a definitive and inhuman law for us. We have to rise up against all forms of power. . . . Power is anything that tends to render immobile and untouchable those things that are offered to us as real, as true, as good.[149]

I interpret the "we" in this passage as denoting a *collective* (Sartre's "group praxis") rather than a *collection* (Sartre's "seriality").[150] Thus the very *possibility* of ethics of the self is here tied to resistance to power understood as a force of authority that seeks to undermine self-making by subjugating it to a fixed and universal law (whether under the guise of science, religion, or reason). Against Rorty (whose philosophy is nevertheless based on the idea that "no aspect of reality should be allowed to become a definitive and inhuman law for us"), but close to the later Sartre, Foucault claims that there is no self-making without resistance to power, without some effort to counter (transcend) the ossifying effects of power (Sartre's "practico-inert") though the reciprocal *rapport à soi* within a group, the "we" in the above passage.

***

By way of conclusion, I would note that, in my view, the main objections to Foucault's ethics of the self are as follows: (1) how to integrate the ethics of the self with social life and the relation to others (reciprocity), particularly when there is a conflict between the two; (2) how the ethics of the self can be a basis for politics, when it immediately concerns the individual "practice of freedom," which necessarily privileges the *souci de soi* over social cohesion; (3) how a modern ethics of the self is not simply the product of bourgeois liberalism rather than its antithesis.

The first problem is that of normativity. Indeed, Foucault is against any such hint of a normative or prescriptive ethics. Nevertheless, when confronted with an extreme example—say, the outcast neo-Nazi individualist—why would his or her *rapport à soi* be any less genuine (creative, inventive) than that of the outcast homosexual who strives to achieve social acceptance? Both are undoubtedly forms of resistance to the prevailing powers that be (although the second has recently been far more successful in gaining recognition). In other words, does the "ethics of the self" have any limit in regard to its specific moral content (as for Rorty, it would be the liberal-democratic idea that we reduce unnecessary suffering, and for Sartre, it would be the maximization of human freedom)?[151]

The second point raises the specter of anarchism: If everyone goes his or her own way, then rather than a "nondisciplinary form of power," we would soon no longer have any organized form of power at all; all order breaks down; there is general chaos, all against all, and so on. While Foucault did at times signal a sympathy for anarchism,[152] he does not defend it explicitly in his philosophical writings. But to hold that virtually any form of government is ipso facto oppressive as an exercise of power over individuals borders on an anarchist position (for what form of government power is Foucault ready to *defend* rather than merely tolerate?), even if Foucault means for the ethics of the self to be a call to vigilance, and even if he eventually "softened" his view on power (separating it completely from physical violence),[153] emphasizing its productive and dynamic potential as a counterbalance to its destructive aspects.

With respect to the third problem, Foucault was always concerned with distinguishing the idea of the ethics of the self from "me ethics," that is, from egotism, *amour-propre*, hedonism, dandyism, and so on. Nevertheless, it is an inescapable fact that the modern political order that most promotes and celebrates the ideal of individual autonomy is the liberal democracy built on the strength of a large and prosperous middle class. If, in fact, Foucault's view of power can be summarized, as he does in an interview conducted in 1980, as simply "limiting the relations of power as embodied and developed in a particular society," as opposed to either exercising power more effectively (i.e., reinforcing power—dictatorship, police state) or overturning (state) power (i.e., revolution—Marxism, anarchism),[154] then it is hard to see much daylight between Foucault and a bourgeois-liberal or even a democratic-conservative position (which also favors limiting the power of government).

Finally, as I have argued in the final part of this chapter, interpretations of Foucault would greatly benefit from a serious comparison with Sartre. This is, in my view, the greatest lacuna in Anglophone scholarship on Foucault in particular,[155] much of which either elides this relationship or takes Foucault too much at his word regarding its salience. If we take, for example, the following statement of Foucault, there is little to distinguish the late Foucault from Sartre (save being a homosexual):

Being homosexuals we are in a struggle with the government, and the government is in a struggle with us. When we deal with the government, the struggle, of course, is not symmetrical, the power situation is not the same, but we are in this struggle, and the continuation of this situation can influence the behavior or nonbehavior of the other. So we are not trapped. We are always in this kind of situation. It means that we always have possibilities, there are always possibilities of changing the situation. We cannot jump *outside* the situation, and there is no point where you are free from all power relations. But you can always change it. So what I've said does not mean that we are always trapped, but that we are always free. Well anyway, that there is always the possibility of changing.[156]

This is a good summary of how Foucault conceives of the power of the ethics of the self: its potential for group praxis ("we") and its dependence on an existentialist concept of freedom and of the "situation"—the freedom/obligation to choose ourselves in every instant, which is our only effective defense against the other's oppressive gaze.

CHAPTER THREE

Derrida in Heidelberg

The specter of Heidegger's Nazism and the question of ethics

Deconstruction is justice.
—JACQUES DERRIDA

The publication (in French) in 2014 of the 1988 encounter between Jacques Derrida, Hans-Georg Gadamer, and Philippe Lacoue-Labarthe is, despite its belatedness—or perhaps even because of it—a most valuable document for understanding the evolution of Derrida's thought at a critical juncture. The "Heidelberg Conference," as it has come to be known,[1] was prompted by the sensational publication in France of Victor Farias's *Heidegger et le nazisme* in 1987.[2] Hence the conference's title: "Heidegger: Portée philosophique et politique de sa pensée" (Heidegger: The Philosophical and Political Import of his Thought). The publication of the conference proceedings allows us to examine anew the question of whether, or to what extent, Derrida underwent an "ethical turn" in his work, as many commentators have alleged, and more importantly, to explore the significance of ethics for Derrida's thought as a whole, as manifested at this pivotal moment. Although, unlike Foucault, Derrida does not offer a neat interpretation of his own intellectual trajectory in terms of phases or shifts, the year 1987 nevertheless has, as noted in my introduction to this volume, a before-and-after quality to it in the development of Derrida's oeuvre and of Theory more generally. For, in addition to the "Heidegger Affair," 1987 was also the year of the "de

Man Affair," which had a comparably sensational effect (but in the United States rather than in France).[3] It is undeniable that the two "affairs," in which Derrida was one of the main subjects of attack, had a real effect on Derrida's psyche and consequently on his thought, or, more precisely, on its orientation. Indeed, Derrida's biographer, Benoît Peeters, concludes a chapter devoted to these polemics thus: "As if in response to the accusations [the Heidegger Affair and the de Man Affair], ethical and political questions would soon move to the center of the stage."[4]

Before launching into an analysis of the conference proceedings, we must first make a distinction or separation between ethical *themes* in Derrida's work (forgiveness, hospitality, justice, the law, etc.),[5] themes that Derrida takes up *after* 1987,[6] and the question of an ethical *dimension* in Derrida's thought more broadly, in particular how his early works—those that have come to define Derrida's signature contribution to philosophy, *deconstruction*— relate to the question of ethics and/or politics.[7] Without such a distinction, the notion of an "ethical turn" in Derrida becomes vague and unwieldly. For example, one critic speaks (in 2005) of Derrida's "decision (some would say belated decision) to engage directly the kind of political, legal, and ethical questions that had for the most part been rather marginal to deconstruction in its early incarnation."[8] This assertion is based on several loaded terms that require careful elucidation. What is the nature of this "decision"? In what sense were ethical questions "marginal" as opposed to "essential" to deconstruction? Does deconstruction itself undergo a radical change if one assumes a "shift" to a more "ethically conscious" orientation? If so, does this imply that deconstruction was initially *deficient*, that it lacked the ethical element (or its effective articulation) that would have made it less open to attack (hence the "belated" nature of the "decision")? On the other hand, this assertion is undoubtedly a correct reflection of how Derrida's more recent work has been *perceived* or *received*, due to Derrida's change in thematic orientation.

It is undeniable that the question of ethics and/or politics in Derrida's thought starts to receive attention only after 1987.[9] In the eighty entries resulting from a word-search combination of "ethics" (as keyword) and "Derrida" (in the title) in the *MLA Bibliography*, seventy-nine (essays, books, book chapters, dissertations) were published after 1987, and exactly one was published prior to that year (in 1985). A word-search substituting the word "politics" for "ethics" yields similarly stark results (126 entries from 1987 to the present; one from 1980). Obviously something happened around 1987 that changed the way in which commentators approached Derrida's work. While one might be tempted to ascribe it solely to Derrida's shift in thematic orientation, it would be impossible to disentangle this shift from the overall change in intellectual climate (i.e., the "political turn") that influenced and shaped it.

There appear to be two basic assumptions regarding the status of ethics in Derrida's oeuvre: (1) It is a mostly belated attempt, post-1987, to come to terms with the ethical and/or political meaning of deconstruction, a meaning that was not articulated or at least not explicitly articulated in the pre-1987 texts; (2) Derrida's work was ethico-political from the start and thus any shift or "ethical turn" is merely apparent (or at best a shift in emphasis). The first proposition is somewhat accusatory, since it presupposes that a *transformation* of Derrida's thought was necessary to fulfill its ethico-political promise (as in the passage cited above). As for the second, it would be hard to find a more unequivocal statement than the following from Marko Zlomislić's 2007 book *Jacques Derrida's Aporetic Ethics*: "This work will provide reasonable and logical arguments based on the evaluation of the objective evidence and will show that Derrida has been concerned with ethics from the beginning of his authorship, with the emergence of his first published texts."[10] Similarly, Tom Cohen, in his preface to a collection of essays on *Jacques Derrida and the Humanities* (a collection that includes Derrida's piece on "the university without condition"), puts forward the premise: "That these essays, virtually or otherwise, would concern themselves less with the polemical contexts of Derrida's past reception—distracting misprisions of 'nihilism,' 'relativism,' or 'linguisticism' and so on—than demonstrate by interrogation and performance the 'affirmative deconstruction' that Derrida has, from the first, insisted was the necessarily transformative premise of his thought."[11] Common to the second approach is the desire to defend or shield Derrida from attacks or misinterpretations that target his thought as ethically disengaged and politically impotent (like those of Edward Said in his 1982 book *The World, the Text, and the Critic*),[12] hence the necessity of asserting a primordial ethical orientation ("from the first") and of denying shifts or turns. One immediately perceives the problem with this second approach when one considers, for example, Gayatri Spivak's invocation (in 1988) of the same concept of "affirmative deconstruction," which, unlike in Cohen's assertion, is seen instead as a sign of a *change in strategy* on Derrida's part[13]: "This study [*Spurs*, 1975] marks [Derrida's] move from the critical deconstruction of phallocentrism to 'affirmative' deconstruction (Derrida's phrase). It is at this point that Derrida's work becomes less interesting for Marxism."[14] This "move" was precipitated, according to Spivak, by the influence of feminist discourse, a discourse that had itself been influenced by deconstruction: "Over the last few years, however, I have also begun to see that, rather than deconstruction simply opening a way for feminists, the figure and discourse of women opened the way for Derrida as well."[15] Thus, feminism was, as it were, returning the favor.

Both approaches I have sketched exhibit important deficiencies, despite being nominally "correct" from a certain perspective. It does not necessarily follow that, because Derrida starts to focus more on ethical and political *themes* in his post-1987 texts, an ethical orientation had been lacking in the earlier texts. Conversely, just because an ethical dimension can be discerned in the early works and that such an orientation was therefore present "from the first," it does not therefore mean that the thematic shift toward ethics and politics is merely apparent, inconsequential, or superficial. What is required is a more nuanced approach that takes into account the shifting contexts of Derrida's thought and its reception.

My effort to identify an "ethical turn" in Derrida's thought should therefore not be taken as an indictment of Derrida's earlier work (any more than it was of Foucault's); it is rather a matter of a *retrospective reorganization* (we saw this very consciously on the part of Foucault). Thus, when Derrida insists at the Heidelberg conference on the ethical dimension of his early groundbreaking work, he acknowledges that this dimension might not have been perceivable due to a change in "code": "From the beginning . . . the questions I addressed to Heidegger were also political questions . . . even if [this questioning] was not in the code in which this is done today."[16] In other words, the very manner of ethical questioning—its protocols, assumptions, and rhetoric—had shifted, making it necessary to recast his earlier work. A few years later, in "Force of Law" (1990), Derrida notes similarly, "There are no doubt many reasons why the majority of texts hastily identified as 'deconstructionist' seem—I do say *seem*—not to foreground the theme of justice (as theme precisely), nor even the theme of ethics or politics."[17] Thus, while it would certainly be wrong to say that Derrida somehow repudiates his first publications by choosing to engage with explicitly ethical themes, it would be equally wrong to impose a rigid form on "deconstruction," as if it were somehow immutable, as if its understanding could not be shaped by extrinsic forces, later emendations, or new frameworks. If deconstruction teaches that meaning is always "to come" (it is never definitive),[18] this applies no less to the meaning of deconstruction itself.

Derrida liked to note that many, if not most, of the texts he wrote after he became well known are the result of being asked to speak on particular occasions about particular topics.[19] Hence, a certain thematic evolution of Derrida's work is *inevitable* (and from this perspective, it is perhaps less internally driven than Foucault's) and is in some sense beyond his control; that is, while Derrida of course chooses which engagements to accept, he cannot choose the nature of the engagements he is offered. Obviously, one does not say the same thing in an era of high structuralism that one says in an era of identity politics, feminist theory, queer theory, international terrorism, and so on; it is a matter of engaging with one's moment, according to the idea of a "philosophy of the present," as elucidated in the previous chapter.[20]

One last note: The vast majority of the studies on Derrida and ethics are based on a perceived confluence between the later Derrida and Emmanuel Levinas's ethical philosophy, to such an extent that one critic has even called for a "disjoining" of Derrida and Levinas.[21] This chapter proposes rather to study, in the context of the Heidelberg conference, the question of ethics in Derrida's relation to Heidegger, arguably the thinker who most occupied or interested Derrida.[22] While there has been much commentary on Derrida's relation to the "Heidegger Affair," these have not taken into account the (only recently available) 1988 conference, which offers a unique window into Derrida's thinking at this pivotal moment.

Derrida in Heidelberg

Writing in *The Gadamer Reader: A Bouquet of the Later Writings* (2007), the editor, Richard E. Palmer, avers that "the Heidelberg encounter was not documented, and a note sent to me from a friend in Heidelberg at the time claimed that nothing of philosophical interest had transpired there."[23] The appearance of the 1988 conference volume proves him wrong on both scores. Nevertheless, Palmer's claim does testify to a certain obscurity or secrecy surrounding the event and its surprising publication more than a quarter century later. The editor of the proceedings, Mireille Calle-Gruber, speaks of an "événement de l'archive" (archive event). Whatever the reasons for its belated appearance, this volume offers a new perspective on a crucial moment not only in Derrida's career but also in French thought more generally.

That the media scandal surrounding Farias's book clearly struck a nerve among French thinkers is reflected in the flurry of publications it provoked. At the beginning of 1988, Lacoue-Labarthe publishes *La fiction du politique: Heidegger, l'art et la politique* (translated in 1990 as *Heidegger, Art, and Politics: The Fiction of the Political*). Taking advantage of the media attention, Pierre Bourdieu offers in March of 1988 a revised version of a text originally written in 1975, *l'Ontologie politique de Martin Heidegger* (translated in 1991 as *The Political Ontology of Martin Heidegger*). The same month, Jean-François Lyotard's *Heidegger et "les juifs"* (translated in 1990 as *Heidegger and "The Jews"*) appears. May sees the publication of Alain Renaut's and Luc Ferry's *Heidegger et les modernes* (translated as *Heidegger and Modernity* in 1991). Although it had been written and submitted for publication *before* the controversy erupted, Derrida's *De l'esprit: Heidegger et la question* (translated as *On Spirit: Heidegger and the Question*),[24] appearing in January 1988, was nevertheless seen through the lens of the Farias provocation (particularly given Derrida's focus in this book on Heidegger's infamous "Rectorship Address" of 1933).[25]

It would probably be an understatement to call the Heidelberg conference "highly charged," for it combined a multitude of intersecting elements related to the polemical aftermath of Farias's book: the fact that Derrida is at the height of his fame and influence; that he would be discussing his most important philosophical progenitor; that he would be engaging with Heidegger's most prominent student and an eminent philosopher in his own right[26]; and, not least, that he would speaking in the very place where Heidegger himself had delivered controversial remarks in the 1930s. Peeters (who had access to the conference materials in an archive) sets the scene thus:

> The debate was held on the evening of February 5, 1988 in front of over a thousand people. In many ways it was exceptional. After a series of confrontations in France, the Heidegger question was finally returning to

Germany, and in a place fraught with memories: it was in this very lecture hall that, on 30 June 1933, Heidegger had given a speech with the title "The University in the New Reich." The audience had come not just to see Derrida, but also Gadamer, already a very old man and a local star; it was also the first time that Derrida and he had spoken to one another since their failed dialogue in 1981. When the speakers entered the hall, the audience applauded in German style, banging on the tables.[27]

The earlier event with Gadamer and Derrida, held at the Goethe Institute in Paris on April 25, 1981, became known as "The Conversation That Never Happened," as Richard Bernstein dubbed it.[28] In Heidelberg, however, they appear determined to have a true "conversation," with Derrida remarking to Gadamer that "at our encounter in Paris, a few years ago, it [the concept of conversation] was already the question. And the conversation continues, as you see."[29]

Appearing alongside Gadamer, whose personal, professional, and philosophical closeness to Heidegger is well known,[30] Derrida is circumspect in describing his own philosophical filiation. Although Derrida had no personal or professional relation to Heidegger (they in fact never met, despite several attempts to bring them together),[31] he and his philosophy are often called "Heideggarian," as if Derrida were an exponent or disciple.[32] Derrida is quick to reject this label, placing himself in the French tradition of a "polemical" relation to Heidegger (Levinas, Sartre). Derrida thus goes so far as to assert that "there were no Heideggerians in France," because "all those who have been marked by their reading of Heidegger had a polemical relation with him, in the noblest meaning of this term: it was an *Auseinandersetzung (explication)* for all."[33] Derrida qualifies his own *Auseinandersetzung* as "uncanny": "From the beginning of my reading of and references to Heidegger, I was completely conscious of the fact that I was in an '*explication*' with him that was nothing if not *uncanny [inquiète]*"— thereby referring obliquely to Heidegger's use of *unheimlich* (uncanny) in *Being and Time*.[34]

Derrida thus prefers to characterize the French relationship to Heidegger as one of "interest," distinguishing those who "declared their interest in Heidegger," such as Derrida himself, Jean-Luc Nancy, Levinas, and Lacoue-Labarthe, from those, like Foucault and Gilles Deleuze, who seemed to hide this influence, even though it had a "decisive" impact on their thought.[35] Indeed, Foucault remarks in his last interview, just before he died: "I've never written anything on Heidegger and only one very short article on Nietzsche. Yet these are the two authors whom I've read the most. I think that it's important to have a small number of authors with whom one thinks, with whom one works, but on whom one doesn't write."[36] Paradoxically, then, it is precisely those who freely and openly acknowledge Heidegger's influence who are held to account for not being sufficiently forthcoming about this relationship.

Derrida sees different forces at work in the French and German responses to Farias's provocation. In France, according to Derrida, the media firestorm was a function of the fact that members of the general public—those who were not knowledgeable about philosophy or Heidegger and who became aware of Heidegger's Nazism only through Farias's book—felt that this information had been withheld from them. They therefore "accused those who took an interest in Heidegger either of not being aware of Heidegger's Nazism, or, having been aware of it, of not transforming what they knew as professional philosophers into a subject of public debate [*en problème commun*]."[37] In other words, the Farias controversy is more about the gap between professional and public knowledge on a matter that interests the public (the idea of a "Nazi philosopher") than it is about Heidegger per se, whose Nazi associations had been well known in French philosophical circles since the 1940s.[38]

With respect to the German context, Derrida finds the denunciations of the French fixation on Heidegger, such as of those of Manfred Frank, "very unjust."[39] He offers two reasons why such accusations have been launched:

1. After the war, because of Heidegger's prior association with the Nazi Party, his philosophy was tainted and thus not widely read in Germany, whereas the French could read him without the baggage of a "guilty conscience," without worrying that they might be seen as reactionary, sympathetic to Nazism, and so on.[40] In addition, many of the French thinkers who took up Heidegger were Jewish, thus placing them at a further remove from what Heidegger represented in Germany. Derrida remarks, "I never felt, for biographical reasons that would be easy to explain . . . any attraction to right-wing ideas, Nazism, etc. Therefore we freely read Heidegger: we are not ashamed to read him."[41] This feeling of freedom—which was not without a sense of responsibility—in the French reading of Heidegger defined the gap with the German reception.

2. Heidegger's taboo status in Germany led to a "desire to accuse, from the other side of the border, those who took on Heidegger."[42] The Germans could therefore wash their hands of the Freiburg philosopher because of their history; they were in this manner relieved of any *obligation* other than that to ignore Heidegger. If it was considered an ethical obligation to refuse to read or discuss Heidegger in Germany, it was also considered an ethical obligation to denounce the attention paid to Heidegger outside Germany. However, from Derrida's perspective, it is precisely because Heidegger's philosophy is tainted by an association with Nazism that philosophers—qua philosophers—have a special duty to engage with it: "It is up to

us to read as rigorously as possible, and as responsibly as possible, Heidegger's texts, *all* of them—the Rector's Address, the political speeches, but also other texts; we must not renounce the political responsibility that must be ours."[43]

As an example of his uncanny, polemical, and otherwise contentious relation with Heidegger, Derrida cites his recently published book *De l'esprit* (which, as mentioned above, was composed before the appearance of Farias's book and thus was not in any way provoked by it):

> In France, I have been accused, on multiple occasions—although I recently devoted a small book to Heidegger's Nazism . . . [where I] began to interpret a certain relation between Heidegger's thought and Nazism—I am reproached for not having denounced Heidegger's Nazism! Although this is the very topic of the book [*je ne parle que de cela*].[44]

It is clear from the outset of the conference that Derrida feels as if, in the polemics surrounding Farias's book, both in France and in Germany, *he* were being called on to defend Heidegger's misdeeds, as if he, although Jewish,[45] were somehow in a vague sense *guilty*, as if, through a retreat into philosophical abstractions (being, presence, undecidability, etc.), he were effectively cleansing Heidegger's philosophy, thereby absolving it from any involvement or association with Nazism.

Thus, beyond the superficial polemics provoked by the media firestorm surrounding Farias's book, Derrida contends that there are nevertheless serious philosophical questions that gain new prominence through this refocusing of attention on Heidegger's Nazism. We can delineate at least three areas of concern: (1) the ethical status of Heidegger himself, especially his silence after the war; (2) the question of the extent to which Heidegger's philosophy is tainted by his Nazism; and (3) the ethical status of deconstruction as revealed in this discussion. I consider these in turn.

The philosophical meaning of Heidegger's silence

Interestingly, the conference participants appear to be less concerned with Heidegger's pro-Nazi activities in 1933 than with his silence after the war. Commentators regularly cite three attenuating factors in connection with Heidegger's prewar activities: (1) Heidegger's momentary but sincere enthusiasm for the Nazi movement was, in its context, unexceptional—many of Germany's leading intellectuals experienced a similar "enthusiasm"; (2) Heidegger seemed to realize his error early on, promptly withdrawing his support for the Nazi Party; and (3) the period in question, the early

1930s, was well *before* the full scope of Nazi evil became actual and evident, before the Second World War and the Holocaust. Thus, from the perspective of the conference participants, what is truly blameworthy, or at least less "forgivable," is the fact that, after the war, Heidegger apparently felt no compunction that would lead him to write about Nazism, the Holocaust, or his political activities in 1933, or to discuss these things in an interview. Derrida remarks that

> most of us are, I think, in agreement that even if we could understand, explain, excuse the engagement of [Heidegger with Nazism in] 1933 and, in a complicated and equivocal manner, some of its consequences in the years that followed, what is *unforgivable* (Lacoue-Labarthe's word), what is a "wound for thought," as Blanchot says, is the silence after the war, the silence about Auschwitz, etc.[46]

Although this might appear prima facie to be merely a personal failing on Heidegger's part, the conference participants see it as possessing an important philosophical dimension.

According to Gadamer, the silence was due to the fact that "Heidegger thought that it [the Nazi movement] was no longer *his* revolution; it had become a decadent revolution for which he felt no responsibility."[47] Thus Heidegger's "mistake" lay in the fact that he did not understand the true nature of this movement or that he had overlooked or was blind to some of its aspects; in short, he was politically naïve; he was duped. But Gadamer does not take this insight to its logical conclusion, namely that Heidegger thought, *initially*, that Nazism was indeed *his* revolution, that it in fact represented the kind of revolution with which he could identify and thus that there are important aspects of Nazism that Heidegger *continued to approve of* (anti-Semitism, for one, as confirmed by various sources),[48] even after his disillusionment. It is these aspects that require further study and interrogation, to the extent that they suggest some coincidence between Heidegger's philosophy and Nazism, a coincidence that Gadamer openly acknowledges, as we will see below.

On the other hand, following Gadamer's explicit logic, it would appear that the reason for the unforgivable silence lies precisely in Heidegger's forgivable 1933 self. In other words, since Nazism was not, or was no longer, *his* revolution, Heidegger no doubt felt that any postwar apology would necessarily be seen as admitting *too much*: as if he were taking responsibility for what Nazism eventually *became*—a genocidal, warmongering state—as opposed to simply a misguided attraction to a (now universally discredited) political ideology. It is one thing to be anti-Semitic and to subscribe to a xenophobic agenda, but it is quite another to countenance or support actual genocide. Today we tend to conflate the two attitudes, regarding the latter as the *foreseeable* result of the former. Thus, Heidegger's error looms larger after the war precisely because of the *fact* of the Holocaust, the fact that unthinkable evil *actually* occurred (and therefore is no longer "unthinkable," in any strict sense). Precisely because the Holocaust *happened*, it appears as a kind of historical proof of the power of anti-Semitism. An "appropriate" apology for Heidegger would therefore be impossible,⁴⁹ for it would entail explaining how Heidegger understood Nazism in the early 1930s, in the face of an historical actuality that has changed the very meaning and parameters of such a discussion.

Derrida, for his part, chooses to see Heidegger's silence as *philosophically productive*. Imagine, Derrida speculates, if Heidegger had issued, after the war, a mea culpa for his actions, in addition to stating that "Auschwitz was the absolute horror [*l'horreur absolue*]."⁵⁰ What would have been the result? Heidegger would have been "absolved," according to Derrida, and we would not have seen the need to further investigate the relation between Heidegger and Nazism. His denunciations and self-denunciations would have closed the inquiry ("il aurait *fermé* les choses"),⁵¹ in addition to being gratuitous (for *everyone* effectively denounces the Holocaust; even the deniers implicitly denounce it, declare it to be evil, in their adamant refusal to admit that it happened). Derrida thus speaks of Heidegger's silence in terms of an "inheritance" and the "*injunction* to think what has not been thought."⁵²

As for the "why" of Heidegger's silence, Derrida hypothesizes that it is a function of Heidegger's inability to articulate a *philosophically* adequate response to the catastrophe:

> I think that Heidegger perhaps said to himself: I can only condemn Nazism if I can do it not only in a way that would be on the level of what I have already said, but also on the level of what happened there. And this he was incapable of doing. And this silence is perhaps an honest way of recognizing this. It is a very audacious hypothesis: I said that I was improvising tonight.⁵³

Heidegger's silence here appears under the guise of humility; it is a recognition of philosophical impotence. Hence the necessity, says Derrida, of reading Heidegger "in the way that he did not read himself."⁵⁴ The polemical reading of Heidegger is, then, one that necessarily includes an ethical reflection on Heidegger's relation to Nazism. Derrida also appears, à la Lyotard,⁵⁵ to invoke the idea of inadequacy in the face of the immensity and "unthinkable" nature of the Holocaust to explain Heidegger's silence. In this manner, the silence can be construed as a kind of "respect" (in the moral-aesthetic sense that Kant gives this term in the third *Critique*).⁵⁶ Although Derrida does not develop this point, by far the most interesting implication of his hypothesis is the suggestion that, in making such an effort of apology, explanation, denunciation, and so on, Heidegger's philosophy might itself have been called into question; for, one would suppose, such an effort would have required a *revision* of his thought. Philosophy, for Heidegger, is not about dispensing timeless wisdom but about *engaging with its moment*; his is a "philosophy of the present." As Laurence Hemming puts it:

> It is Heidegger's extraordinary power to set the present times in relation to the whole of history that gives us thoughtful pause even when we are confronted with Heidegger's claims about the inner greatness of the movement that gave us National Socialism: it was after all the revolutionary movement itself, and its trajectory, its whither and whereunto, that Heidegger was trying to understand.[57]

Thus, Heidegger's early engagement with Nazism can be seen as being as inevitable as his later silence, since speaking out would have involved admitting not only an ethical error but also a philosophical one. Heidegger is perhaps more interested in saving his philosophy than he is in saving himself, as indicated in a much-cited passage from the 1949 lecture "The Question Concerning Technology," which was deleted from the published version: "Agriculture is now a motorized food industry, the same thing in its essence as the production of corpses in the gas chambers and the extermination camps, the same thing as blockades and the reduction of countries to famine, the same thing as the manufacture of hydrogen bombs."[58] Here, it would appear that Heidegger was attempting to reveal an anti-Nazi element in his thought. But the very fact that this passage was withheld from publication goes again to the question of Heidegger's silence.

Philosophy and Heidegger's Nazism

If, as Gadamer remarks, "it is clear that one cannot disassociate Heideggerian philosophy from the fact of the extermination that took place in our century" and that there are "serious affinities between Heidegger's philosophical position and certain tendencies of [the Nazi] movement,"[59] then how can the relation between Heidegger's *philosophy* and Nazism be described? This is indeed the question that lurks behind the "scandal" of Farias's book, and the participants at the Heidelberg Conference are keen to address it.

The participants generally agree that, while a simple or blanket condemnation of Heidegger's philosophy is an extreme to be avoided, the relation between Heidegger's thought and Nazism is nontrivial and requires exploration. Thus, none of the participants would appear to agree with the position put forward by Richard Rorty in his review of Farias's book, which effectively puts all the Nazism on the side of Heidegger the man, thereby erecting a wall between Heidegger's Nazism and his philosophy. I briefly consider Rorty's view, since it throws the main issues into relief.

In his review, Rorty calls Farias's book "an excellent antidote to the evasive apologetics that are still being published."[60] From Rorty's perspective, a "good reason" for caring about Heidegger's Nazism is simply practical-ethical: "It pays to realize that the vast majority of German academics, including some of the best and brightest, turned a blind eye to the fate of their Jewish colleagues, and to ask whether we ourselves might not be capable of the same sort of behavior."[61] A "bad reason" for caring about Heidegger's Nazism, according to Rorty, is to indict his philosophy. Rorty thus contests the "notion that learning about a philosopher's moral character helps one evaluate his philosophy. It does not, any more than our knowledge of Einstein's character helps us evaluate his physics."[62] Rorty notes that the logician and mathematician Gottlob Frege was "a vicious anti-Semite and proto-Nazi,"[63] but that this was considered philosophically irrelevant. The reason why we tend to conflate the moral character and intellectual achievements of philosophers, as opposed to mathematicians or physicists, is because "philosopher" often means "ideal human being who perfectly unites wisdom and kindness, insight and decency." In other words, the role of the philosopher in society is often supposed to be that of a kind of exemplar or sage. Indeed, Rorty remarks that Heidegger "carried over into philosophy the attitude characteristic of religious prophets: that their own voice is the voice of some greater power (God, Reason, History, Being), a power that is about to make all things new, to bring on a new age of the world."[64] If one gives up this misguided view of the philosopher, then "the greatness" of a Frege or a Heidegger "is unsullied by their moral indecency."[65]

The main problem with Rorty's argument, from my perspective, is twofold: (1) The distinction he makes between "character" and thought is not pertinent in the way he thinks it is; and (2) the non-distinction he effects between philosophy and the sciences (or mathematics) with regard to ethics is not tenable. With regard to the first issue, it is not simply a question of moral character per se (an *extrinsic* relation—e.g., a philosopher can be unethical or even commit a crime, but this would have little bearing on the *thought* of a philosopher), but rather a question of how Heidegger's philosophy itself reveals certain affinities with Nazism (an *intrinsic* relation). Thus, one could easily expand the notion of "moral character" to include views, attitudes, and activities that have intellectual content (as in the Greek *êthos*, explored by Foucault),[66] in which case there would be a necessary overlap with a thinker's philosophical positions. In Heidegger's case, many of his philosophical pronouncements have political and cultural resonances that go far beyond the technical matters of academic philosophy.

As for the second issue, while a case could be made that certain areas of philosophy such as logic and the philosophy of science have no necessary moral or political dimension and thus could be considered separate from a philosopher's political commitments, this is not the case for much of what is known as Continental philosophy, which is much more holistic than its Anglo-American counterpart—with its hyper-compartmentalization of philosophy into subdisciplines that have little or no overlap, which effectively ghettoizes ethics. Thus, while I agree that the political activities of a physicist have nothing to do with the content of physics research itself (even if it might have something to do with the *uses* of such research—the atomic bomb, for instance), or that Frege's anti-Semitic views have nothing to do with the type of philosophy he pursues (logic, mathematics), it would be hard to maintain this stance with regard to the kind of philosophy Heidegger espouses, namely *cultural* philosophy, that is, a philosophy of the present, a philosophy that strives to seize its moment rather than eternity, a philosophy in which an ethico-political dimension is thus at least implied, even if it is not overtly acknowledged; for it is a matter of asking, as Rorty says, "What we should do with ourselves?" (See Chapter 4.) Thus, one could make the case that it would have been difficult or impossible to be the kind of (German) philosopher Heidegger wanted to be without taking a strong stand on Nazism. I thus think that Rorty's own view on what philosophy should be—*practical* world-interpreting rather than theoretical world-reflecting—militates against his desire to separate Heidegger's philosophy from his Nazism. In short, if we read Heidegger the way Heidegger called for his philosophy to be read, then Heidegger would be subject to the moral critique waged against his philosophy.

A more difficult but related question is how to treat some unfortunate moral attitudes of a philosopher whose ethical thought we find otherwise compelling and important.[67] If we indicted Heidegger's philosophy for its Nazism, then would we not have to indict Aristotle because of his acceptance of slavery? No doubt! However, the difference between Heidegger and Aristotle is that there was no social evolution regarding the acceptability of slavery during Aristotle's lifetime, like there was against Nazism and anti-Semitism in the latter half of the twentieth century. Heidegger was thus expected to reconcile his earlier views and actions with the new social dispensation, something that could not have been expected of Aristotle's view of slavery, Kant's views on race, and so on.

In *Heidegger and "The Jews"* (1988), Lyotard takes a similar approach to Rorty, exhorting us to "not mix Heidegger's thought with his 'politics' and the sociohistorical context in which it was played out. Remember that thought exceeds its contexts (something Farias forgets)."[68] Lyotard thus stresses the poststructuralist credo of the irreducibility of interpretation to a single hermeneutic protocol. But even if we allow that thought exceeds its contexts (but how could it exceed *every* context, context as such?), it nevertheless still has a context from which it emerged, and it is this context that is at issue.

On the other side of the argument is Tom Rockmore's elaborately and exhaustively articulated thesis (1992) that "Heidegger's philosophical thought and his Nazism are inseparable."[69] His case is based not on a general argument about philosophy, like Rorty's, but rather on the peculiarity of Heideggerian philosophy, the seeming *inevitability* of its turn to Nazism:

> Heidegger's understanding of ontology commits him to a turn to politics, centered on the concept of human authenticity, which demands realization

> in a political context, as a condition of the authentic thought of Being. Heidegger's turn to Nazism was an obvious attempt to seize a supposedly propitious moment. . . . Heidegger's attempt to seize the day . . . should not be invoked to explain his adherence to National Socialism as a mere error of judgment, as a simple mistake, as the kind of mistake anyone, so to speak, could make. The reason is obvious: unlike everyone, or his academic colleagues, or even other philosophers, Heidegger possessed an important philosophical theory, and it is this theory itself which led him from the ivory tower inhabited by German intellectuals toward the political arena.[70]

Putting aside the question of the propriety of Rockmore's interpretation of Heidegger's thought (the examination of which would take us too far afield),[71] the argument suffers, in my view, from a Heideggercentric analysis of the question of the relation between Nazism and philosophy. Far from inhabiting an "ivory tower," many leading German thinkers and academics offered philosophical support to the Nazi regime, prime among them Alfred Bäumler and Carl Schmitt, whose intellectual and personal involvement with Nazism was more fervent, far-reaching, and unrepentant than that of Heidegger. Heidegger was not exceptional but was part of a current of elite German thought that gravitated toward the Nazis. Moreover, the notion of "inseparability" is belied by the very fact that Heidegger's philosophy has generated a steady stream of voluminous scholarship, only a small part of which is concerned with Nazism and much of which is associated with left-leaning scholarship. To the extent that a thinker's ideas are deemed *useful* beyond the original context, they effectively escape its constraints (in this more limited sense, I agree with Lyotard).

In his *Heidegger, Philosophy, Nazism* (1997), Julian Young accepts Rockmore's "inseparability" proposition, but turns the argument on its head:

> Taking on board the wisdom of those who insist on the inseparability of man and philosophy, I have sought to de-Nazify both. None of Heidegger's philosophy, I have argued, is implicated, either positively or negatively, in fascism, and neither, therefore is the essential man. . . . I have argued that Heidegger's political involvement was inconsistent with the deepest philosophical position he had *already worked out*, at least in the essay "The Essence of Truth" in 1930.[72]

Young's conclusions are based on the assumption that by 1935, Heidegger "had moved into fundamental opposition to Nazism" and that that represented a return of sorts to his "essential" thought, as distinguished from Heidegger's "parochial" thinking (a distinction Young adapts from Habermas), that is, his nonphilosophical attitudes, which unfortunately "invad[e] those texts which are properly classified as philosophical."[73]

This last point would appear to put into question the inseparability between the personal and the philosophical that forms the basis for Young's assertions; indeed, Young's thesis depends on a sleight of hand, on seeing the "essential man" as involving the philosophical rather than the parochial Heidegger—a tenuous assertion at best.

At the conference, Derrida carves out an approach that reveals more of an ethical concern than either Rorty or Lyotard, while steering clear of the "inseparability" thesis. Thus, whereas Derrida grants that using Heidegger's association with Nazism to simply dismiss Heidegger's philosophy is a bad idea, he nevertheless considers the relation to have a genuinely *philosophical* dimension, even insisting that those who comment on or use Heidegger have a special *responsibility* to explore this relation. This view thus goes much farther in Rockmore's direction than Rockmore gives him credit for (Rockmore aligns Derrida's position with those who see Heidegger's supposed *Kehre* [turn] as tantamount to a denazification).[74] For, on the one hand, Derrida laments that many of those who denounce Heidegger seem to do so not on the basis of study but rather on ancillary considerations (i.e., their condemnation is not philosophical in nature): "We have a right to ask those who want to make a quick judgment on the relation between the philosophical text and a political behavior that they at least start to try to read [Heidegger]."[75] Moreover, contra Rockmore, Derrida suggests that any strictly "political" interpretation will obfuscate Heidegger's singular contributions to philosophy, contributions that have little or nothing to do with Nazism per se and that were elaborated before the Nazi period (e.g., Heidegger's magnum opus *Being and Time*, published in 1927)[76]: "There are immense resources in Heidegger's text."[77] While Derrida notes that such an assertion risks giving the impression that he is "defending" Heidegger, he merely wants to argue against treating Heidegger's philosophy as if Nazism were its dominant or defining feature and against the tendency to reflexively tie thought to real-world engagements.

One potential weakness of this approach is the extent to which (as Rockmore contends) Heidegger uses earlier positions to support Nazi-era pronouncements, that is, the extent to which Heidegger's sees the rise of Nazism in the 1930s, at least initially, as, in some sense, the *fulfillment* of the thought he had been pursuing since the 1920s. There is also the problem of an inevitable overlap in vocabulary and rhetoric between political and philosophical discourse during this period, which provided a framework for Heidegger's more controversial texts (e.g., the attempts by far-right ideologues such as Bäumler to translate the philosophical ideas of Nietzsche into the support of Nazism).[78]

In short, Derrida proposes to treat the relation between Heidegger's philosophy and Nazism as both significant and irreducible. As Derrida puts it, what can "the experience of Heidegger's thought have in the way of affinity, synchrony, common roots [*communauté de racines*] with this still unthinkable thing we call Nazism?"[79] Unfortunately, Derrida does not develop this point in detail at the conference—no doubt because he had endeavored to do precisely this in his book *De l'esprit*. Still, the statement is instructive. It identifies three modalities of contact between Heidegger's thought and Nazism: (1) *affinity*—this includes Heidegger's intellectual attraction to Nazism, the proximity of his thought to right-wing ideas, and the commonality of themes (such as *Schicksal* [fate] and *Geschick* [destiny])[80]; (2) *synchrony*—the historical context that situates the affinity as one of effective engagement (as opposed to being a proto-Nazi or a post-Nazi affinity), given that the formative period of Heidegger's philosophy is exactly coextensive with the founding, ascension, and reign of the Nazi Party (1920–45); (3) *common roots*—Nazism itself draws on major figures of German philosophy, including Johann Gottlieb Fichte, Nietzsche, and Oswald Spengler, many of whose ideas were also influential on Heidegger; even if one argues that the Nazis "twisted" these ideas (particularly in the case of Nietzsche), much of the influence falls within a legitimate interpretive relation. In other words, there is some properly philosophical overlap with Nazism that cannot be simply reduced to anti-Semitism, racism, the desire for world domination, and so on.[81] Further, Derrida asserts that "a certain active reading of Heidegger can help us get closer to a way of thinking about what we condemn [in Heidegger]."[82] Here we come to the idea of a "left-orientated" reading of Heidegger that uses Heidegger's text to articulate an anti-Nazi (antitotalitarian, antifascist) position. Thus, the polemical reading of Heidegger is also an ethical reading. Indeed, this ethical-polemical reading would appear to be the point of departure for what Derrida calls "deconstruction."

The ethics of deconstruction/ deconstructive ethics

It is at the Heidelberg conference that, seemingly for the first time in such a direct manner, Derrida states explicitly, categorically, and without qualification that deconstruction is in fact an ethical enterprise: "Deconstruction, for example . . . is an exercise of responsibility. . . . And it is not because deconstruction deconstructs that it is irresponsible. On the contrary: I think that it is an exercise of responsibility to remain vigilant in the face of inherited concepts of responsibility."[83] However, the question remains, as Christina Howells puts it: "Can deconstruction do any more than question ethical systems and beliefs? Can it ever pass beyond the negative phase?"[84] In other words, is remaining "vigilant" the sole ethical function of deconstruction (or the sole function of deconstruction *tout court*), a function that places it close to Foucault's concept of the ethics of the self as the site of resistance to power (i.e., the recognition that "everything is dangerous"), as we saw in the previous chapter?

Derrida notes that many accuse deconstruction, due to its axiomatic use of notions of undecidibility, aporia, double bind, and so on, of being "a politics of neutrality, of indifference, of indecision," lamenting that

> when we say that ethics, that the way in which we define ethics today trembles due to a lack of foundation, or when we say that we no longer know with any certainty what it means to be responsible, the violence to which we are subjected is: so, you are promoting an immoral discourse, an irresponsible discourse![85]

In other words, depriving ethics of a foundation is seen as an attempt to undermine ethics itself. Derrida retorts:

> I say *exactly the opposite*: there is no possible responsibility that does not submit to this undecidibility [*qui ne fasse l'épreuve de l'indécidabilité*], and this impossibility. I think that an action, a discourse, a behavior, that does not undergo this terrifying test of undecidibility [*qui ne traverse pas cette terrifiante épreuve de l'indécidabilité*], with all its *double binds*, all its conflicts of which one could give examples, is simply the tranquil operation of a program, more or less tranquil. The program could be Nazi, democratic, or this or that . . . but if we do not undergo this terrifying test of undecidability [*si on ne traverse pas cette terrifiante épreuve de l'indécidabilité*] there is no responsibility.[86]

Derrida thus seeks to turn the tables on his adversaries, implying that those who do not subject ethical concepts to a deconstructive or subversive reading—that is, those who cannot face up to ethics' lack of an *a priori* ground—are simply accepting the status quo, the established morality, whether it be that of a democracy or a totalitarian state (Sartre's "practico-inert" and the "tranquility" of Heidegger's "they-self"). To say that we should only put morality to the test in certain extreme situations misses the point of deconstructive ethics as vigilance; for democracy can always turn into fascism, as it did in Germany in 1933 (the Nazis won a democratic election and then promptly dismantled all the apparatuses of democracy). Derrida effectively asserts that there is no ethics without deconstruction, that deconstruction is "essential" to ethics, because ethics fundamentally involves "undecidability" or radical singularity, the lack of a firm basis on which to base ethical decisions, thus prefiguring the famous dictum he proffers in "Force of Law" (1990): "*Deconstruction is justice.*"[87] In an interview conducted in the early 1990s, Derrida avers, "However careful one is in the theoretical preparation of a decision, the instant of the decision, if there is to be a decision, must be heterogeneous to the accumulation of knowledge. Otherwise, there is no responsibility. . . . The decision, if there is to be one, must advance towards a future which is not known, which cannot be anticipated."[88] There are important echoes here of Sartre's description of ethical decision as analogous to the creative condition of art in his famous lecture "L'existentialisme et l'humanisme" (which we touched on in the previous chapter): "There is this in common between art and morality, that in both we have to do with creation and invention. We cannot decide a priori what it is that should be done."[89] Sartre and Derrida (and perhaps Foucault as well) are saying essentially the same thing: that ethics is not a matter of preexisting or immutable principles but of self-invention in the moment of decision.[90]

If, as the catastrophes of the twentieth century have demonstrated, the traditional concepts of responsibility have failed us, then deconstruction can be aligned with a certain *pragmatism*, since it is a matter of finding a notion of responsibility that *works* in the *present*. Derrida notes that the Kantian concept of responsibility, as it was inscribed in European thought and institutions, "did not prevent Auschwitz."[91] The traditional notion of responsibility is therefore "insufficient."[92] We require a notion of responsibility that can take into account the recent horrors and can respond to the ethical challenges of the present, all while remaining radically open to the singular and the new:

> I hold that . . . even when it calls into question this axiomatic of subjectivity or of responsibility, or when it calls into question certain axioms of Heideggarian discourse, it [deconstruction] is not an abdication of responsibility; it is—as I see it in any case—the most difficult responsibility that I can assume. And to entrust myself to [*me fier à*] traditional categories of responsibility appears to me, today, to be, precisely, irresponsible.[93]

But how can an engagement with Heidegger's philosophy in particular help with the renewal of ethics, particularly in view of Heidegger's anti-subjectivism? Noting that "*Dasein* is a responsible being,"[94] Derrida sees Heidegger's shift from a subject-centered (epistemological) to a being-centered (ontological) philosophy as merely a starting point[95]:

> The discourse of Heidegger on this topic does not satisfy me. No doubt, he helped me go from a concept—let's say, of a Kantian, intentionalist, volontarist notion of responsibility—toward another type of response; for Heidegger, the response that he makes of the *Ruf* [call] and the *Gewissen* [conscience], of the originary *Schuldigsein* [guilt], displaces the question of responsibility toward something else, toward the question of being, and I know that it is by taking this route, without stopping where Heidegger stopped, that we must redefine [*redéfinir*] this responsibility.[96]

Through the idea of responsibility as response to the call of being,[97] Heidegger points the way toward a new ethics, even if he was incapable of formulating it himself. If there is something to be learned from Heidegger's engagement with Nazism, it is that his philosophy *did not prevent* such an engagement, even if it cannot necessarily be considered a cause of or to be inextricable from it (although this latter point is the subject of great contention, as mentioned above).

Nevertheless, despite Derrida's call for a "redefinition" of ethical responsibility, he still underlines the difficulty of such an undertaking in current idioms: "I cannot define [responsibility] in moral or political terms in the contemporary sense of these terms, because these terms are still, for me, the names of open problems."[98] It is, however, unlikely that these "open problems" would ever cease to be such so as to allow Derrida to precisely define, for the present, the concept of responsibility in the ethical and political sense—even if later texts, such as "Force of Law," with its emphasis on radical singularity (singular justice versus normative law),[99] and *The Gift of Death*, with its reference to Heidegger's discussion of responsibility in *Being and Time*,[100] gesture in this direction. Indeed, at the conference, Derrida appears to anticipate the work he will later undertake, as when he reflects that "I think that the question is that of responsibility; I think that the Heideggerian mediation of this question is a necessary one; it's one I thought that I would never be able to stop probing, and thus the question of responsibility remains open."[101]

As paradoxical as it may seem, it is clear that Derrida sees his path to thinking about ethics—to ethical thought—as necessarily going *through* Heidegger. If Derrida's thought represents a deconstruction of Heidegger's deconstruction of Western metaphysics, as Derrida himself has described his work,[102] then Derrida's ethical thought must also be seen as a certain development of Heideggarian thinking, namely as a thinking *with* but also—and simultaneously—*against* Heidegger. The polemical reading of Heidegger is simply the ethical reading of Heidegger that Heidegger himself makes possible, namely an ethics beyond subjectivism and foundationalism. To answer Howells's question, then, about the possibility of deconstruction getting beyond a "negative phase" with regard to ethics, one might say that this "negativity"—thinking without foundation—is simply the groundless ground on which any ethical act, thought, or attitude is, qua singularity, rendered intelligible or possible.[103] Hence, as Richard Bernstein avers, "Derrida's ethical-political horizon *is* a 'point of departure' for virtually everything he has written."[104] For is not Derrida's "deconstruction of Western metaphysics" (i.e., rationality) essentially a strategy of showing how supposedly value-neutral hierarchies (truth) are in fact value-creating forms of exclusion or subordination (ethics)? Nevertheless, one can still ask if Derrida has not given us an "Ethics of Ethics," that is, the kind of metaethical positioning Derrida ascribed to Levinas in an early essay ("Violence and Metaphysics"),[105] even if, in the end, Derrida's ethical thinking is quite distinct from that of the author of *Totality and Infinity*.

CHAPTER FOUR

Richard Rorty's "cultural politics"

Ironist philosophy and the ethics of reading

Richard Rorty's famous dichotomy between the public and the private, in which ironist (non-foundationalist) philosophy, like high-modernist literature, is relegated to the private realm, would appear to doom any attempt to theorize ethics or politics from a Rortean perspective. Indeed, Rorty proclaims in his 1989 book *Contingency, Irony, Solidarity* that "theory [i.e., philosophy] has become a means to private perfection rather than to human solidarity."[1] By this, Rorty means that "ironist theorists like Hegel, Nietzsche, Derrida, and Foucault seem to me invaluable in our attempt to form a private self-image, but pretty much useless when it comes to politics."[2] Those who see these thinkers as socially beneficial assume, falsely, that we can "hold self-creation and justice . . . in a single vision."[3] By the same token, however, Rorty also rejects the non-ironist, Enlightenment perspective on politics: that knowledge of what binds us all together—for example, universal rationality—is necessary for the creation and maintenance of a liberal-democratic polity. He thus criticizes philosophers in the Kantian-Enlightenment tradition, such as Jürgen Habermas, whose idea of intersubjectivity as "communicative reason" is, for Rorty, a misguided effort to impose nonempirical, regulative norms on the public sphere. According to Rorty, the "social glue" holding modern democratic societies together is simply the "consensus that the point of social organization is to let everybody have a chance at self-creation to the best of his or her abilities, and that that goal requires, besides peace and wealth, the standard 'bourgeois freedoms.'"[4]

In his final publications, however, Rorty would appear to have significantly revised the view promulgated in 1989 and maintained throughout the 1990s. Rorty's emphasis on "philosophy as cultural politics,"[5] as the final installment (2007) of his *Philosophical Papers* is entitled, and his suggestion, in a late essay, that ironist literature can indeed foster human solidarity, are seemingly at odds with his strict dichotomy between the public and the private as well as his critique of the ethico-political possibilities of the ironist, non-foundationalist philosophical tradition. Indeed, what Rorty proposes under the rubric of "philosophy as cultural politics" is hardly distinguishable from the idea of a "philosophy of the present" explored in the previous two chapters with regard to Foucault and Derrida (and Heidegger implicitly). This is especially apparent when we consider that Rorty has, throughout much of his career, described his approach to philosophy as "holding one's own time in thought"[6]—a thesis inspired by a passage in Hegel's *The Philosophy of Right*: "Each individual is in any case a *child of his time*; thus philosophy, too, is *its own time comprehended in thought*."[7] In the preface to his 2007 collection, Rorty expressly links this idea to "cultural politics":

> Like my previous writings, they [the essays collected in *Philosophy as Cultural Politics*] are attempts to weave together Hegel's thesis that philosophy is its time held in thought with a non-representationalist account of language. . . . Dewey agreed with Hegel that philosophers were never going to be able to see things under the aspect of eternity; they should instead try to contribute to humanity's ongoing conversation about what to do with itself. The progress of this conversation has engendered new social practices, and changes in the vocabularies deployed in moral and political deliberation. To suggest further novelties is to intervene in cultural politics. Dewey hoped that philosophy professors would see such intervention as their principal assignment.[8]

The idea of philosophy as an "ongoing conversation" vaguely recalls the section "Philosophy in the Conversation of Mankind" in Rorty's first book *Philosophy and the Mirror of Nature*,[9] thus seemingly supporting Rorty's claim that "readers of my previous books will find little new in this volume."[10] However, readers familiar with Rorty's oeuvre will in fact find that the preface marks a significant departure from much of his earlier thought: (1) in the idea that philosophy should "*intervene* in cultural politics" instead of remaining in the private realm (ironist philosophy) or suffering political irrelevance (Habermas); (2) in that philosophy should promote "changes in the *vocabularies* deployed in moral and political deliberation," a stipulation that appears to bridge the divide between individual and collective self-creation; (3) in that philosophy as "its time held in thought" should primarily be about what *collective* purposes to give ourselves ("humanity's ongoing conversation about what to do with itself"), which would appear to conflate the self-questioning of autonomous intellectuals (irony) with mundane consensus building (solidarity). It is thus difficult to see how Rorty's late notion of "cultural politics" can possibly fit within the sharp public/private dichotomy he had cultivated throughout his career.

More specifically, then, how are we to square Rorty's vision of "philosophy as cultural politics" with his critique of the political dimension of Foucault's "ethics of the self" (discussed in Chapter 2)? And how to relate Rorty's 1989 praise of Derrida for having had the "courage to stop trying to bring together a quest for private autonomy and an attempt at public resonance and utility"[11] to his 2003 statement that "we prefer to describe Heidegger and Derrida as offering us imaginative neologisms that help us hold our time in thought"?[12] This juxtaposition of quotations from disparate moments in Rorty's career certainly suggests some kind of evolution or even a volte-face on the question of what "holding one's time in thought" means with respect to the ethico-political implications of philosophy.

To address these conundrums, I shall focus on two of Rorty's late essays, "The Decline of Redemptive Truth and the Rise of a Literary Culture" (given as a lecture in 2000, published in 2007 under the title "Philosophy as a Transitional Genre")[13] and "Redemption from Egotism: James and Proust as Spiritual Exercises" (given as a lecture in 2001, published in 2010),[14] which can be seen as representative of Rorty's final thought on the vocation of philosophy and the public/private diremption.

Rorty's "literary culture"

An important part of Rorty's philosophy, beginning at least with *Contingency, Irony, Solidarity*, is the idea of a "poeticized culture,"[15] a notion that is posited as an antidote to a culture that worships something nonhuman, whether the Truth or the Divine—what Rorty sarcastically terms the "One Right Description."[16] It functions as both a descriptive, analytical statement of current tendencies as well as a prescriptive statement that lays out Rorty's hope for the future. Thus Rorty's elucidation of what he terms a "literary culture" (inspired by C. P. Snow's "two cultures")[17]—namely "a culture in which the novel has become the central vehicle of moral instruction"[18]—in his essay "Philosophy as a Transitional Genre" should be seen as largely a restatement and further development of his idea of a poeticized culture. (Rorty also sometimes employs the term "postmetaphysical culture" as a synonym for "literary culture" and "poeticized culture.")[19]

In "Philosophy as a Transitional Genre," Rorty argues that there have been three main stages of human development, all of which can be characterized in terms of redemption: redemption by religion, redemption by philosophy, and redemption by literature/art. The decisive break occurs, according to Rorty, between a philosophical and a literary culture, since both philosophy and religion are characterized by redemption by an absolute or a nonhuman reality, whereas, in a literary culture, the redemption is distinctively human; it is effected by human self-making or self-transcendence. As Rorty describes it:

> The intellectuals of the West have, since the Renaissance, progressed through three stages: they have hoped for redemption first from God, then from philosophy, and now from literature. Monotheistic religion offers hope for redemption through entering into a new relation to a supremely powerful non-human person. Belief—as in belief in the articles of a creed—may be only incidental to such a relationship. For philosophy, however, beliefs are of the essence. Redemption by philosophy is through the acquisition of a set of beliefs which represent things in the one way they really are. Literature, finally, offers redemption through making the acquaintance of as great a variety of human beings as possible. Here again, as in religion, true belief may be of little importance.[20]

Rorty here exalts creativity and practical ethics ("the acquaintance of as great a variety of human beings as possible") over truth as the organizing "principle" of our post-metaphysical, intellectual culture. The kind of creative self-invention that defines a literary culture is, for Rorty, the only valid concept of human autonomy. Rorty therefore rejects the Kantian notion of autonomy as rational self-legislation, in favor of a quasi-existentialist conception (minus the *angst*). Indeed, Rorty notes in the same essay that "autonomy, in this un-Kantian . . . sense, is pretty much the same thing as Heideggerian authenticity."[21] The Rortean autonomy embodied in a literary culture thus represents a sort of an amalgam of Nietzschean self-overcoming and Heidegger's idea that we (*Dasein*) must rise above (seek redemption from) the inauthentic "they-self" (*das Man*, social conformity), both in ourselves and with respect to others. Autonomy is about distinguishing ourselves from the vulgar crowd, from the social dynamic that comforts and controls the self. As Heidegger observes in *Being and Time*:

> In this inconspicuousness and unascertainability, the they [*das Man*] unfolds its true dictatorship. We enjoy ourselves and have fun the way *they* enjoy themselves. We read, see, and judge literature and art the way *they* see and judge. But we also withdraw from the 'great mass' the way *they* withdraw, we find 'shocking' what *they* find shocking. The they, which is nothing definite and which all are, though not as a sum, prescribes the kind of being of everydayness.[22]

This passage exposes the pejorative and historical (as opposed to the value-neutral and structural)[23] sense of *das Man* as the exemplary figure of twentieth-century mass culture, which has reduced individuals to mindless imitation, what Heidegger calls "the everyday lostness in the they."[24] The they-self is thus a "negative" ontological disposition, insofar as it denotes a loss of creative perspective on our own possibilities (authenticity).

Rorty sees the genre of the novel in particular as a privileged way of attaining or regaining this creative perspective on ourselves. In *Contingency, Irony, Solidarity*, Rorty expresses this Heideggerian contrast between authenticity and *das Man* as that between novels that restrict themselves to "the range of purposes presently statable within some familiar, widely used, final vocabulary" (i.e., conformity to the social norm) and novels that seek to work out "a *new* final vocabulary" (i.e., realize heretofore unimagined possibilities).[25] Of course, this presupposes that, as one commentator remarks, "The human self is not adequately or inadequately expressed in a vocabulary; rather it is created by the use of a vocabulary."[26] (This is also the assumption of Foucault, setting the stage for his "ethics of the self").[27] That is, the self is socially *constructed* but not socially *determined*—at least not completely. We have the possibility of transcending our acculturation (when supported by the proper sociopolitical system, i.e., the "standard bourgeois freedoms").

Where Rorty departs from Heidegger (and from Foucault, for that matter) is with regard to the direction of (Western) culture more generally. Words such as "progress" and "hope," so often found in Rorty, are nearly completely absent from Heidegger's oeuvre, which features many dark and brooding passages, such as the following from *Introduction to Metaphysics*: "We have said that the world is darkening. The essential episodes of this darkening are: the flight of the gods, the destruction of the earth, the standardization of man, the pre-eminence of the mediocre."[28] (And this is from a 1935 lecture course, thus *before* the disasters of WWII and the Holocaust.) Whereas Heidegger in effect sees the triumph of the *das Man*, Rorty, on the contrary, sees our post-Nietzschean age, dominated by a literary culture, as one that is *defined* in some sense by authenticity, by increasing "self-reliance" (even if Rorty also sounds a pessimistic note regarding economic developments)[29]:

> I hope that what I have said so far has given some plausibility to my thesis that the last five centuries of Western intellectual life may usefully be thought of first as progress from religion to philosophy, and then from philosophy to literature. I call it progress because I see philosophy as a transitional stage in a process of gradually increasing self-reliance. The great virtue of our new-found literary culture is that it tells young intellectuals that the only source of redemption is the human imagination, and that this fact should occasion pride rather than despair.[30]

Although the passage would appear to suggest a general *cultural progress* (i.e., progress that is social as well as individual), Rorty specifically singles out "the intellectuals," for only they are in search of redemption. The "intellectuals" have, by and large, given up the search for redemptive *truth*, "the need to fit everything—every thing, person, event, idea and poem—into a single context, a context which will somehow reveal itself as natural, destined, and unique,"[31] settling instead for redemption by the imagination, that is, self-creation/autonomy—the search for novelty rather than eternity.

Despite the recent decline of the humanities in general and departments of literature in particular, one might yet ask if this kind of inculcation of "young intellectuals" is not what university courses on literature, and on the novel in particular, are designed to accomplish—unless the approach to the text is formalist in orientation, in which case the existential significance is often elided. Thus, specifically in terms of literary criticism, Rorty's notion of a "literary culture" presupposes a particular (some might say reductive) approach to the literary text, one for which, incidentally, the textualism based on philosophers Rorty otherwise admires is strikingly ill suited. This explains why, while extoling Derrida as a thinker, Rorty always felt that the use to which Derrida's writings were put in literary studies was detrimental both to the understanding of Derrida's philosophy and to literary studies itself. In his 1984 essay "Deconstruction and Circumvention," Rorty avers that, insofar as "deconstruction" is understood as a "method of reading texts," "neither this method, nor any other, should be attributed to Derrida."[32] It would appear that, for his part, Rorty embraces a kind of "humanistic" approach insofar as it proposes to treat the literary text as a deeply human relation to the social and historical world. This is similar in some ways—surprisingly—to the approach of Edward Said and his brand of "secular" criticism (as articulated in *The World, the Text, and the Critic*),[33] although with a far more ambiguous relation to the "political." We will return to the political implications of Rorty's approach to literature below, after discussing his specific reflections on the novel.

Rorty's invocation of "the intellectuals" in "Philosophy as a Transitional Genre" smacks of a certain elitism, and one that would appear to be out of step with his egalitarianism:

> Most human beings, even those who have the requisite money and leisure, are not intellectuals. If they read books it is not because they seek redemption but either because they wish to be entertained or distracted, or because they want to become better able to carry out some antecedent purpose. They do not read books to find out what purposes to have. The intellectuals do.[34]

Thus, while intellectuals and nonintellectuals might read the same books, they do not read them the same way or with the same goal; in other words, they do not perceive books as possessing an *existential significance*. For the intellectual, reading imaginative literature, preeminently the novel, is a matter of finding "a *new* final vocabulary." But unlike Heidegger's (or Theodor Adorno's) indictment of the corrupting influence of mass culture, Rorty (like Foucault's practical division between the *oi prôtoi* and the *oi pôlloi*, the elite and the many, in the "ethics of the self") sees a largely neutral and fluid border between intellectuals and nonintellectuals, as befits an egalitarian society. Responding to a question about the role of higher education, Rorty remarks that "getting acquainted with the imaginative power of men like Shakespeare, Mozart, St. Paul, Jefferson, Pericles, Plato, Napoleon, and the like is probably the best way to get people to use their imaginations."[35] To the extent that university enrollments have greatly expanded since the 1960s, one could say that our culture is increasingly "intellectual."

It would certainly appear that, by its very nature, a literary culture would have a better shot at large-scale social transformation than a philosophical culture. Proust is obviously easier to read, is more enjoyable, requires less background knowledge, and has a far wider appeal than Kant (or Hegel, Nietzsche, Heidegger, Derrida, etc.). Moreover, it is possible that readers who might initially be interested only in the purely aesthetic or recreational aspect of *Remembrance of Things Past* might nevertheless discover an existential significance in spite of themselves. Such individuals might experience a *conversion*, similar to what René Girard describes in the last chapter of his *Deceit, Desire, and the Novel*.[36] The novel is thus more like religion than philosophy in terms of the breadth of its cultural relevance and the depth of its impact on the individual.

Nevertheless, despite the social significance implicit in his embrace of the novel as moral education, Rorty insists in this essay that redemption by the imagination—the adoption of a new final vocabulary—can be a matter only of private self-creation, thereby falling back on his 1989 position:

> But those of us who rejoice in the emergence of the literary culture can counter this charge [a rejection of argument in favor of oracular pronouncements] by saying that although argumentation is essential for projects of social cooperation, redemption is an individual, private, matter. Just as the rise of religious toleration depended on making a distinction between the needs of society and the needs of the individual, and on saying that religion was not necessary for the former, so the literary culture asks us to disjoin political deliberation from projects of redemption. This means acknowledging that their private hopes for authenticity and autonomy should be left at home when the citizens of a democratic society foregather to deliberate about what is to be done.[37]

The problem, as we noted above, is how to understand the final sentence of the passage, regarding democratic deliberation about "what is to be done." For this question is also at the center of "philosophy as cultural politics" as expressed in the preface, in which Rorty speaks about "humanity's ongoing conversation about what to do with itself," which implies "changes in the vocabularies deployed in moral and political deliberation"[38]—that is, a reflection on ends, not just means. According to the passage cited above, Rorty seemingly holds that what goes on in the public sphere can happen only within a fixed and settled paradigm (a final vocabulary) and that propositions about "what is to be done" cannot result in existential reflections on (sociopolitical) purposes and projects (a shift in final vocabulary). But if this were true, then how to explain actual paradigm shifts from, say, monarchy to democracy or communism, or from democracy to fascism, or existential decisions regarding going to war, colonial ambitions, the abolition of slavery, mass education, and so on? Or perhaps Rorty should be taken as making the *strictly ethical* point that projects of redemption *should* be restricted to the private realm, even if they are *in fact* often found in the tumultuous transitions from one political order to another—that since we have reached the ideal political order for the promotion of individual projects of self-creation (bourgeois liberalism), we should simply rejoice in the fact that paradigm shifts on the cultural-political level are no longer necessary or even desirable: "I don't think that there will be any big intellectual revolutions from now on. The educated political classes of all countries are going to be thinking in terms of the European Enlightenment, and civilization is going to be Eurocentric."[39] But this solution is hardly satisfactory, as I will explore below.

Finally, does the embrace of a "literary culture" imply that Rorty has simply abandoned philosophy? For if philosophy is a "transitional" genre,[40] then does this not mean that philosophy itself has been transcended? If so, what, then, are we to make of Rorty's own text, written in the *genre* of philosophy? Even if Rorty's text can be considered metaphilosophical, it does not thereby escape philosophy (Kant's *Critique of Pure Reason* is as much metaphilosophy as it is philosophy). One possible response is that the advent of a literary culture has not so much supplanted philosophy as it has changed its nature; philosophy takes on a new meaning in a context in which it occupies no central or even a specific place:

> From within a literary culture, religion and philosophy appear as literary genres. As such, they are optional. Just as an intellectual may opt to read many poems but few novels, or many novels but few poems, so he or she may read much philosophy, or much religious writing, but relatively few poems or novels. The difference between the literary intellectuals' readings of *all* these books and other readings of them is that the inhabitant of a literary culture treats books as human attempts to meet human needs, rather than as acknowledgements of the power of a being that is what it is apart from any such needs. "God" and "Truth" are, respectively, the religious and the philosophical names for that sort of being.[41]

"Literature," then, is the relativistic (ironic) standpoint from which all cultural products are viewed (which is, in fact, the working assumption of Theory as practiced in literature departments).[42] But this assertion does not address, and might even be said to obfuscate, the concept of "philosophy as cultural politics," which, it would seem, appeals to a specifically philosophical approach to culture that cannot simply be subsumed under the literary (or art).

The ethics of (novel) reading

In *Contingency, Irony, and Solidarity*, Rorty makes a distinction between "books which help us become autonomous" and "books which help us become less cruel,"[43] a distinction that derives from his private/public dichotomy. (Rorty thinks that we need only one guiding moral principle in a liberal democracy: the recognition that "cruelty is the worst thing we do.")[44] Thus, on the one side, there are the "elitist" (high-modernist) texts such as Henry James's *The Ambassadors* (1903) and Proust's *Remembrance of Things Past* (1913–27). These serve only *private* self-invention (autonomy). On the side of "books which help us become less cruel," we find two sorts: (1) "books which help us see the effects of social practices and institutions on others,"[45] like Harriet Beecher Stowe's *Uncle Tom's Cabin* (1852) and Victor Hugo's *Les misérables* (1862); and (2) books that serve as a "warning . . . against the tendencies to cruelty inherent to searches for autonomy,"[46] such as the haunting works of Vladimir Nabokov and George Orwell. As Rorty points out, this contrast is typically construed according to the traditional distinction between autonomous art (aestheticism) and committed (ethically engaged) art. Rorty wants to displace the essentialist overtones of this debate into a Nietzschean question of *utility* (what is good for life),[47] thereby contrasting books that serve individual self-making with those that serve the common good. In particular, Rorty wants to disabuse us of the Kantian idea that authentic aesthetic experience involves "disinterested contemplation." We must not, as Rorty puts it, confuse the "quest for autonomy with a need for relaxation and pleasure."[48] For in contrast to the aestheticists, the ironists have "doubts about the final vocabulary they employ"[49] (even if some versions of aestheticism, such as the dandyism of Oscar Wilde, involve some notion of self-making). In other words, the difference is an *existential* one.

What is especially interesting about Rorty's typology from the point of view of this chapter is that one type (or rather subtype) would appear to bridge the divide between the public (solidarity) and the private (autonomy), namely books, like those of Nabokov and Orwell, that "dramatize the conflict between duties to self and duties to others."[50] Something similar can be observed in the second essay under consideration in this chapter, "Redemption from Egotism: James and Proust as Spiritual Exercises," in which Rorty revisits the question of the significance of the novel for contemporary moral and intellectual life.

Like "Philosophy as a Transitional Genre," the main aim of "Redemption from Egotism" is to contrast religion and philosophy with a culture oriented toward novel reading. The essay thus represents a further development of the notion of a literary culture, but with one very important difference: the seemingly obligatory reference to the private/public diremption is noticeably absent. In fact, Rorty here appears to want to transcend this dichotomy. Instead of relegating Proust to the private realm of self-creation, as he did in his

1989 book, Rorty will suggest that the ironist novels of Proust and James can in fact promote social responsibility through the activation of individual autonomy, a position that places him very close indeed to Foucault's "ethics of the self."

We should note that Rorty is speaking not so much about the novel genre as such, but about how novel *reading* affects us, makes us who we are. Thus, as mentioned above, he is not interested in questions of genre or style—that is, poetics, formalist analysis. He also professes to be against what goes under the banner of Theory in departments of literature, for it threatens the autonomy of literature:

> [Harold Bloom] believes—rightly, in my opinion—that the dominance in U.S. departments of literature first of "theory" and then of "cultural studies" has made it more difficult for students to read well. For such attempts to give politics or philosophy hegemony over literature diminish the redemptive power of works of the imagination.

As this passage suggests, the literary critic who most typifies the approach to literature Rorty favors is Harold Bloom (or at least the later Bloom; the earlier Bloom was steeped in Theory).[51] Works by Bloom such as *Shakespeare: The Invention of the Human* (1998) and *How to Read and Why* (2001), which appeared just prior to the writing of the essays we have been discussing, are clearly an influence on Rorty's formulations, even if Rorty had already worked out much of his thinking on the significance of literature in *Contingency, Irony, Solidarity*. The first paragraph of "Redemption from Egotism" reads: "Harold Bloom is America's wisest, most learned, and most helpful student of literature. He has recently published a book called *How to Read and Why*. In it he says that 'The ultimate answer to the question "Why read?" is that only deep, constant reading fully establishes and augments an autonomous self.'"[52] Of course, both Rorty and Bloom have a common source in Nietzsche's individualist aesthetics. But it is the specifically *existential* significance of literature that, for Rorty and Bloom, triumphs over the narrowly aesthetic. As Rorty avers:

> For cultists like myself, remembering our first reading of these authors is central to the story we tell about our own growing up. They helped make us the people we are, and our gratitude remains intense. Insofar as we consider any books sacred, their novels count as such. So we find it irritating and misleading to find them brought under the category of "the aesthetic" as opposed to "the moral" or "the spiritual." We can of course acknowledge that there are beautiful passages in these novels, and that they are triumphs of literary craftsmanship. But these facts are no more essential to our relation to these books than the prose of the King James Version is to the Christian's relation to Christ, or the architecture of Nara and Kyoto is to the religious life of the Japanese Buddhist.[53]

According to Rorty, then, the very notion of literary *value* is inextricably tied to moral-existential self-understanding, to "authentic" being-in-the-world. Rorty's theses are not limited to the novel, however: "In our own time, ethnography, historiography, and journalism continue to broaden our sense of the possibilities open to human lives."[54] It is simply that the novel is *best* suited to assist us "in grasping the variety of human life and the contingency of our own moral vocabulary."[55] This is due to the novel's unparalleled ability to represent human figures (types as well as singular individuals) that have an isomorphic relation to the world of experience. Thus it is preeminently the *realist* (or modernist-realist) novel that best fulfills the specifically human (or secular-humanist) potential of the genre, as Rorty understands it.

There is, however, some tension with the concept of realism—its mimetic aspect—in Rorty's thought. Given his abhorrence of the philosophical concept of truth as correspondence to reality, Rorty would appear to be against any version of realism that is understood as a "mirroring" of reality:

> I think "rendering reality" is the wrong compliment to pay to [Henry] James (although I admit that it is one he was inclined to pay himself). Whenever a novelist creates a character with a set of self-descriptions and a moral outlook that we never before imagined, we can of course say, if we like, that an aspect of reality has been captured that had not previously been so well captured. But it is the novelty of the character and the utility of our acquaintance with her that justifies our praise, rather than the fidelity of representation. We did not know that aspect was there to be represented before we met Dimitri Karamazov or Charlotte Saint, nor that a moral dilemma could be regarded as Fanny Assingham does before we overheard her talking about it with her husband.[56]

While Rorty does not directly refute the concept of "fidelity of representation" in this passage, he nevertheless suggests that such a concept is mostly irrelevant to what he wants to argue. What interests him most is the novel's ability to *redescribe* reality in ways that create new human possibilities and that lead to a reappraisal of our moral assumptions. Rorty's "novelty" is not, then, in any strict sense opposed to mimesis; in fact, it would appear that the kind of novelty Rorty promotes is a function of realistic representation itself. Even if it is not primarily informed by the idea of mimesis as world-reflecting (Plato) or as the presentation of everyday reality in a tragic, serious, or problematic manner (Auerbach's "mixture of styles"),[57] Rorty's Nietzsche-inspired "aestheticism" is nevertheless parasitic on Aristotle's contention, in the *Poetics*, that "it is not the poet's function to relate actual events, but the *kinds* of things that might occur and are possible in terms of probability or necessity" (1451a-37–38)[58] and on Auerbach's idea that realism represents a secularization and assimilation of Christian intuitions regarding egalitarianism and moral worth.[59] Thus (with a nod to

Aristotle), a literary description would be less useful for our self-development if: (1) it bore no relation to a shared reality (consensus belief), if we could not recognize it as a *human possibility*; or (2) it merely presented reality (actuality) or repeated prior descriptions of the world (which no longer relate to *possibilities* as such). And (with a nod to Auerbach) the literature of self-creation also presupposes the egalitarian concept of an individual capable of self-actualization as a subject of history. Hence Rorty's aversion to nonmimetic or highly idiosyncratic works, such as those by Franz Kafka, since he feels that these are of little use for our self-development. (During a discussion of this essay held at Stanford University in the early 2000s, which I attended, Rorty dismissed Kafka as an "oddball.") Thus only a "novelty" tempered by mimesis is useful and therefore redemptive.

Rorty describes at length the many virtues of novel reading, both in general and by using the specific examples of Proust and James, two authors who exemplify for him the greatest potential of the genre. Although Rorty does not enumerate these virtues in any systematic way, I think that the following summary will be helpful in clarifying his position:

1. Novel reading offers escape from *egotism*, which Rorty defines as "self-satisfaction": the assumption that "all the knowledge necessary for deliberation, all the understanding of the consequences of a contemplated action that could be needed . . . that one is now fully informed, and thus in the best possible position to make correct choices"[60] ("egotism" is basically the bad faith/self-deception of Heidegger's they-self)—(this also recalls Sartre's formulation that "there is this in common between art and morality, that in both we have to do with creation and invention. We cannot decide a priori what it is that should be done").[61]

2. It permits us to get to know what a *variety* of unfamiliar people are like, thereby increasing understanding and *tolerance* (Tzvetan Todorov comments that, according to Rorty, "what novels give us is not new information but a new capacity for compassion with beings different from ourselves")[62]; this applies to *both* committed and ironist literature, unlike what Rorty argued in *Contingency, Irony, Solidarity*.

3. It encourages us to wonder if we are sufficiently aware of the needs of others; the novel thereby offers a specifically *moral education*: "The hegemony of the novel can be viewed as an attempt to carry through on Christ's suggestion that love is the only law"[63] (this view coheres with Auerbach's contention that the triumph of the realist novel is based on a working out of the Gospels' aesthetico-moral dialectic between *sublimitas* and *humilitas*).[64]

4   It allows us to take an ironic distance from our unexamined assumptions about the world—our *idées reçues*—thus setting the stage for the possible adoption of a *new* final vocabulary.
5   It enlarges the imagination; we are thus able to envisage new possibilities, as opposed to the simple codification of existing norms that moral philosophy/didactic literature offers.
6   It instills *practical* knowledge rather than theoretical knowledge, that is, in Rorty's parlance, "knowing-how" (gaining familiarity with concrete situations) as opposed to "knowing-that" (application of preestablished principles or theories).[65]
7   It enables us to see our lives as a work of art; it thus gives us a sense of an *existential* and not a merely aesthetic "exaltation," and satisfies our "longing for shapeliness"[66] (as in Foucault's "styles of existence"[67] and in the following passage of Nietzsche: "*One thing is needful.*—To 'give style' to one's character—a great and rare art! It is practiced by those who survey all the strengths and weaknesses of their nature and then fit them into an artistic plan until every one of them appears as art and reason, and even weaknesses delight the eye").[68]
8   It provides an *example* of "creative self-overcoming"; that is, as a vehicle of the author's self-overcoming, the novel incites the reader to achieve a similar self-overcoming; one imitates the originality itself rather than the product of the originality (as in Nietzsche's inversion of the *imitatio Christi* in the *The Antichrist*: "In reality there has been only one Christian, and he died on the Cross").[69]

The upshot of all of this is that

> it is by causing us to rethink our judgments of particular people that imaginative literature does most to help us break with our own pasts. The resulting liberation may, of course, lead one to try to change the political or economic or religious or philosophical status quo. Such an attempt may begin a lifetime of effort to break through the received ideas that serve to justify present-day institutions.[70]

This statement appears to directly contradict the assertion quoted above (from the roughly contemporaneous "Philosophy as a Transitional Genre") that "the literary culture asks us to disjoin political deliberation from projects of redemption." Indeed, the statement sounds very Foucauldian (minus the term "liberation," which Foucault sees as distinct from "freedom"),[71] particularly the idea that self-creation (Foucault's "ethics of the self") can support the critique of institutions (or what Sartre called the "practico-inert"—the status quo).[72] Along with the 2007 preface to *Philosophy as Cultural Politics*, this is the closest Rorty comes to breaking out of his ironist cage: a declaration that, generally speaking, reading ironist novels can have/should have a real-world, sociopolitical impact. That is, insofar as these novels are uniquely calibrated to effect an escape from "egotism," ironist literature allows for a reconsideration of our final vocabulary and, through this effort, a reconsideration of collective purposes and ideas of justice. In short, novel reading is a practice of "cultural politics," a term he cites once in the essay.[73] "Redemption from Egotism" is thus more in tune with the preface to *Philosophy as Cultural Politics* than is "Philosophy as a Transitional Genre," and in my view it should have been substituted for the latter in this collection.

I am not the only commentator to notice this shift in position, which I consider to be tantamount to an "ethical turn" (interrupted by Rorty's death from cancer in 2007), such as was observed in Foucault. In a recent book, *Romanticism and Pragmatism: Richard Rorty and the Idea of a Poeticized Culture* (2015), Ulf Schulenberg observes (concerning the "Egotism" essay) that "James and Proust are not only useful for private purposes of self-fashioning, they also indirectly contribute to moral reflection in a liberal democratic culture." Thus "the strict separation between private irony and social hope cannot always be maintained."[74] However, even if Schulenberg recognizes that Rorty's "discussion of Proust and James in 'Redemption from Egotism' complicates the categories that he introduced in *Contingency, Irony, and Solidarity*,"[75] he nevertheless tends to downplay the significance of this shift from the earlier position, making it sound as if it were an exception to the rule rather than a new rule. I contend, however, that Rorty has in fact reconsidered some of his major tenets; he appears to have reached the conclusion that what he once called the "firm distinction between the private and the public"[76] obfuscated the significance of novel reading for "cultural politics." Like Sartre's shift from *Being and Nothingness* to *Critique of Dialectical Reason*, Rorty aims to broaden the individualist existentialism of his earlier work to include a collective-cultural dimension. Although he professes not to like Sartre's *Critique* (even if he admires much of Sartre's oeuvre),[77] his key notion of "solidarity" nevertheless recalls its notion of "group praxis" almost verbatim. From a late interview: "[Solidarity] is accepting reciprocal responsibility to other members of the group for the sake of a common purpose."[78]

Another interesting viewpoint on Rorty's "ethical turn" is expressed by Colin Koopman, who argues in a 2013 essay that while Rorty appears, at times, to want to abandon philosophy, to wash his hands of it, he is simply "seeking to nudge things over from *professional philosophy* toward *cultural criticism*."[79] Koopman thus makes a distinction between "two conceptions of philosophy across Rorty's thought": One involves debunking the outlandish claims of "professional philosophy" (both Analytic and Continental) as "making pretty grand world-historical promises on their own behalf," whereas the other involves philosophy conceived as "cultural criticism," namely as "an exercise that is of abiding value for modern liberal democracies like America."[80] According to this scenario, Rorty's late call for "philosophy as cultural politics" is where he had wanted to end up all along: "Here in one of his very last writings [the preface to *Philosophy as Cultural Politics*] printed just months before he passed away, the indefatigable critic of foundationalist philosophy offered a final, and incisively concise, characterization of the positive role that he hoped philosophy might yet come to play."[81] Thus Rorty can be said to ultimately believe in a positive and socially committed role for philosophy, even if much of current philosophy had disappointed him on that score.

The problem with this analysis (well argued and convincing as far as it goes), is that it does not take into account the conflict with Rorty's cardinal idea of the public/private split, which disqualifies ironist, non-foundationalist philosophy from taking any public role. Is it possible for Rorty to promote the idea of "philosophy as cultural politics" while maintaining that we must "stop trying to combine self-creation and politics, especially if we are liberals" and that "liberal political discourse would do well to remain as untheoretical and simpleminded as it looks"?[82] The main problem for me is not whether or not Rorty thinks philosophy in general is socially valuable but whether the kind of philosophy he favors, in particular ironist philosophy, is useful for the public sphere or only for private self-invention, as he had maintained throughout the bulk of his career.

What I am calling Rorty's "ethical turn" in the 2000s may in fact be a response of sorts to Richard Shusterman's blistering critique of Rorty in a chapter entitled "Postmodern Ethics and the Art of Living," from his book *Pragmatist Aesthetics: Living Beauty, Rethinking Art*. Although the book was published in 1992, it was reissued in a second edition in 2000, which may have prodded Rorty to take a second look. (Rorty certainly read the first edition, since Shusterman refers to his reaction to it in his introduction to the second edition.) In his chapter, Shusterman takes Rorty to task for his conflation of self-creation with uniqueness or originality: "Even if the ethical goal of narrative self-creation be modeled on the creation of a work of art, it still does not follow that such creation must be radically novel and altogether unique." This is because art can be aesthetically satisfying without "radical and idiosyncratic originality."[83] Shusterman thus considers Rorty's "radical individualism" to be narrowly elitist and counterproductive, for it ultimately devolves into a state of "non-autonomy, a bondage to the new and individualistic."[84] Shusterman thus also sees Rorty's public/private dichotomy as untenable, criticizing Rorty for his "extreme privatization of morality," for "failing to recognize how deeply and ineluctably the public ethos structures the very conception of our diverse quests for private perfection."[85] Ultimately, for Shusterman, Rorty's conception of individual self-creation is simply an intellectual version of "capitalist America," with its "breathless production and accumulation of new vocabularies and new narratives."[86]

I see much of value in Shusterman's polemic, particularly his critique of the public/private split that structures so much of Rorty's thought. However, if he wants to indict Rorty's ideal of self-creation, he also needs to tell us what is wrong with this same ideal as expressed in Nietzsche, Heidegger, and Sartre, not to mention Foucault, whose philosophy he seems to favor. In this vein, I do not think that Shusterman understands Rorty's specifically *existential* conception of aesthetics (as Hayden White notes, "I think that the task of Theory nowadays is to free art from aesthetics").[87]

I also agree, as noted above, that Rorty's seeming elitism is problematic in addition to being out of step with his broader egalitarianism (Shusterman does not bring the latter point into his discussion). It is indeed difficult to separate out the intellectuals from the rest of culture, as if there were little or no interaction between the two (and this is especially true with respect to university students). For if most of the "intellectuals" as Rorty describes them (i.e., those who seek redemption) shift to a "literary culture," then would this not have a powerful effect on the culture at large (e.g., through opinion columns, television commentary, Internet blogs, Hollywood movies, etc.)? In other words, cannot the "progress" that the "literary culture" represents also be construed as social progress? For is not one of the functions of a literary culture to persuade some of the nonintellectuals to become self-creating individuals and thereby, by dint of sheer numbers, have a sociopolitical impact? Not to mention the fact that, as Schulenberg puts it, "Rorty seems to hold that only in his ideal poeticized culture would one achieve full human maturity and dignity."[88] I do not think Rorty would maintain that full human dignity is for the intellectuals alone. Indeed, as cited at the beginning of this chapter, Rorty had remarked in *Contingency, Irony, Solidarity* that "the point of social organization is to let *everybody* have a chance at self-creation to the best of his or her abilities." It is indeed difficult to reconcile this egalitarian ideal with the elitist observation (in "Philosophy as a Transitional Genre") that "most" are nonintellectual social conformists (Heidegger's *das Man*). Finally, when Rorty speaks about holding "our *time*" in thought, how can he not be referring to the general direction of an entire culture, rather than the musings of the intellectuals?

Rorty addresses these concerns somewhat in a late interview ("On Philosophy and Politics"), in which he suggests that ironist philosophy may indeed have an *indirect* effect on public discourse: "The philosophers whom I admire (Donald Davidson, Jacques Derrida, for example) are also the ones for whom I should like to claim social utility—very long-run social utility, of the sort that can be attributed to changes in the intellectual atmosphere which eventually benefit society as a whole."[89] This suggestion is, indeed, a far cry from the trenchant pronouncements on the public/private split in *Contingency, Irony, Solidarity* and in writings as late as "Philosophy as a Transitional Genre." With regard to the public/private dichotomy, Rorty would appear to want to have his cake and eat it too.

I conclude by observing that in some of his last writings and interviews, Rorty's conception of individual self-creation and of its potential impact on society is little different from that we find in Foucault's "ethics of the self"—an idea that, as we saw in Chapter 2, Rorty had relentlessly criticized throughout much of his career. Like Foucault, the self is for Rorty a "practice of freedom"[90]; for it is by becoming aware of our historical contingency and of the productive and constraining power of language that we can attain a creative perspective on our possibilities. Even the subtitle of the essay we have been discussing—"James and Proust as Spiritual Exercises"—recalls Pierre Hadot's and Foucault's efforts to define an alternative to theoretical knowledge in the idea of philosophy as a way of life.[91] To be fair, Rorty did not have access to most of the relevant material concerning the "ethics of the self" until Foucault's seminars were published in the 2000s (and most appeared after Rorty's death). In addition, Rorty may not have noticed that, in a few of his late interviews, Foucault had, in fact, moved closer to the liberal-reformist position Rorty favors.[92] Finally, it should be said that the confluence between the existential-aesthetic and the ethical in both thinkers is a testament to the abiding influence of the Nietzschean-Heideggerian-Sartrean view of the individual vis-à-vis society.

: ARGUMENT CHARACTERIZATION

2.2.12 Pragma-Dialectics

Already established, in the thirties and forties of the twentieth century, was the Erlangen
School, which preceded Pragma-Dialectics in its important feature of ‘dialectics’ - but
without the pragmatic component. For the Erlangen School, the adversary in the dialectics
was not a real person, but an ideal adversary (Kamlah and Lorenzen, 1984).

Then came Pragma-Dialectics, which was originated in the Netherlands as an empirical
approach to the study of real-life reasoning and argumentation. Both ‘pragma’ and
‘dialectic’ refer to the way in which linguistic exchanges take place between real
individuals. However, Pragma-Dialectics makes an important distinction between how
argumentation does take place, and how it ideally should take place. Both of these aspects
are studied by Pragma-Dialectics.

Pragma-Dialectics originated from the Amsterdam School of Argumentation Theory,
founded by Frans van Eemeren and Rob Grootendorst. For the last forty years, it has been
developed by these two and their collaborators, in a huge body of work - see for instance
van Eemeren and Grootendorst (1984), van Eemeren and Grootendorst (1992), van
Eemeren and Grootendorst (2004), van Eemeren, Grootendorst, Jackson, and Jacobs
(1993), van Eemeren, Grootendorst, and Kruiger (1987), van Eemeren, Grootendorst, and
Snoeck Henkemans (2002), van Eemeren (2001), van Eemeren (2002), van Eemeren
(2009), van Eemeren (2015), and van Eemeren (2018). In this book, we will follow mainly
the 2004 book of van Eemeren and Grootendorst.

According to pragma-dialectics, argumentation is an activity of reason indicating that the
arguer has considered the topic from various perspectives (van Eemeren, Grootendorst,
and Snoeck Henkemans, 2002, p. xii).

CHAPTER FIVE

From *Metahistory* to *The Practical Past*

Hayden White's existentialist philosophy of history

In choosing our past, we choose a present; and vice versa.

—HAYDEN WHITE[1]

The influence of existentialist thought—particularly that of Jean-Paul Sartre—on Hayden White has not, in my view, been adequately appreciated or understood in the large and growing secondary literature on White's oeuvre.[2] This is particularly true of the reception of his magnum opus *Metahistory: The Historical Imagination in Nineteenth-Century Europe* (1973),[3] his most widely read work, which continues to be seen by both detractors and admirers as primarily a contribution to literary theory, rather than, as F. R. Ankersmit observes, "the unparalleled success story of all twentieth century philosophy of history."[4] The emphasis on the literary-formalist over the specifically philosophical import of *Metahistory* and White's other writings has had the effect of obscuring White's larger project: namely, the reorientation of historical studies from a pseudo-scientific discipline that claims objectivity to an endeavor—either academic or "practical"—that must come to terms with its intrinsically creative and ethical vocation. This chapter explores how White's approach is rooted in existentialist theory, in particular in Sartre's idea of "choosing the past," which, I contend, can be seen in retrospect as being one of the guiding threads of all of White's work, from his first important essays of the 1960s to his most recent book *The Practical Past* (2014), in which the ethico-existential aspect is most explicit.

White and Sartre: Choosing the past

We begin our investigations with the consideration of two key early essays by White (both written when White was a professor of medieval history at the University of Rochester, where he taught from 1958 to 1968): "The Burden of History" and "What is a Historical System?"[5] The first, published in the recently founded journal *History and Theory*,[6] would become one of White's best-known texts.[7] Its polemical tone established White as a prominent critic of academic historiography, a reputation that would only be enhanced with the publication of *Metahistory* in 1973.[8] Although less well known, "What is a Historical System?"—originally presented at a conference in 1967, but only published five years later—is no less important to the understanding of White's intellectual trajectory.[9] Both essays reveal the strong influence of Sartre's existentialist manifesto *Being and Nothingness* (*L'être et le néant*, 1943), a book that was formative for many American intellectuals educated in the late 1940s and 1950s.[10]

Sartre's existentialist philosophy revolves around a fundamental dialectic between "being-for-itself" (*l'être-pour-soi*, human consciousness—or *transcendence* in a situation) and "being-in-itself" (*l'être-en-soi*, the inert, the nonconscious—or *facticity* in a situation). Sartre holds that because we are never reducible to our facticity (which includes our past), we are always essentially and inescapably "free," free to *choose* ourselves, but also *obliged* to choose ourselves in every moment, for even to refuse to choose is still a "choice"; passivity is therefore an illusion. (In Sartre's sense, "to choose" does not necessarily entail the ability to obtain but only the *autonomy* of choice. As Sartre says, "Success is not important to freedom."[11]) Hence, existence is a kind of *burden* (we are responsible for it)—just as White will argue in his essay that history is a "burden" in this onto-existential sense. The desire to flee our ontological responsibility is what Sartre calls "bad faith" (self-deception): It involves either refusing our facticity (ignoring our limitations) or refusing our transcendence (relinquishing freedom). In historiographical terms, one could call the first type *negationism*, the denial of facts; and the second type *objectivism*, the denial of choice or responsibility. White treats mostly the second type in his essay; the first type will be addressed in his later work as he comes under attack for his putative "relativism."[12]

In a section of *Being and Nothingness* entitled "My Past," Sartre outlines several positions that will find their way into White's thought. Using the French Revolution as a historical example, Sartre distinguishes between historical *fact* ("The Bastille was taken in 1789"),[13] which is immutable, and historical *meaning* ("a revolt without consequence ... or ... the first manifestation of popular strength"),[14] which is a function of the choices made by later interpreters. "Thus," writes Sartre, "human history would have to be *finished* before a particular event, for example the taking of the Bastille, could receive a definitive *meaning*."[15] Historical actors and historians *choose* or *decide* to see two events as related or unrelated according to their volitional aims and factical predispositions. Thus, to return to Sartre's example, the revolutionary National Convention, "anxious to create a famous past of itself," sought to transform the taking of the Bastille into "a glorious deed" (though from another perspective, the same event could easily be seen as desultory)—a designation it has retained in the form of the *fête nationale*, Bastille Day.[16] (Since the royalist perspective was extinguished and no longer holds sway, there is no genuine alternate history in French national consciousness, but in principle, of course, there could have been.) Through such rituals, modern France effectively chooses itself, constantly, as the embodiment of the ideals of the French Revolution and, in so doing, projects a certain future. The reverse is also true: By projecting these ideals as its most desirable future, modern France effectively chooses the French Revolution as *its* past (the past it has chosen to fulfill or actualize), rather than, say, the *Ancien Régime* or the Napoleonic Empire. In the same way, one could say that modern Germany refuses its Nazi past as *its* past, as the past whose spirit it wishes to embody and perpetuate, but it does not thereby deny the facticity of Nazism of the Holocaust, which would be a form of bad faith, that is, revisionism or negationism.[17] In Sartrean terms, transcending one's past does not in the least involve its denial.

This operation is best illustrated by what Sartre says about the personal past and the existential "project":

> Now the meaning of the past is strictly dependent on my present project.... I alone in fact can decide at each moment the *bearing* of the past. I do not decide it by debating over it, and in each instance evaluating the importance of this or that prior event; but by projecting myself toward my ends, I preserve the past with me, and by action I *decide* its meaning. Who shall decide whether the mystic crisis in my fifteenth year "was" a pure accident of puberty or, on the contrary, the first sign of a future conversion? I myself, according to whether I shall decide—at twenty years of age, at thirty years—to be converted.[18]

Sartre's point here—a point he first sketched in his early novel *Nausea* (1938)—is that the past is meaningless in itself; it only takes on meaning when it is volitionally related to the present, that is, to present *choices*, which, for Sartre, entail a choice of *being* (according to Sartre, we are defined by our chosen actions, not by a preexisting "essence," as in his famous slogan, "existence precedes essence"). Sartre, in effect, collapses the distinction between an internal (subjective) and an external (objective) perspective in historical studies, for the historian is, in fact, in the same predicament as the historical actor: Both are effectively *making history* in both the literal and figurative sense.[19] Sartre notes that "the historian is himself *historical*; that is . . . he historicizes himself by illuminating 'history' in the light of his projects and of those of his society."[20] In other words, whether under the guise of "professionalism" or of "objectivity," the historian cannot escape the fundamental freedom that inheres in every individual's and society's relation to its past and in the ends toward which the individual or collective orients itself as a function of its project. The irreducible element of futurity in choice has the effect of blurring the distinction between history and philosophy of history: All history writing is essentially a projection into the future through the past, even if only philosophy of history does so explicitly (i.e., in good faith).[21]

Summarizing Sartre's view in "The Burden of History," White writes, "We choose our past in the same way we choose our future. The historical past therefore, is, like our various personal pasts, at best a myth, justifying our gamble on a specific future, and at worst a lie, a retrospective rationalization of what we have become through our choices."[22] White will effectively adopt this existentialist view, including the merging of the perspective of the "personal past" with that of the historical past (and this becomes even more explicit in White's analysis of the "practical past" in his most recent work).[23] Indeed, the idea that "we choose our past in the same way we choose our future," that we realize our present aspirations by projecting them backward as well as forward, would become a major theme in White's work. By suggesting that his fellow historians considered the past as pure facticity, as an "in-itself," White was essentially accusing them of "bad faith" in the Sartrean sense. The bad-faith historian refuses to see his or her activity as part of a living project; he or she sees the past *as past*, as irremediably over and done with and as disconnected from the present (the idea of the "fixity of the past")[24]; nevertheless, the past is still conceived as a "burden" in the sense that it weighs on the present as having determined it factically. White thus advocated for the "transformation" of historical studies, so "as to allow the historian to participate positively in the liberation of the present from the *burden of history*."[25] By this, White meant that instead of regarding our past as simply a chain of linear causes that lead inexorably to the present, we should instead conceive of our past as a vast *storehouse of possibilities* from which we are *obliged to choose*, even if not every possibility is realizable in the present (due to our factical limitations).

We turn now to "What is a Historical System?" in which White fleshes out what had only been suggested in the "The Burden of History." Proposing that history be considered on the analogy of a biological organism (i.e., as coming into being, maturing, and dying), White collapses the distinction between historians and historical actors, recalling, as noted above, Sartre's dissolution of the difference between the historical and the personal past. The ostensible aim of the essay was to show that "historical systems differ from biological systems by their capacity to act *as if they could choose their own ancestors*."[26] That is, biological systems are genetic, whereas historical systems are genetic in only a nominal or fictional sense, since these involve not actual (or merely) physical generation but ideal relationships: "The historical past is plastic in a way that the genetic past is not. Men range over it and select from it models of comportment for structuring their movement into the future. They choose a set of *ideal ancestors* that they *treat* as *genetic progenitors*."[27] As an example, White cites the development of medieval Christian civilization, culminating in the Holy Roman Empire. The break with pagan-Roman culture occurred when men decided to consider themselves as being the descendants of the Judeo-Christian part of their past, effectively abandoning the Roman worldview and cultural practices, and thereby becoming wholly "Christian": "When in short they began to honor the Christian past as the most desirable of a future uniquely their own, and ceased to honor the Roman past as *their* past, the Roman sociocultural system ceased to exist."[28] Although White does not mention it in this essay, his idea of the historical system stems from an early fascination with Martin Luther's revolt against the Catholic Church, which replaced an almost millennium-and-a-half-old tradition with a return to textual Christianity and the simplicity of origins. Protestants thus do not regard Catholics as their progenitors but instead see themselves as coinheritors of the original Christianity of the Gospels and of the ministry of Peter and Paul in the first century AD.

At the end of the essay, White sums up his argument in terms that recall the Sartrean language of "The Burden of History": "In choosing our past, we choose a present; and vice versa. We use the one to *justify* the other. By constructing our present, we assert our freedom; by seeking retroactive justification for it in our past, we silently strip ourselves of the freedom that has allowed us to become what we are."[29] That is, we are not determined by our past so much as we choose it. It was traditional historical inquiry that White saw as "stripping [us] of our freedom," since, in its "bad faith" (*la mauvaise foi*), it refused to see in its "justification" of the present the result of a choice of historical being.

White and Heidegger: The practical past

At this point, I think it would be helpful to recall the discussions of this problematic in Martin Heidegger's *Being and Time*—a strong influence on Sartre—which will allow us to better elucidate the stakes involved in the idea of "choosing the past" from the perspective of existentialist philosophy. In Division II of *Being and Time*, Heidegger uses the Kierkegaard-inspired concept of "repetition" or "retrieve" (*Wiederholung*) to describe the constitutive historicity of *Dasein* (human existence):

> *Retrieve is explicit handing down*, that is, going back to the possibilities of Da-sein that has been there. The authentic retrieve of a possibility of existence that has been—the possibility that Da-sein may choose its own heroes—is existentially grounded in anticipatory resoluteness. . . . The retrieve of what is possible neither brings back "what is past," nor

does it bind the "present" back to what is "outdated." ... Rather retrieve *responds* to the possibility of existence that has-been-there. ... Retrieve neither abandons itself to the past, nor does it aim at progress.³⁰

The essentials of Heidegger's existential conception of history are contained in this passage: (1) the idea that *Dasein* can "choose its own heroes," that is, it can choose its own models from the past as possibilities for the present (White echoes this idea in a previously quoted passage: "Men range over [the historical past] and select from it models of comportment"); (2) the idea of the repetition/retrieve (*Wiederholung*) of a past conceived as that which "has been" (*Gewesenheit*)—that is, a past that retains its relation to the present—as opposed to the "outdated" (i.e., objectified) past (*Vergangenheit*) severed from the present; (3) and that repetition/retrieve is also a *response* to the past; in other words, it is the manifestation of an *interpretive* attitude, which is not a desire to relive the past, to merely identify with past actors (retrieve/repetition does not "abandon itself to the past"), but to make it new, open-endedly, that is, without thereby assuming a particular teleology (such as progress or decline). This, for Heidegger, constitutes an *authentic* relation to one's past. Thus, as Richard Rorty notes, *Wiederholung* is an essential element of self-creation: "As Heidegger emphasized, to achieve authenticity in this sense it is not necessarily to *reject* one's past. ... What matters is to have seen one or more alternatives to the purposes that most people take for granted, and to have chosen among these alternatives—thereby, in some measure, creating yourself."³¹

In his ethical reading of Heidegger, Gianni Vattimo offers a lucid reinterpretation of Heidegger's concept of authentic historicity:

> There is no history of Being other than that of human praxis; and there is no objective structure other than that of history considered as previous, that is, as interpreted for and by the present, a history that, as *Being and Time* teaches, is never *vergangen* (gone) but always only *gewesen* (what has been). That is, the past is not an immutable datum ... but a call, a message that always addresses itself to the projectural capacity of the one who receives it and who actively interprets it. What is "real" is not in any way objective Being, but only that which has been produced by other beings existing before us, themselves active interpreters, involved in a process that might have developed differently.³²

Vattimo thus proposes a "radical reading of Heidegger," which translates into a "radical historicism," that is, a historicism that results from an "ontology of the present" (i.e., a "philosophy of the present") and from its triple function of "inheriting-interpreting-transforming."³³ Vattimo contrasts the notion of the past as objective Being with the past conceived as *praxis* (a move that leads Vattimo in a recent book to link Heidegger to Marx),³⁴ thereby recalling Heidegger's cardinal distinction (elaborated in Division I of *Being and Time*) between *Vorhandenheit* ("presence-at-hand" or "objective presence") and

Zuhandenheit ("readiness-to-hand" or "handiness"). On this conception, the past is primarily *Zuhandenheit*, a practical past, a past always already interpreted in the context of its relationality to the present and the future, and only secondarily or derivatively *Vorhandenheit*, the objective apprehension of the past, that is, the past of the traditional, Rankean historian (whose approach, for Heidegger, entails an impoverished vision of the past because of its detachment from being-in-the-world).

In his most recent work, *The Practical Past* (2014), White has sought to develop a similar distinction, that between the "practical past" and the "historical past," a distinction he derives from the British philosopher and political theorist Michael Oakeshott.[35] The concept of the "historical past" matches up with Heidegger's critique of scientific objectivity, of the primacy accorded to "theory" as a mental activity that detaches objects from their practical contexts, considering them in isolation and for their own sake, existing by and for themselves. White writes:

> The historical past is a theoretically motivated construction, existing only in the books and articles published by professional historians; it is constructed as an end in itself, possesses little or no value for understanding or explaining the present, and provides no guidelines for acting in the present or foreseeing the future.[36]

In short, the "historical past" has only a scholarly utility; it does not help us to interpret ourselves with a view toward realizing our goals in the present. But unlike Heidegger's concept of practical utility, White's notion of the "practical past" stems from a more Kantian conception of the "practical," with its ethico-political implications (without losing sight, of course, of the Nietzschean-Sartrean conception of the past as not something to be merely studied, categorized, examined, etc., but rather as something to be *used* for distinctively human ends): "The practical past is made up of all those memories, illusions, bits of vagrant information, attitudes and values which the individual or the group summons up as best they can to justify, dignify, excuse, alibi, or make a case for actions to be taken in the prosecution of a life project."[37] Here again we find the existentialist language of the "project," thereby connecting White's current thinking with the impulses that came out of the writing of "The Burden of History" and "What is a Historical System?" in the mid-1960s.

Not surprisingly, White associates the "practical past" with philosophy of history, thus underscoring the fact that for White, all *authentic* history is philosophy of history. Aligning philosophy of history with literary genres such as the historical and realist novel, which also bear a "practical" relation to the past, White observes:

> It has to be said that, whatever else it may be, philosophy of history belongs to the class of disciplines meant to bring order and reason to

a "practical past" rather than to that "historical past" constructed by professional historians for the edification of their peers in their various fields of study.[38]

Now the idea of the "practical past" is certainly not a new thought in White's work, even if it does effectively bring philosophy of history back into the forefront of White's reflections, after having languished for some time in the background. In fact, the idea of the practical-historical is rooted in White's earliest university studies, in the example of his undergraduate mentor William J. Bossenbrook at Wayne State University (an inspiring figure who also taught Arthur Danto and Harry Harootunian). Describing the intellectually formative (and not merely inspirational) influence of his teacher, White recounts:

> [Bossenbrook] consistently sustained the illusion that the study of history was the most important intellectual task that a morally responsible man could undertake. Perhaps this was because he always portrayed the great historians of the past as actors in the dramas of culture, not as mere passive commentators on events that had already run their courses.... We concluded that thought and action were not mutually exclusive alternatives, but only different aspects of the single seamless web of human involvement.[39]

This passage, written in 1968, before any of the books for which he is now famous had been published, offers what I consider to be the best succinct statement of White's philosophy of history: historical writing as *praxis*—as the shaping both of historical reality and of the community that historical writing serves. White's insistence on the *activity* of the heroic (and "morally responsible") historian/philosopher of history versus the *passivity* of the traditional, objectivist (value-neutral) historian is simply a somewhat romanticized version of a leitmotif that runs throughout his oeuvre.[40] For White's philosophy of history is inextricable from a "philosophy of the present" (explored in Part I of this volume); that is, from an understanding of the role of history in individual and collective self-making and self-transcendence.

Existentialism in *Metahistory*: Tropology and emplotment

We now turn to White's groundbreaking monograph, *Metahistory: The Historical Imagination in Nineteenth-Century Europe*. This multifaceted work endeavors to address several related aims simultaneously, from a historical account of the evolution of historical consciousness in the nineteenth century to a tropological account of the "deep structure" of historical thought. Though it is most famous for the Vico-inspired, fourfold theory of tropes (metaphor, metonymy, synecdoche, irony) developed in an extensive introduction, *Metahistory* is also, and perhaps foremost, a sustained defense of the philosophy of history genre. On the one hand, it infused new life into philosophy of history by making it amenable to the new, linguistically oriented approaches in the humanities; on the other, it deconstructed the cardinal opposition between straight history and philosophy of history that had resulted in the excommunication of the latter from academic historiography. The first goal was achieved by the performative nature of *Metahistory* itself: *Metahistory* demonstrated that a tropological philosophy of history was possible by its very elaboration. In this sense, it is less important to learn that, as White writes, "Marx apprehended the historical field in the Metonymical mode,"[41] which *in itself* is not very illuminating, than to learn that this kind of reflection can be considered as part of a *tropological system* that defines historical consciousness as such.[42]

The second goal involved showing that the tropes structured all historical discourse and thus that, at the deepest or most fundamental level, straight history and philosophy of history are one ("The possible modes of historiography are the same as the possible modes of speculative philosophy of history").[43] But, of course, only a metahistorical approach can account for this fact, thereby surreptitiously establishing its priority. White's *Metahistory* was in effect a metametahistory,[44] since it involved the condition of possibility of historical and philosophical-historical discourse itself, even if this condition was conceived as tropological rather than as logical-conceptual. (White's move was not unlike Jacques Derrida's deconstruction of the opposition between speech and writing: Both terms of the opposition are shown to inhere in a common structure, a structure that can only be described by one of the terms, "writing" or "arche-writing," though Derrida's "arche-" sounded paradoxically more transcendental than White's "meta-.") As Harry Harootunian observes, White "[laid] to rest the claims of the philosophy of history by shifting its ground to linguistic protocols that would demonstrate how 'empirical history' was no more exempt from the mediations of linguistic prefiguration than was philosophy of history."[45] Thus, in his preface to *Metahistory*, White argues that the differences between straight history and philosophy of history are more superficial than essential, that "there can be no 'proper history' which is not at the same time 'philosophy of history,'"[46] meaning that, in addition to the common tropological structure, all history writing inevitably embodies theoretical presuppositions that concern history-in-general and that condition any elaboration of the historical particulars. Proper or straight history is philosophy of history that does not recognize itself as such (because of its unconscious conformity to prevailing norms); philosophy of history, on the other hand, "contain[s] within it the elements of a proper history," choosing rather to emphasize the "conceptual construct" over the historical data.⁴⁷ Thus, from the perspective of each of the opposing poles, straight history is criticized for its *insufficiency* of meaning and philosophy of history for its *excess* of meaning.

It is in this sense that Saint Augustine can be considered to be the "founder of the philosophy of history," as Christopher Dawson, a mid-twentieth-century British Catholic historian and thinker who deeply influenced White, observed in his 1951 essay "The Problem of Metahistory." This is because "[Saint Augustine] does not discover anything from history, but merely sees in history the working out of universal principles. But we may well question whether Hegel or any of the nineteenth-century philosophers did otherwise. They did not derive their theories from history, but read their philosophy into history."⁴⁸ The philosopher of history endows history with an extrinsic meaning-structure, whereas the historian proper, post Ranke,⁴⁹ sees historical meaning as inhering in the historical particulars themselves. Nevertheless, Dawson refused the opposition between "metahistory" and "pure history," arguing that "if history had been left to these pure historians, it would never have attained the position it holds in the modern world. . . . It was only when history entered into relations with philosophy and produced the new type of philosophical historians . . . that it became one of the great formative elements in modern thought."⁵⁰ Thus every *great* historian is in some sense a *philosopher* of history. Though Dawson may not have coined the term "metahistory," he was perhaps the first to give it a positive meaning in his conclusion that "all historiography is . . . pervaded by metahistorical influences"⁵¹—the methodological starting point of White's *Metahistory*.

Dawson was reacting to the low esteem in which philosophy of history was held during the first half of the twentieth century, particularly in the Anglo-American context. He felt that academic historians had become increasingly disconnected from the philosophical roots of their discipline, from the grand visions that had made history "formative" for modern thought. Suspecting that the animosity toward metahistory was due more to the particular philosophical views advocated by metahistorians than to the metahistorical approach *per se*, Dawson observes that

> historians today are in revolt against the metahistory of Hegel and Croce and Collingwood, not because it is metahistorical, but because they feel it to be the expression of a philosophical attitude that is no longer valid; just as the liberal historians of the eighteenth century revolted against the theological metahistory of the previous period.⁵²

In an essay published the same year as his *Metahistory* titled "The Politics of Contemporary Philosophy of History" (1973), White echoes this sentiment, writing that "the term *metahistorical* is really a surrogate for 'socially innovative historical vision.' What the philosophers and the historians themselves call 'straight' history is the historical vision of political and social accommodationists."⁵³ Seen in this light, the distinction between straight history and metahistory or philosophy of history is really that between a conformist and a radical-revolutionary approach to history. Straight history, then, is simply *successful* metahistory; it no longer appears as socially innovative, its philosophical meaning having been assimilated to the point of no longer being perceived as such. (Put in the terms of Sartre's *Critique of Dialectical Reason*, analyzed in Chapter 1: Straight history manifests the *practico-inert*, whereas philosophy of history is *praxis*; as it ossifies, philosophy of history devolves into the *practico-inert* of straight history.)

One of the most important and enduring of White's ideas put forward in *Metahistory* is that of the aesthetic concept of "emplotment," a term of his coinage. Though it sounds as if it were hatched by a literary theorist, the term is in fact designed to reveal something that is specific to historiography (for it would be a redundant concept in literary theory). By "emplotment," White meant that the historian and the philosopher of history use conventional (i.e., preexisting and culturally conditioned) narrative forms to organize and tell a story about the past, or, to put it more succinctly: Stories are *made*, not found. Traditional historiography, on the other hand, had always held that the story is to be *discovered* or *uncovered* in the amassed data, that the facts tell their own story. But this view, if carried to its logical conclusion, presupposes that there are an infinite number of possible stories, none of which bear any formalizable (i.e., plot) resemblance to any other. White holds that this is an illusion, that it is impossible to construct a narrative, whether composed of real or imagined elements, utterly bereft of conventional form (plot type) or of "storiness" itself (i.e., as having, as Aristotle said, a beginning, a middle, and an end). In other words, there is no such thing as narrative-in-general, only particular *kinds* of stories, which White reduces, following Northrop Frye, to the four archetypes of romance, tragedy, comedy, and satire.

Thus, to say that the historian or philosopher *emplots* the story that he or she wants to tell about the past is not to say that he or she selects the kind of story that best fits the facts, but rather that the *choice* of narrative form is in fact a way of "choosing the past"; in other words, there are a multiplicity of ways of emplotting the same elements, none of which, formally speaking, can be said to correspond better to "historical reality" than any other, since historical reality itself is an effect of such a discursive choice. Thus, although White's tropological grid might have appeared at first glance to be rigid and deterministic, it was actually meant as a corollary to Sartre's dictum that we are "condemned to be free." For once we see the tropological apprehension of historical reality as constituted by a *choice* (among different tropological apprehensions) that we are *condemned* to make ("condemned" because we cannot think discursively and thus historically outside of the tropes), we can then unburden ourselves from the idea of corresponding to a nonlinguistic reality, from the illusion of representing historical reality "as it really was" (the Rankean ideal). White writes that "we are indentured to a *choice* among contending interpretative strategies in any effort to reflect on history-in-general; . . . the best grounds for choosing one perspective on history rather than another are ultimately aesthetic or moral rather than epistemological."[54] The phrase "we are indentured to a choice" is clearly a paraphrase of Sartre's "we are condemned to be free." However, White's superimposition of the moral and the aesthetic dimensions that inform and ultimately constitute any "choice of interpretative strategy" already transcends the Sartrean problematic (at least insofar as it was developed in *Being and Nothingness*).[55]

White's idea of emplotment was quite revolutionary, for historians generally believed that, even if they used novelistic techniques to make their accounts more (aesthetically) effective or (epistemologically) convincing, these were on the order of mere form rather than content, which, they believed, remained unaffected by such "embellishments." As White observes:

> The form of the historian's discourse (its form as a story) was conceived to be contingent and detachable from its contents (information and argument) without significant conceptual or informational loss. And this on two possible grounds: either the story told in the discourse was a mimetic image of a concatenation of events which, once established as facts, could be shown to have actually manifested the same form as the story told about it; or, the story told about the events was simply an instrument or medium of communication used by the historian to convey information about an uncanny subject-matter to a lay audience deemed incapable of comprehending it in its historiologically processed form.[56]

White thus contends that there is a "content of the form," as one of his essay collections was titled,[57] that the aesthetic form inevitably conveys a moral and ideological content, forming a totality with the putative "content," from which it is in the end indistinguishable.

The rapprochement White effected between historical and fictional narrative on the level of form was, unsurprisingly, considered a threat to the quasi-scientific objectivity that historians saw as legitimating their discipline as the search for the truth of the past. The idea that every narrative contains an inexpugnable element of fiction (the very conventionality of form that preexists and conditions any narrative process) appeared to strip history of its status as an empirical, fact-driven discipline.[58] If "all stories are fictions,"[59] as White liked to say, then how could the historian effectively separate his activity from that of the novelist? And if fictionality (which, for White, is simply another name for figuration) is fundamental to historicity, then how are we to conceive of "historical reality," the concept of which supposedly differentiated modern historical inquiry from mythical thought?

Existential figuralism

White's response to these questions involved arguing, following Erich Auerbach's demonstration in his magnum opus *Mimesis: The Representation of Reality* in *Western Literature*, that "realism" in historical writing is at bottom an ethico-aesthetic concept. White illustrates this idea in his exploration of *figural realism*, the title White gave to his 1999 collection of essays. In *Metahistory*, however, White had spoken about figuration in terms of "*prefiguring* the historical field"; that is, the figures/tropes set out the basic modes of apprehending historical reality, the representation of which (the historical account) was the fulfillment of the figure/trope that structured it. This conception of "prefiguration" was *compositional*; that is, it is what accounted for the historian's *construction* of the historical referent, which exists only as an effect of discourse (since it is no longer observable except as trace, residue, ruin, remnant, etc.). But no "prefiguration" is inherently more "realistic" than any other.

In his later work, however, White will use the concept of prefiguration as *projectional*; this involved seeing the prefiguration-fulfillment relation as a function of a temporally realized project. White comes to view the very *act* of narration as a means of "choosing the past," thus uniting his earlier existentialist view of historical meaning with his later, specifically narrativist and Auerbach-influenced approach. This idea, elaborated in his article "Auerbach's Literary History: Figural Causation and Modernist Historicism" (and collected in *Figural Realism*), takes as its starting point Auerbach's literary-historical reinterpretation of the Christian concept of *figura* (on which Auerbach had written an eponymous essay in 1939), which White saw as the unacknowledged methodological principle underlying Auerbach's *Mimesis*.[60]

The concept of *figura* derives from the Christian hermeneutic tradition. According to this notion, persons and events in the Old Testament are said to *prefigure* persons and events in the New Testament, the latter being the *fulfillment* of the former. It thus differed from prophecy, which projects forward. Figural interpretation, also called "typology" (the relation between the "type" and its fulfillment in the "antitype"), projects *backward*, treating earlier events *as if* they had been destined to be fulfilled in later ones. This type of interpretation had the advantage of preserving the reality or literalness of events that might otherwise be taken as having a merely allegorical or symbolic significance. Figural interpretation was thus a prototype of nineteenth-century historiography, of a way of generating specifically *historical* meaning. White quotes Northrop Frye in this context: "What typology really is as a mode of thought, what it both assumes and leads to, is a theory of history, or more accurately of the historical process: an assumption that there is some meaning and point to history, and that sooner or later some event or events will occur which will indicate what that meaning or point is, and so become an antitype of what has happened previously."[61] In the Christian context, however, there was an assumed teleology to this interpretive process: The earlier event was thought to actually *cause* or be intrinsically connected to the later event (often occurring centuries later) as part of a divine plan. Christian-figural interpretation was thus, *in theory*, a way of understanding or perceiving God's project, even if *in practice*, it was a very *human* project of self-actualization that was being performed; for Christian typology, inevitably and in effect, involved *choosing the past*. White called this aesthetic and secularized analog to the Christian *figura* "figural causation." One can thus perceive how the Christian *figura* could become the prototype of the existentialist concept of historicity outlined above. As White writes:

> Plot-meaning is a way of construing historical processes in the mode of a fulfillment of a fate or a destiny considered, not as an instance of mechanical or teleological causality, but as contingent on the interplay of free will (choice, motives, intentions), on the one hand, and historically specific limits imposed upon the exercise of this free will, on the other.[62]

In more explicitly Sartrean terms, then, plot-meaning is a combination of facticity ("historically specific limits") and transcendence/freedom ("free will"). White thus narrativizes the existentialist/Christian-figural concept of projection: the generation of narrative meaning (emplotment) is simply a function of the prefiguration-fulfillment dynamic, codified in such literary devices as "foreshadowing," "dénouement," "formal patterning," "flashback," and so on.

The first specifically philosophical articulation of the dynamic of figuralism is no doubt Søren Kierkegaard's concept of *repetition*. In his eponymous book, Kierkegaard writes that "the dialectic of repetition is easy, for that which is repeated has been—otherwise it could not be repeated—but the very fact that is has been makes the repetition into something new."[63] White observes that Kierkegaard's concept of

> repetition—"not the simple repeating of an experience, but the recreating of it which redeems or awakens it to life"—names the process productive of the type/antitype relationship by which a later event, text, period, culture, thought, or action can be said to have "fulfilled" an earlier one.... "Fulfillment" here is to be understood as the product or effect of a kind of reverse causation—a kind of causation peculiar to historical reality, culture, and human consciousness, by which a thing of the past is at once grasped by consciousness, brought into the present by recollection, and redeemed, made new.[64]

Figural causation is thus a kind of "reverse causation," and in this sense, history, like the Sartrean "project," is an act of redemption; one redeems the past by choosing it, by choosing to actualize it in and for the present, thereby making it "new," or making it anew.

The difficulty for the modern historian in countenancing such an idea of "reverse causation" is succinctly addressed by Gabrielle Spiegel, who observes that White is

> secularizing typological notions of the relationship between figures and events separated by centuries in a way that, I suspect, few contemporary

historians would understand or accept. For the notion of "fulfillment" suggests that an earlier event/person/type in some (perhaps only "figural") sense *causes* its much later, distanced realization, hence bypassing immediate local contexts as principles of explanation.[65]

However, it is not so much that White's figuralism "bypasses" immediate or local contexts; rather it superimposes itself on them as their condition of possibility. Certainly, White privileges narrative explanation over mechanical or efficient-causal explanation in historical accounts. (And "causality" is, of course, itself a highly contested term in philosophy.) He argues that *narrativization* (to which even nonnarrative history must ultimately succumb) underlies the creation of any specifically *historical* meaning, even if the examination of "antecedent causes" provides useful *information* for the construction of historical narratives.

White does not deny that the examination of nexuses of efficient-causal relations can offer insights into how or why something happened the way it did, just as one would naturally take into account such relations in the investigation of the causes of a car crash or of the results of an election. But to "explain" a car crash in purely causal-physicalistic terms (as one entity of a certain shape and size, making contact with another at a certain velocity, a certain angle, and in certain weather conditions, etc.) does little to "explain" such an event in terms of the human-moral factor involved, even if a strictly objective description is considered adequate for the physical or exact sciences. Thus no one "explains" the results of an election by saying that one candidate got more votes than another or by describing the voting technology, even if these are valid causal explanations. Insight into human events requires *understanding*, *imagination*, and ultimately *interpretation*, and, for White, interpretation in history is nothing but figuration.

Thus to "explain" a car crash or an election is to say what it *means*; such explanation is thus indissociable from the *act* of interpretation, with all that the term "act" entails (i.e., the moral, the volitional, the practical). Putatively "empirical" descriptions tend to suppress, deemphasize, or even eliminate the role of the will in meaning making or interpretation. They proclaim their objectivity under the self-deceptive (and perhaps even self-serving) guise of passivity. As White observes at the end of his introduction to *Tropics of Discourse*, ours is "an age which has lost its belief in the will and represses its sense of the moral implications of the mode of rationality that it favors. But the moral implications of the human sciences will never be perceived until the faculty of the will is reinstated in theory."[66] Indeed, in his major works, White fuses Sartre's existential voluntarism with Auerbach's redemptive figuralism. Historians as well as historical agents effectively choose their own past and, by this very act, their own present. In short, "choosing the past" is an irreducibly ethical act.

CHAPTER SIX

Hayden White and the ethics of historiography

In a special issue of *Rethinking History* (2013) commemorating the fortieth anniversary of Hayden White's *Metahistory: The Historical Imagination in Nineteenth-Century Europe,* Gabrielle Spiegel speaks of a "new interpretation of *Metahistory* as essentially an ethical, rather than literary, intervention into historical writing,"[1] citing Herman Paul's work as well as my own as examples of this trend.[2] Indeed, over the past forty years, commentators have been more intrigued by the polemics of White's "poetics of history"—his rapprochement between history and fiction elaborately developed in his tropological and narratological analyses—than by any ethical considerations his work might imply or suggest. In fact, White's unfortunate reputation as a radical postmodern relativist—still prevalent in some quarters—has all but branded him an amoralist whose thought is incapable of distinguishing between a neo-Nazi revisionist and a responsible historian of the Holocaust.

While the previous chapter studied the ethical implications of White's existentialist stance, this chapter explores the role ethics plays in White's epistemological critique of historiography. In the first part of the chapter, I analyze how the question of ethics figures in *Metahistory*, focusing on how White's vaunted formalism coheres with his plea, in the conclusion to this work, to transcend formalism's inherent irony and nihilism. In the second part, I examine how the question of Holocaust representation, which became the object of intense debate in the 1990s, subjected White's thought to a specifically ethical critique.

The ethics of *Metahistory*

In his *Metahistory*, White offers a two-pronged epistemological critique of modern historiography. On the one hand, he puts into question the essential opposition between straight history and philosophy of history, arguing that straight history inevitably expresses a view of history itself and that all attempts to "make sense of history-in-general" have "a common [metahistorical] origin."[3] On the other, he dismisses the essential opposition between literature and history, contending that the latter is as dependent on conventional narrative forms as the former and that, unlike the isolated facts out of which a narrative is fashioned, narrative itself is not subject to empirical verification (i.e., narrative forms cannot be judged according to a correspondence model, since they preexist the data to which they are being applied). Both aspects of White's metahistorical critique derive from his identification of history with historical *writing*: the view that history is a particular (and in some sense peculiar) discursive practice that produces its object (the "mimesis effect")[4] rather than an empirical-scientific activity that aims to uncover the ontological plenitude of a found past (historical objectivism).[5] Qua epistemological critique, the principal aim of White's *Metahistory* is demystification: It endeavors to demonstrate what historians are doing *in fact* (emplotment, recourse to preexisting plot types) despite their *beliefs* to the contrary (letting the facts "speak for themselves"; uncovering the "true story" of events as they "really were").[6] Thus, in this sense, it would be absurd to interpret *Metahistory* as a program for writing history in a particular manner; it merely describes the contingent, tropological-narratological basis on which *any* history is necessarily constructed.

On one level, White's demystification of historiography, his exposure of historiographical bad faith, is strictly analytical or descriptive. But there is another self-deceptive aspect of historical objectivism that White highlights in *Metahistory*: namely, that which concerns the *attitude* of the historian. The dispositional basis of the objectivist approach to historiography is that of the disinterested, value-neutral search for the truth, an attitude White labels "ironic," for it negates or disavows all personal investment in the results of one's activity. One is merely "following the facts wherever they lead." The objectivist historian believes that he or she is unearthing the plot inherent in the historical record and that his or her personal predilections, political views, and institutional role have no *substantive* impact on the historical account itself (that is to say, "disinterested" does not mean that one has no personal *reactions* to historical events, simply that these are not supposed to get in the way of the search for the truth). But if, as White contends, history is emplotted—if the plot is *imposed* on the historical data rather than *found* in it—then narration necessarily involves an interpretive *choice* that is not determined by the facts alone. Thus, whereas the objectivist historian sees his or her account as *determined* by the facts, White argues that he or she—without realizing it—is in fact *choosing* one interpretive strategy over another. Analytically speaking, then, there is no difference between an objectivist historian and a demystified Whitean historian with regard to their actual activity (both are emplotting their narratives). The difference lies in their *attitude* toward their activity. The question is, can or to what extent does a change in attitude—namely from objectivist (scientistic) to creative (ethico-aesthetic)—lead to a change in historiographical practice?

In an often-quoted passage from the preface to *Metahistory*, White observes that, since we are "indentured to a *choice* among contending interpretative strategies in any effort to reflect on history-in-general . . . the best grounds for choosing one perspective on history rather than another are ultimately aesthetic or moral rather than epistemological."[7] The use of "best grounds" implies a prescriptive (ethical) rather than an analytical posture. White is exhorting the historian to break out of his or her epistemological straitjacket and realize his or her "moral and aesthetic aspirations" (as he puts it in the conclusion), thus suggesting that a change in attitude would indeed result in a change in practice and not simply in a more lucid or analytically correct view of historiography. This is confirmed in the afterword to White's most recent book *The Practical Past* (2014), in which he observes that "identity is forged of *acts* of choice, decision, and performance on aesthetic and ethical grounds (although I would combine these two kinds of faculty under the name of 'practice')."[8] While, from an analytical point of view, "best grounds" would appear to imply that White is allowing some space for interpretive choice to be legitimately based on purely epistemological factors (i.e., on the idea that the facts alone *determine* one's historiographical approach), we must not be led astray. For White simultaneously holds that (1) the demand for the scientization of history represents in fact a statement of *preference* for a specific modality of historical conceptualization, and that (2) "there are no apodictic epistemological grounds for the preference of one mode of explanation over another."[9] In other words, the grounds for "historical conceptualization" are *in fact* moral or aesthetic, irrespective of the epistemological justifications the historian may adduce. In the conclusion, White similarly writes that "when it is a matter of choosing among different alternative visions of history, the only grounds for preferring one over the other are *moral* or *aesthetic* ones."[10] That is, the historical objectivist is self-deceived if he or she believes that his or her historical vision is guided by the facts, when it actually conditions them (i.e., it provides the interpretive frame from which the facts take their meaning).

The vacillation between the two phrasings of "only grounds" (in the conclusion) and "best grounds" (in the preface) is emblematic of the somewhat ambiguous relation between the descriptive and the prescriptive, the analytical and the ethical, in *Metahistory*. For what White must mean by "best grounds" is that, even if the historian accepts that interpretive choice is in fact informed by ethical and aesthetic concerns, the historian should not simply resign himself or herself to this truth (as kind of a necessary evil), but rather *embrace* it as an affirmation of his or her essential freedom. Only thus can White's metahistorical critique lead to a transformation of historical practice. This methodological ambiguity between practice and praxis is where the tension between the ironic-postmodernist and the ethical-humanist-existentialist sides of White's thought comes to the fore. If, as Hans Kellner remarks, irony "eliminate[s] [the historian's] status as a free and interested party,"[11] how to get from irony to ethics? How can White's ironic stance on the analytical level, which tends toward disengagement, conduce to an ethically and socially responsible attitude? In short, how to escape the nihilism of the ironic attitude? The problem of nihilism is in fact the bane of all post-Nietzschean thought: Heidegger seeks to overcome it in the resoluteness of *Dasein* and the mystery of Being, Foucault in the willful resistance to an amorphous power, Derrida in the notion of an undeconstructable justice, Rorty in the private/public split (private irony vs. public consensus), Gianni Vattimo in the reinterpretation of nihilism in the name of an ethical hermeneutics.[12]

In his conclusion to *Metahistory*—actually in the last paragraph of the work—White articulates the problem thus:

> If we wish to transcend the agnosticism which an Ironic perspective on history, passing as the sole possible "realism" and "objectivity" to which we can aspire in historical studies, foists upon us, we have only to reject this Ironic perspective and to will to view history from another, anti-Ironic perspective. Such a recommendation, coming at the end of a work which professes to be value neutral and purely Formalist in its own reflections upon historical thinking in its classical age, may appear inconsistent with the intrinsic Irony of its own characterization of the history of historical consciousness. I do not deny that the Formalism of my approach to the history of historical thought itself reflects the Ironic condition from within which most of modern academic historiography is generated. But I maintain that the recognition of this Ironic perspective provides the grounds for a transcendence of it. If it can be shown that Irony is only one of a *number* of possible perspectives on history, each of which has its own good reasons for existence on a poetic and moral level of awareness, the Ironic attitude will have begun to be deprived of its status as the *necessary* perspective from which to view the historical process. Historians and philosophers will then be freed to conceptualize history, to perceive its contents, and to construct narrative accounts of its processes in whatever modality of consciousness is most consistent with their own moral and aesthetic aspirations. And historical consciousness will stand open to the re-establishment of its links with the great poetic, scientific, and philosophical concerns which inspired the classic practitioners and theorists of its golden age in the nineteenth century.[13]

This paragraph, emphatically placed at the end, changes the meaning of *Metahistory*. It endows it with an explicitly ethical consciousness that can be read retrospectively into the work. The key to this ethical consciousness is the placement of irony, or rather its displacement. White identifies the "ironic" perspective on history *both* with the kind of value-free formalism of the kind employed in *Metahistory* (a formal agnosticism or an agnosticism toward all possible forms) and with the value-free, empiricist-objectivist view of the world that had become the credo of historical studies in the twentieth century.[14] With respect to irony itself, White distinguishes two types or levels: (1) irony as one master trope among other master tropes (i.e., the precritical or prefigurative tropes of metonymy, metaphor, synecdoche); (2) irony as *meta*-trope, the trope on the basis of which tropology itself is elaborated. It is the meta-trope of irony that, by heuristically enabling a multiperspectival treatment of historical discourse, permits both the exposure and the overcoming of the ironic attitude itself, insofar as it is stripped of its hegemonic pretensions and is revealed to be "only one of a *number* of possible perspectives on history." In short, White's metahistorical irony reveals itself to be merely *methodological* rather than substantive—a means to an extrinsic end rather than an end in itself.

White had foreshadowed this move earlier in *Metahistory*, at the beginning of the chapter on Benedetto Croce, in which he observed that "although philosophy of history remains Ironical with respect to any given historian's work, its aim is to expose to consciousness, to criticize, and to eliminate the possibility of an Ironical historiography."[15] This, then, is also the purpose of the philosophy of history that is White's *Metahistory*: to transcend irony through irony. If *Metahistory* zealously pursues a radical perspectivism, it is precisely to overcome the nihilism of the surrender to irony that resulted in a false objectivity. In this sense, White's project also recalls that of Nietzsche, of whom he observes:

> Even Nietzsche, who viewed all products of thought Ironically, purported to save historical thinking for life by reducing it to the same fictional level as science and philosophy, grounding it in the poetic imagination along with these, thereby releasing it from adherence to an *impossible* ideal of objectivity and disinterestedness.[16]

Thus, White, like Nietzsche, seeks to "save" historical thinking from the "*impossible* ideal of objectivity and disinterestedness" by grounding it in the poetic imagination and by redefining its purpose as a means of individual and collective self-creation. Just as Nietzsche sought to combat the debilitating nihilism he saw as symptomatic of his age,[17] White, too, aims to counter the objectivist nihilism of professional historiography in the late twentieth century.

However, while White finds in Nietzsche's life-affirming aestheticism a valuable starting point, he ultimately sees Sartrean existentialism as a more effective antidote to irony (as we saw in the previous chapter). Hence White's rhetoric of "choice." If choice is *in fact* inimical to the detached, ironic attitude, it is because it necessarily involves value. The value-neutral perspective adopted on the analytical level as it relates to the specification of form gives way to the value-laden perspective that informs or accrues to the *choice* of form, even if no plot type is intrinsically more ethically attuned or aesthetically appropriate than any other. Thus, White can say, as he does in *The Practical Past*, that "history reads us moral lessons, whether we would have it or not, simply by virtue of the casting of its accounts of the past in the form of stories."[18] In other words, we *cannot not* make moral choices when writing history, since emplotment (narrative choice) represents a moral as much as an aesthetic choice.

Nevertheless, this is often the basis for the ethical objection to *Metahistory*: Is not the Nazi historiographer *free* to emplot his narrative as he sees fit, prefiguring the historical field using the tropes he considers most adequate to his worldview? Of course, but that is like asking if the Nazi also perceives the world according to the categories of the understanding and the forms of intuition as outlined in Kant's first *Critique*. From a metahistorical perspective, emplotment is simply what every historian does, Nazi or not. This objection thus conflates or equates *Metahistory*'s descriptive assertions, which indeed argue for an epistemological relativism, with moral relativism. Such a confusion is what allows Dirk Moses to observe that White's "Nietzschean-inspired vision of history is inadequate because it cannot gainsay that a genocidal vision of history is immoral."[19] Of course, analytically speaking, *all* metahistorical choices are equally contingent, and on this level White's relativistic tropology is no more "amoral" than Derrida's *différance* or Foucault's "power," all of which are quasi-transcendental assertions of the way in which history, meaning, and values, respectively, are *in fact* created. This is why White endeavors to transcend irony, precisely to reach a place where ethical judgment becomes meaningful. It is for this reason that Sartre, more than Nietzsche, provides the impetus for White's metahistorical ethics.

A more pertinent way of posing the ethical objection to *Metahistory* is expressed by Gabrielle Spiegel:

> [If] the drive behind White's work is a certain freedom to choose one's past in order to serve the present that one desires—and that such choices represent existential preferences—then how does one address the ethical issue of some, including whole nations like the Germans [under the Nazis], who choose to live *judenrein*, in the name of creating a better, purer, and more desirable society.[20]

Spiegel's objection involves the motivation or attitude of the historian, the ethical implications of *choosing the past*. She attacks the very idea of an existentialist ethics as intrinsically contradictory or absurd. Why is one not free to choose evil without being accused of bad faith? In an interview with Sartre, Simone de Beauvoir asked him about his conception of good and evil. His response is instructive: "Essentially, the Good is that which is useful to human freedom, that which allows it to give their full value to objects it has realized. Evil is that which is harmful to human freedom."[21] In other words, the maximization of human freedom is the only (regulative) principle one needs. This statement would appear to imply two things with respect to White's metahistorical ethics. On the individual level, the historian who maximizes freedom realizes the sublimity of his or her creative or poetic capacity over the illusion of objectivity. On the collective level, the maximization of freedom refers to a community's capacity to reinterpret and recreate itself, without thereby suppressing the freedom of any other community. On the collective level, then, freedom is never absolute or realized in a vacuum; it is a matter of a *contest* of interpretations.[22] Historiographical ethics thus demands the taking into account of competing freedoms—often a zero-sum game in which affirmation of one group's freedom (self-interpretation as self-creation) necessarily entails the suppression of another's (e.g., Israel-Palestine). But this is simply to say that where there can be no net increase in human freedom a truly "just" outcome is impossible.

Metahistorical ethics and the question of Holocaust representation

In 1990, Saul Friedlander convened a conference at the University of California, Los Angeles, which proved to be a watershed event in Holocaust historiography. It was titled "Nazism and the 'Final Solution': Probing the Limits of Representation,"[23] and its participants included some of the most recognizable names in historiography and Theory: Perry Anderson, Carlo Ginzburg, Martin Jay, Dominick LaCapra, Eric Santner, Anton Kaes, Berel Lang, Geoffrey Hartman, and, of course, Hayden White. If this event was about defining a new ethics of historiography guided by the example of the Holocaust, White's reputation as an unrepentant, amoral relativist appeared to provide the perfect foil.

Indeed, the figure of Hayden White hovers over many of the essays like a dark cloud (Friedlander's evenhanded introduction being the exception). I shall discuss just one of these critiques of White's work, that of Carlo Ginzburg. Taking his cue from White's 1982 essay "The Politics of Historical Interpretation: Discipline and De-Sublimation,"[24] Ginzburg begins by citing White's observation that "there are no grounds to be found in the historical record itself for preferring one way of construing its meaning over another,"[25] to which Ginzburg retorts mockingly "no grounds?"[26] However, White does not say "no grounds" *tout court*, but rather, "no grounds to be found *in the historical record itself*"—that is, no *epistemological* grounds. White also stipulates that he is speaking about *interpretation* or *emplotment* ("construing its meaning"), not the establishment of facts. As observed above, White does envision other grounds for preferring one *interpretation* over another, namely ethical and aesthetic grounds, but Ginzburg makes no mention of this.

Ginzburg then turns to White's comparison of the work of Holocaust denier Robert Faurisson with the Zionist interpretation of the Holocaust in an effort to demonstrate that White's concept of truth is both contradictory and immoral.²⁷ White's comparison of these two heterodox accounts is based on his standard distinction between fact and interpretation:

> The distinction between facts and meanings is usually taken to be the basis of historical relativism. This is because in conventional historical inquiry, the facts established about a specific event are taken to be the meaning of that event. Facts are supposed to provide the basis for arbitrating among the variety of different meanings that different social groups can assign to an event for different ideological or political reasons. But the facts are a function of the meaning assigned to events, not some primitive data that determine what meanings an event can have.²⁸

Thus, according to White, Faurisson's revisionist account is rightly condemned on epistemological grounds for its denial of established facts, but the Zionist account cannot be so judged; for in the latter case, it is a matter of interpretation, not of fact. As Ginzburg quotes White: "It's truth [that of the Zionist view], as historical interpretation, consists precisely in its *effectiveness* [Ginzburg's italics] in justifying a wide range of current Israeli political policies that, from the standpoint of those who articulate them, are crucial to the security and indeed the very existence of the Jewish people."²⁹ Ginzburg believes he has caught White in a contradiction because of the use of the word "truth." But again, White is distinguishing epistemological truth (factuality or correspondence to reality) from (as in this case) interpretive truth ("as historical interpretation"), namely *figural* truth, the agreement between the figure and its fulfillment. As White observes in *Figural Realism*, "All stories are fictions. Which means, of course, that they can be true only in a metaphorical sense and in the sense in which a figure of speech can be true."³⁰ Disparate facts are not in and of themselves *effective*; facts alone cannot define a people's destiny.³¹ To attain a specifically historical meaning, facts require emplotment, interpretation, that is, *rhetoric*—tropic and figural processes. Rhetoric is by definition *effective* discourse. Ginzburg quotes White (italics by Ginzburg): "The effort of the Palestinian people to mount a politically *effective* response to Israeli policies entails the production of a similarly *effective* ideology, complete with an interpretation of their history endowing it with a meaning that it has hitherto lacked."³² By underlining the word "effective," Ginzburg is simply making White's point: that historical interpretation or emplotment is a matter of rhetoric, that its "truth" is of a different order than that of science or logic.

White's comparison recalls Heidegger's contrast (in *Being and Time*) between truth-as-world-disclosure (interpretation) and truth-as-correctness (fact). Both the Israeli Zionists and the Palestinians are using history as a means of self-creation, of self-interpretation, an effort that, qua world-disclosure, is "ontological" (in Heidegger's sense) rather than epistemological in nature and thus cannot be judged according to logical or scientific notions of truth or falsity. These self-interpretations can claim to be "true" to the extent that they are *effective* in symbolizing the aspirations of their community, that is, insofar as they activate figures that, in the minds of the intended audience, find fulfillment in its collective ideology and project.[33]

Ginzburg either fails to discern or refuses such distinctions. In what he imagines to be a *coup de grâce*, he writes, "We can conclude that if Faurisson's narrative were ever to prove effective, it would be regarded by White as true as well."[34] Ginzburg apparently takes "true" here to be epistemological truth, in which case the sentence would be a non sequitur. White has never asserted such an absurdity. No matter how effective Faurisson's narrative (Faurisson's interpretation), it would not change the status of the factual record. On the other hand, let us assume that Ginzburg means interpretive truth, figural truth. If so, the question is better posed thus: Does a deficient factual record impact the effectiveness, positively or negatively, of Faurisson's narrative (i.e., of its capacity to express the self-interpretation of a community, say that of the Nazi or neo-Nazi community)? No doubt Faurisson believes that it does; for what other motivation could there be to deny a specific part of the factual record—as opposed to factuality in general, like a "postmodernist" would. Revisionists are not relativists; they believe (albeit in bad faith) that they have a legitimate claim to factual truth. Nevertheless, would a deficient factual record not lead to a deficient interpretation, to a less *effective* interpretation? It might, if in denying facts one loses credibility with one's contemporaries. By mixing lies with interpretive projection, totalitarian regimes actually lessen or undermine the effectiveness of their revisionist histories—hence the recourse to a police state to maintain control.[35]

Of course, on a deeper level, what *counts* as a fact is itself dependent on a prior world-disclosure (or "precritical" projection, to use White's terminology),[36] in our case that of the scientific-naturalist view of the world. What counted as historical "fact" in medieval Europe was very different from what counts as fact in a contemporary context. We no longer permit miracles and witchcraft to serve as factual elements in the historical account; they are simply described with an ironic distance. Thus, in the most general sense, all facts are dependent on a prior interpretation. However, this does not thereby collapse White's fundamental distinction between fact and interpretation.[37] Meta-interpretations or metahistorical apprehensions determine what counts as fact and truth in a given context, but these interpretative frames are not themselves subject to epistemological conditions of true or false. As White writes, "The plot structures used to fashion the different stories are not in the nature of propositions that can be submitted to tests of verification or falsification in the way that 'singular existential statements' [i.e., facts] can be tested."[38] In a recent book (*Meaning, Truth, and Reference in Historical Representation*, 2012), Frank Ankersmit makes a similar point: "We must clearly distinguish between statements about representations (that can be true or false) and representations themselves (that cannot be propositionally true or false)."[39]

Which brings us once again to the question of the relation between irony and ethics. According to Ginzburg,

> [White] argues that his skepticism and relativism can provide the epistemological and moral foundations for tolerance. But this claim is historically and logically untenable. Historically, because tolerance has been theorized by people who had strong theoretical and moral convictions. . . . Logically, because absolute skepticism would contradict itself if it were not extended also to tolerance as a regulating principle.[40]

To follow Ginzburg's argument, one would first have to establish whether or to what extent White is a "skeptic" or a "relativist." White is no more a "skeptic" than is Heidegger, who famously observed that what Kant called the "scandal of philosophy," the thesis of skepticism regarding the existence of external reality, needed to be reversed, that the real "'scandal of philosophy' does not consist in the fact that this proof [of the existence of external reality] is still lacking up to now, but *in the fact that such proofs are expected and attempted again and again*."[41] In other words, skepticism is based on objectivism, on a metaphysical-realist or correspondence theory of truth, a position that, as we have seen, White, like Heidegger, rejects. As for relativism, White admits to being a pluralist with regard to the view that no single, overarching perspective on reality or history can claim epistemological priority. But this does not thereby render *moral* judgment impossible or moot. On the contrary, moral judgment is returned to the realm of ethical responsibility (choice), from which it had become estranged by the supposedly "value-neutral" perspective of historical objectivism.

What Ginzburg is attempting to formulate—without realizing it—is the question, discussed above, of how White can transcend irony by means of irony, of how irony can lead to ethics. For White, as we have seen, irony leads to ethics by revealing that epistemological justifications cannot be self-validating, that lurking behind such justifications lie moral apprehensions that science cannot fathom—or afford to ignore.

# PART THREE
Literature

CHAPTER SEVEN

The ethics of conversion

Metaphysical desire in René Girard and Jean-Paul Sartre

The affinities between the thought of René Girard and Jean-Paul Sartre are rarely noted and even more rarely commented on.[1] This is no doubt due, in large part, to Girard's reputation for being "anti-Sartre."[2] And yet, Girard's earliest essays, those published in the 1950s and 1960s, were often concerned with existentialist themes and with Sartre's works in particular.[3] Even Girard's well-received first book, *Mensonge romantique et vérité romanesque* (1961, translated in 1965 as *Deceit, Desire, and the Novel*),[4] contains numerous references to Sartre, more than any other philosopher discussed in the book. In a 2008 preface to a collection of his early essays, Girard observes, "As I reread these essays I am struck by their Sartrean tone. Jean-Pierre Dupuy saw the importance of bad faith [*la mauvaise foi*] for the elaboration of the mimetic hypothesis. Sartre was thus for me more important than Hegel. The first philosophy book I understood was *Being and Nothingness*."[5] As this passage suggests, Sartre's *Being and Nothingness*, in particular its cardinal notion of *bad faith*, was a formative influence on Girard, including on the formulation of his mimetic theory of desire, the cornerstone of his thought.

This chapter explores some commonalities between Sartre and Girard, in particular how their shared understanding of human desire as ontological lack—what Girard calls "metaphysical desire" and Sartre the "desire to be God"—reveals a common ethical dimension in the idea of *conversion*: In Girard, it is found in the conversion from deviated to horizontal transcendence, and in Sartre, in the conversion from bad faith to authenticity.

I thus argue that Girard's quasi-religious concept of conversion is modeled to a great extent on Sartrean authenticity, a relation that allows us to see how Girard's theory is more existentialist, and Sartre's philosophy more Christian-religious, than either would care to admit.

Metaphysical desire

To better situate it in terms of Sartre existentialist philosophy, let us briefly recall Girard's theory of mimetic desire, first outlined in his *Deceit, Desire, and the Novel*. Girard focuses on the novel (namely Cervantes's *Don Quixote*, Stendhal's *The Red and the Black*, and Proust's *The Remembrance of Things Past*) to articulate his theory, for he believes that the great writers have a better understanding of human desire than do the philosophers, the psychologists, or the social scientists. Thus, Girard does not offer us a theory of literature, or a theory that makes use of literature for some nonliterary end, but rather offers us literature *as* theory.[6]

On Girard's account, desire does not have its origin in the self or in the object, but in a third party.[7] That is, we do not desire something spontaneously or for its intrinsic qualities, but according to another person; we imitate the Other's desire. Girard distinguishes two types of mimetic desire, *internal mediation* and *external mediation*, a distinction that has both a historical and a structural-systematic significance. In traditional and premodern societies, societies that are based on rigid hierarchies and strict lines of authority, the distance between models and imitators tends to be very large or even absolute (the models may also be mythical or derive from an earlier civilization). In such contexts, social mediation is a function of hierarchy; there is thus relatively little possibility for mediators and imitators to become rivals or otherwise come into conflict with one another. Girard calls the type of mediation that predominates in these societies *external*, since the mediator generally lies outside the imitator's social, temporal, or practical sphere (as in Don Quixote's imitation of the knight-errant).[8] External mediation most often takes the form of explicit veneration or admiration. Within a specific caste or peer group, however, the propensity for imitation to lead to rivalry is ever present due to the social and spatial proximity of the actors. Girard terms this type of mediation *internal*, for it involves relations within a given sphere that often give rise to conflict. In internal imitation, the mediator is both a model and an obstacle. He embodies the double bind "Imitate me; do not imitate me"; that is to say, with a single gesture he designates the object to be desired even as he reserves it for himself. In a world where class distinctions have weakened and no longer place limitations on desire—that is, our modern, egalitarian world—imitation, particularly of the internal variety, is far more widespread and pervasive, even if modern societies nevertheless institutionalize types of imitation that are openly expressed, such as economic competition, creative inspiration,[9] or the notion of the "role model." The more the individual frees himself from the formal expressions of authority (tradition, religion—the imitation of transcendental models), the more his imitation turns toward his neighbor, thereby multiplying the interfaces and increasing the intensity (as in Stendhal's analysis of "*la vanité*" and Proust's portrayal of "snobbery"). This condition generally goes unperceived because the imitation of our peers is most often hidden or disavowed. Girard also speaks of "mediated desire," for there is always a level of *social mediation* between my desire and its object. That is, even if Girard most often focuses on concrete (literary) examples that involve specific interpersonal, triangular relationships, the "third party" can just as well be the social itself, particularly when a social ideal is embodied in a particular person/character.[10]

As suggested in the above-cited preface from 2008, there is a direct relation between the theory of mimetic desire as expounded in his first book and Sartre's notion of bad faith in *Being and Nothingness*. Girard continues: "According to Sartre, bad faith [*la mauvaise foi*] is fundamentally mimetic: the café waiter imitates the waiter who preceded him; he plays at being a café waiter, a bit like Don Quixote plays at being a knight errant."[11] Let us recall Sartre's example of the café waiter:

> Let us consider this waiter in the cafe. His movement is quick and forward, a little too precise, a little too rapid. He comes towards the patrons with a step a little too quick. He bends forward a little too eagerly; his voice, his eyes express an interest a little too solicitous for the order of the customer. Finally there he returns, trying to imitate [*essayant d'imiter*] in his walk the inflexible stiffness of some kind of automaton while carrying his tray with the recklessness of a tightrope-walker. . . . All his behavior seems to us a game. . . . But what is he playing? We need not watch long before we can explain it: he is playing at *being* a waiter in a cafe.[12]

The word "imitate" is explicitly used in the passage to describe the operation of bad faith. By endeavoring to imitate the ways of the café waiter, he strives *to be* a café waiter. Sartre thereby identifies *imitating* with *being*. But to imitate is, of course, not to be; it is the *desire* to be, the desire to be the Other, the model (though Sartre does not put it in terms of alterity). The essential role of imitation in this example thus emphasizes Sartre's point that, in terms of "human reality" (Sartre's translation of Heidegger's *Dasein*), to be is not to be. In Sartre's paradoxical formulation: "I . . . am what I am not and am not what I am."[13] Or, put another way: My essence is not to have an essence. (This is what Sartre means by the famous phrase "existence precedes essence": to exist means to be a contingency that conditions and thus ultimately negates all stable identity, determination, definition, etc.) The café waiter cannot really "be" a café waiter, for then the waiter would be an essence, a "being-in-itself" (*être-en-soi*, the self-identical, an object devoid of consciousness) in Sartre's terminology. But human consciousness, what

Sartre calls "being-for-itself" (*être-pour-soi*, noncoincidence with itself) is free of any ontological (pre)determination, is free to be what it chooses to be; indeed, it is "condemned to be free," condemned to choose its being in every moment. The failure to accept, or the impulse to flee from, this ontological responsibility is what Sartre calls "bad faith" (*la mauvaise foi*), a kind of self-deception or self-delusion.[14]

Although he rarely theorizes it explicitly, the concept of bad faith/self-deception is fundamental to Girard's conception of the psyche and to his theory of mimetic desire. Girard defines bad faith as the "obvious fact that we are not always clearly aware of our deepest motivations."[15] As in self-deception, the dynamic of mimetic desire presupposes a minimal awareness of its operation; otherwise its truth would not be so violently repressed or denied, as in internal mediation (mimetic rivalry). Girard thus sees mimetic desire in terms of bad faith and bad faith in terms of mimetic desire.[16] They are in fact two sides of the same coin.

The identification of imitating with being is what, in his first book, Girard will call "metaphysical desire," a term that is virtually impossible to understand unless its Sartrean provenance is recognized. This notion is clearly derived from Sartre's idea of desire as ontological lack. According to Sartre, individual consciousness, "being-for-itself," is essentially a transcendence (negation, freedom) constituted by lack, a lack of a plenitude of being, the plenitude of the "being-in-itself" (the self-same or the thingly object). In short, being-for-itself always desires being-in-itself; it desires a being that coincides with itself and is not defined by (does not suffer from) lack. Only an in-itself, an object *for* a consciousness, possesses a fullness of being that lacks nothing. Thus to *desire* is to lack being; it is to recognize one's essential incompleteness or self-alienation. As Sartre writes, "The existence of desire as a human fact is sufficient to prove that human reality is a lack.... Desire is a lack of being."[17] Desire is in fact desire for being; is it not mere psychological lack; it is an *existential* (or onto-existential) concept. Hence Girard's Sartrean-existential language in *Deceit, Desire, and the Novel*: "The desire is aimed at the mediator's *being*."[18] And lest anyone think that Girard eventually abandoned the explicitly Sartrean formulations of his first book, that Girard's remarks in his 2008 preface were simply an intellectual reconstruction of his mind-set in the 1950s, let us recall what Girard averred in an interview conducted in 1996: "All desire is a desire for being."[19]

Desire is desire for a *plenitude* of being—this amounts to a desire for the negation of desire. This impossible, self-negating desire, which is simply the impossibility of desire itself, is what Sartre calls the "impossible synthesis of the for-itself with the in-itself."[20] This synthesis is impossible because the for-itself, qua consciousness, can never, *by definition*, be an in-itself, an essence that coincides with itself, a fullness of being that lacks nothing. The only being that can be both a for-itself and an in-itself is *God*, according to Sartre. Thus, Sartre reasons, we all desire to be God; that is, we all desire that desireless state of self-sufficiency and autonomy that only a deity can enjoy. Let us recall what Sartre has to say about God:

> Is not God a being who is what he is—in that he is all positivity and the foundation of the world—and at the same time a being who is not what he is and who is what he is not—in that he is self-consciousness and the necessary foundation of himself? The being of human reality is suffering because it rises in being as perpetually haunted by a totality which it is without being able to be it, precisely because it could not attain the in-itself without losing itself as for-itself. Human reality therefore is by nature an unhappy consciousness with no possibility of surpassing its unhappy state.[21]

Both Girard and Sartre see the same existential angst that is the lot of a human reality defined by an impossible desire. Human consciousness will always be "unhappy" because of the unbridgeable divide between the lack that it is and the totality it desires. This "being *haunted* by a totality" that it lacks is the very essence of Girard's concept of "metaphysical desire." Thus, both Sartre and Girard interpret human reality in terms of a fundamental but impossible desire to be God. In Sartrean terms, "Every attempt of the for-itself to be an in-itself is by definition doomed to failure."[22] In Girardian terms, the desire for the Other's godlike autonomy is a contradiction that is doomed to failure. Girard observes (in *Deceit, Desire, and the Novel*) that "Hegel's unhappy consciousness and Sartre's project to be God are the outcome of a stubborn orientation toward the transcendent, of an inability to relinquish religious patterns of desire when history has outgrown them."[23]

Hence Girard's analysis of *narcissism*: Anyone who merely projects an aura of self-sufficiency or autonomy will appear to be godlike. In an essay entitled "Narcissism: The Freudian Myth Demythified by Proust," published in 1962 (thus around the time of his first book), Girard notes how Proust's narrator experiences an intense attraction to a group of girls (*une bande à part*) who ignore him, realizing that it is because they ignore him that they fascinate him. The flaunting of the narcissist's lack of desire—the aura of self-sufficiency projected by the narcissist—captivates the observer, who dreams of the autonomy of which the narcissist appears to be a shining example. Desiring the Other's autonomy is a contradictory enterprise doomed to fail, thereby confirming the narcissist's superiority and increasing his or her prestige. This process is described vividly by Proust, using religious metaphors. Girard comments:

> Throughout the novel, the desires—innocent as well as perverse—of Marcel and of the other characters are described in *quasi-religious* terms. Behind the coveted something, there is always a someone endowed with an almost *supernatural prestige*. Marcel yearns after a kind of *mystical communion*, with an individual or with a group, dwelling, he believes, in

a superior realm of existence and entirely separated from the vulgar herd. This *metaphysical* desire takes a different form in the various stages of the novel.[24]

"Metaphysical desire" is thus, for Girard, a perversion of the religious attitude. It is therefore with an eye toward Sartre (by way of the early-twentieth-century-philosopher Max Scheler) that Girard titles the second chapter of *Deceit, Desire, and the Novel* "Men Become Gods in the Eyes of Each Other."[25] In Girard's formulation, it is the Other, as the model of ontological self-sufficiency, who plays the role of God.

Thus, what I am endeavoring to argue is that in his notion of "metaphysical desire," Girard effectively replaces the Sartrean God with the Other. As Girard observes in the same 2008 introduction cited above:

> What Sartre calls "essence" is existential imitation. I am close to him in this regard, but pushing Sartre's analyses to their logical conclusion means seeing the Other as a concrete model: the essence of the café waiter is this Other who showed me how to be a waiter; I observed him playing his role, and he was my model. Everything in Sartre is expressed in terms of existence and essence, not enough in terms of Self and Other. In my view, this is absolutely impossible: alterity is inextricable from all that I perceive as mine, as Me.[26]

Therein lies the fundamental difference between Sartre and Girard: the displacement of ontology by alterity. In Sartre, the dialectic of existence and essence, of the for-itself and the in-itself, overshadows the role of the Other in defining human reality. For even if Sartre does proffer anti-solipsistic arguments (as in his celebrated analysis of shame)[27] and even if he, like Girard, theorizes Self-Other relations in terms of conflict (in the remarkable section of *Being and Nothingness* entitled "Concrete Relations with Others"), Sartre ultimately privileges the ontological interpretation of Self-Other relations, which means that alterity, instead of being primordial, as it is for Girard (as well as for Emmanuel Levinas, for that matter), is relegated to a secondary and contingent status.

Conversion and authenticity

In the conclusion to *Deceit, Desire, and the Novel*, the *bad faith* of metaphysical desire is counterposed to an *authentic* attitude toward transcendence (Girard explicitly uses the Sartrean term *authenticité*). This is also described by Girard as the difference between "deviated transcendence" (bad faith) and "vertical transcendence" (authenticity). This relation between vertical and deviated transcendence can also be thought in terms of the relation between the figurative-secular and literal-religious levels of signification. Indeed, the conclusion develops more explicitly and to a greater extent the religious implications of Girard's theory of mimetic desire, and it does so—in a Sartrean manner, but ultimately against Sartre—by exploiting the essential ambiguity of religious terminology. As Girard observes concerning Proust: "The metaphor, therefore, should reveal the metaphysical significance of desire. . . . In Proust's masterpiece the sacred is not merely another metaphoric domain; it is present whenever the author deals with the relationship between the subject and his mediator."[28]

Indeed, throughout the conclusion, Girard's rhetorical operation is similar to what he describes in the opening paragraphs of his essay "Racine, Poet of Glory" (published just three years after *Deceit, Desire, and the Novel*): "[Racine] reinvigorates metaphors by bringing together the two domains of language to which they owe their existence as metaphors." This procedure involves a "reinsertion" of the metaphor "back into its literal context."[29] Thus, by bringing together the figurative (secular) and literal (religious) meanings, the novelistic conversion in effect reinserts secular metaphors into their literal-religious context, thereby revealing or renewing the profound meaning of the religious terminology. Girard observes that "common language goes from the sacred to the rhetorical, and Racine goes from the rhetorical to the sacred."[30]

In his conclusion, Girard also goes "from the rhetorical to the sacred." In this movement, Girard is being far more literal in his conclusion than many readers are aware. For, in articulating a concept of conversion, the conclusion in fact establishes or performs Girard's own conversion, an "intellectual conversion," as he called it.[31] Girard elaborates in a late essay:

> Great literature literally led me to Christianity. This itinerary is not original. It still happens every day and has been happening since the beginning of Christianity. It happened to Saint Augustine, of course. It happened to many great saints such as Saint Francis of Assisi and Saint Theresa of Avila who, like Don Quixote, were fascinated by novels of chivalry. . . . In my case, it was not Virgil or even Dante who guided me through hell, but the five novelists I discussed in my first book: Cervantes, Stendhal, Flaubert, Dostoevsky, and Proust.[32]

The literary or novelistic conversion, the journey "through hell," as he calls it, leads Girard to a personal conversion to Christianity. Girard never relinquished the idea that one of the most effective paths to religion is through the great works of *secular* literature.

Hence Girard's (seemingly untenable) claim, in *Deceit, Desire, and the Novel*, that "all novelistic conclusions are conversions."[33] By this, he does not mean that all novels end with a conversion scene. Girard is using the term "novelistic" in a quasi-technical sense, opposing it to "romantic": "Romantic" novels perpetuate the illusion that desire is autonomous, unmediated, and will lead to personal fulfillment; "novelistic" novels reveal the truth of desire—that desire will lead not to self-fulfillment but to alienation, despair, and spiritual death.[34] The romantic desire to transcend religion results in a parody of the sacred: "The negation of God does not eliminate transcendency but diverts it from the above to the below. The imitation of Christ becomes the imitation of the neighbor."[35] The greatest novels are necessarily "novelistic," in Girard's view, since their greatness is in large measure a function of their perspicacity in understanding human relations and in effecting a "conversion" of their authors and readers. The "novelistic" conclusion, then, is where the unmasking of desire leads to an effective renunciation of the world, of the idolatry of the Other:

> Repudiation of the mediator implies [equals] renunciation of divinity, and this means renouncing pride. . . . In renouncing divinity the hero renounces slavery. Every level of his existence is inverted; all the effects of metaphysical desire are replaced by contrary effects. Deception gives way to truth, anguish to remembrance, agitation to repose, hatred to love, humiliation to humility, mediated desire to autonomy [desire according to the Other to desire according to the Self], deviated transcendency to vertical transcendency.[36]

In renouncing (or negating) a false divinity (deviated transcendence, the desire to be God), the hero discovers the path to authenticity: "*Authentic* conversion engenders a new relationship to others and to oneself."[37] (The English translation, "true conversion," obscures the Sartrean language, which is both conscious and strategic.) Therefore, according to the conclusion, the transformative experience of novelistic conversion is not the result of some positive discovery concerning the nature of the divine, of love, or of humility; it derives from the overcoming of bad faith/mediated desire. A self that has transcended the world will have only one real desire: the authentic desire for God—not the Sartrean God, but the imitation of Christ. This transcendence of the world is also a reconciliation *with* the world, an abandonment of negative attitudes (such as hatred, resentment, vanity, egotism, etc.): "The novelistic denouement is a reconciliation between the individual and the world, between man and the sacred."[38]

The contrast between the specifically Christian virtues (humility, love [*caritas*], inner peace) and corresponding vices (pride, hatred, anguish) in the above-quoted passage is not coincidental. Girard maintains that a novelistic conversion is nominally "Christian" in the sense that an affirmation of Christian values is inextricable from a critique of worldly desire. Thus, an atheist can live by Christian principles without contradiction and may even be more "Christian" than a believer: "The repudiation of a human mediator and renunciation of deviated transcendency inevitably calls for symbols of vertical transcendency whether the author is Christian or not."[39] Girard is thus careful to emphasize the "universality" (the secular nature) of figures of conversion that are deployed in novelistic conclusions, despite their apparently Christian provenance.

The word and the idea of conversion are also present in Sartre's posthumously published *Notebooks for an Ethics*, which asserts that "*conversion* may arise from the perpetual failure of every one of the For-itself's attempts to be. Every attempt of the For-itself to be In-itself is by definition doomed to fail."[40] In other words, Sartrean conversion results from the recognition of the impossible desire to be God (Girard's metaphysical desire). As we saw in Chapter 2 on Foucault, conversion is not merely a religious concept; it is rather an ethical one at bottom. Thus, in *The Care of the Self*, Foucault makes the seemingly Girard-sounding statement that "to convert to oneself is to turn away from the preoccupations of the external world, from the concerns of ambition."[41] Sartre is thus in some sense continuing this Greek tradition of conversion (*epistrophê*) in his existentialist theory, while including Christian elements as well. In the following commentary on Sartre by David Detmer, one could insert Girard's name for Sartre and "metaphysical desire" for "bad faith":

> Sartre sees bad faith, the futile quest to be God, interpersonal conflict, and misery to be, as it were, our natural or default condition. This is why a radical conversion from the situation toward which our ontological condition inclines us is needed. Here again we find in Sartre's philosophy an atheistic analogue to Christian doctrines—in this case that of original sin. It is as if he were saying that we are in a fallen state, and stand in need of salvation! This, I propose, is the key to understanding Sartre's footnote placed at the end of his discussion of bad faith, in which he tells us that we can "radically escape bad faith," but that it requires "a self-recovery of being which was previously corrupted." This self-recovery, which Sartre calls "authenticity," requires a radical conversion from the project of being-God to a project based on freedom.[42]

Sartre's existentialist concept of conversion (authenticity) is thus structurally analogous to Girard's quasi-religious (and nominally Christian) notion of novelistic conversion, which itself is based on Sartrean authenticity. By interpreting the Sartrean God as the concrete Other, as a deviated transcendence, Girard in effect reveals how a Christian conception of conversion is at work in Sartre's philosophy, even as an examination of Sartre's thought reveals an existentialist dimension in Girard's mimetic theory. This Sartrean-secular-existentialist dimension will also inform Girard's analysis of religion in *Violence and the Sacred* and *Things Hidden Since the Foundation of the World*, even if many commentators on Girard have yet to recognize it.

CHAPTER EIGHT

The ethics of realism

Literary history and the sublime in Erich Auerbach's *Mimesis*

Since the early twentieth century, literary history has been criticized for ignoring the text, or more precisely, for focusing on the context at the expense of the text. Successive waves of critical orthodoxies—Russian formalism, New Criticism, structuralism, poststructuralism, New Historicism—have declared it to be either provincial or irrelevant. Despite these attacks, literary history is still considered an important methodology in Continental Europe, particularly in the editing of the national literature. However, in the American academy, which prizes intellectual innovation over conservation and tradition, literary history has long been all but moribund.[1]

In the early part of the twentieth century, a group of German scholars developed a new kind of literary history, Romance philology, which distinguished itself by its combination of astonishing erudition, stylistic interpretation, and grounding in German philosophy and intellectual history. The chief exponents of this tradition—Ernst Curtius, Karl Vossler, Leo Spitzer, and Erich Auerbach—attempted to revitalize literary history by providing it with a methodology that would rescue it from the pedantry of nineteenth-century historicism.[2] But the intentions of these critics were also ethical and humanistic: to valorize a common European tradition—even a common humanity—in the wake of the devastation wrought by the Second World War. In his late work *Literary Language and Its Public in Late Latin Antiquity and in the Middle Ages* (1958), Auerbach observes, forebodingly, that

> European civilization is approaching the term of its existence; its history as a distinct entity would seem to be at an end, for already it is beginning to be

engulfed in another, more comprehensive unity. Today, however, European civilization is still a living reality within the range of our perception. Consequently . . . we must today attempt to form a lucid and coherent picture of this civilization and its unity. I have always tried, more and more resolutely as time went on, to work in this direction, at least in my approach to the subject matter of philology, namely literary expression.[3]

Auerbach's magnum opus, *Mimesis: The Representation of Reality in Western Literature*,[4] written during his exile in Turkey and published just after the war (1946), was meant to be this "lucid and coherent picture of [European] civilization and its unity."

While this group of German philologists was influential in the United States during the postwar period, only Auerbach's work has retained its relevance.[5] This is due to the unparalleled success of his *Mimesis*, which continues to be widely studied and discussed seventy years after its initial publication.[6] There are perhaps several reasons for the success of *Mimesis*, the most obvious being Auerbach's custom of introducing every chapter with a close reading of a representative and canonical work. Auerbach's way of drawing out the essence of an entire period from the reading of a single text is a hermeneutic tour de force that has few if any rivals.

There is, however, another reason for the success of *Mimesis*: its structural and ethical approach to literary history.[7] *Mimesis* is the story of realist representation in language, defined not in ontological terms as a verbal approximation of reality (correspondence of mind to world—*adequatio intellectus et rei*), but in ethico-aesthetic terms as the serious presentation of human reality in its aspects that are most common or ordinary.[8] *Seriousness*, with respect to the mode of presentation, and *everydayness*, with respect to what is presented, are the two fundamental conditions of what Auerbach calls "realism." Although there is much debate about what Auerbach exactly means by this term—his distaste for theoretical or conceptual vocabulary is well known—the structural import is clear. In every instance of realistic representation, Auerbach uncovers the same underlying pattern: *Stilmischung*, the mixture of styles, which represents the breakdown of *Stiltrennung*, the hierarchical division/separation of style/subject matter (elevated style for heroes, kings, and nobles; comic style for low-born characters). The principal turning points in the history of realistic representation—sublime realism (*sermo humilis*, the Gospels), figural realism (the literature of late antiquity and the Middle Ages), and historical realism (the nineteenth-century French novel)—all share a common structure. Thus Auerbach's putative "relativism" is, I believe, overdone, not least by Auerbach himself. Discussing his methodology, Auerbach writes, "Historical relativism . . . is a radical relativism, but that is no reason to fear it. . . . In the historical forms themselves, we gradually learn to find the flexible, always provisional, categories we need."[9] This assertion, however, is not borne out by Auerbach's actual practice.[10] Given the fact that *Mimesis* is a survey of what goes under the rubric of Auerbach's conception of realism, rather than a survey of what types of literature were held to be realistic according to the standards of the period that produced them (e.g., the notion of verisimilitude in French neoclassicism), the amplitude of possible variations is restrained by a unifying thesis imposed from the outside.[11]

Although the mixture of styles will take on the different forms mentioned above, its initial definition as the combination of *sublimitas* and *humilitas* in the Gospels will remain valid throughout Auerbach's history. Auerbach explicitly excludes any interpretation of the mixture of styles that would enclose realism within the middle or intermediate style.[12] He aims toward a concept of *high* literature, in which realistic genres such as the novel, traditionally disparaged as formally defective, are revalued for their profound grasp of the human condition. To achieve this end, Auerbach seeks to maintain a dynamic tension between the high and the low, the sublime and the mundane, throughout his exposition of realistic representation in Western literature. The sublime is thus an essential element in Auerbach's concept of realism.

Readers may find this assertion surprising, for Auerbach's use of the sublime in *Mimesis* has attracted relatively little attention.[13] Although the term "sublime/sublimity" (*das Erhabene* in German, *sublimitas* in Latin, *hypsos* in Greek) and its synonyms, "high," "lofty," and "elevated," can be found throughout *Mimesis* and are at the core of his concept of the mixture of styles, Auerbach is rarely mentioned in critical discussions of the sublime,[14] nor is the sublime much of a topic in Auerbach studies. The reason for this oversight, I believe, lies in the impression that for Auerbach the sublime is not a critico-aesthetic category but simply names a particular style, the grand or elevated style of the Greek and Latin systems of rhetoric. Seen in this light, the term is of little critical interest and can have no broader implications for Auerbach's conception of realism.

This line of thinking is deficient in two respects. First, it is clear that Auerbach uses the term *sublime* (*Erhabene*) in ways that go far beyond the stylistic meaning; second, the stylistic meaning is itself misleading due to Auerbach's rather expansive concept of style, which is often indistinguishable from what today we would call *tone* or *genre*.[15]

Auerbach's notion of sublimity clearly derives from Longinus's *Peri hypsous* (*On the Sublime*) and, to all appearances, is not mediated by eighteenth-century discussions of this notion. Although we find only a single mention of Longinus in *Mimesis*, Auerbach comments at length on *Peri hypsous* in a chapter entitled "Camilla, or, The Rebirth of the Sublime"[16] from his *Literary Language and Its Public in Late Latin Antiquity and in the Middle Ages* (published posthumously in 1958), which Auerbach considered a "supplement" to *Mimesis*.[17] In this book, Auerbach characterizes the subject of Longinus's treatise as the lofty or sublime style:

> The most important among the theorists of the Imperial Age, the unknown author of the Greek treatise *On the Sublime* [*Peri hypsous*], who probably

lived in the first half of the first century AD, spoke impressively on the matter. The lofty style, he says in substance, is not, like the middle style, intended to please and persuade but to fire with enthusiasm and to carry away.[18]

This interpretation of Longinus is peculiar in that, first, it presents itself as a commonplace, and secondly, it directly contradicts the interpretation of Nicolas Boileau in the preface to his 1674 translation of *Peri hypsous*, which introduced Longinus into European intellectual culture and made *le sublime* a fashionable term.[19] Auerbach was certainly aware of Boileau's preface (he refers to it in *Mimesis*), yet he fails to mention the apparent divergence in conception.

Let us recall Boileau's interpretation of Longinus. In his preface to the 1674 edition,[20] Boileau announces that the sublime is not a type of style corresponding to the categories of classical rhetoric; rather it is a critical *concept*, one that allows us to conceptualize moments of transcendence in the verbal arts:

> It must be observed then that by the Sublime he [Longinus] does not mean what the Orators call the Sublime Style, but something extraordinary and marvelous that strikes us in a discourse and makes it elevate, ravish and transport us. The sublime style requires always great Words, but the sublime may be found in a Thought only, or in a Figure or Turn of Expression. A thing may be in the Sublime Style and yet not be Sublime, that is, have nothing extraordinary or surprising in it.[21]

Prima facie, Auerbach's conception would appear to be diametrically opposed to this reading of Longinus's treatise ("orators" is clearly a metonymy for rhetoric). However, looking closely at Auerbach's chapter on the sublime (in *Literary Language and Its Public*), we see that he makes a similar distinction between the true sublime and that which resembles it only superficially. Near the end of this chapter, he observes that Longinus's treatise represents a reaction against the type of elevated style that Auerbach dubs "rhetorical sublimity." He associates this vapid form with Senecan tragedy and the writings of Ovid, who "allowed himself to be beguiled by rhetorical devices and tricks."[22] Longinus similarly inveighs against rhetorical artifice: "Sublimity and emotion are a defense and a marvelous aid against the suspicion which the use of figures engenders. The artifice of the trick is lost to sight in the surrounding brilliance of beauty and grandeur, and it escapes all suspicion."[23] Echoing the well-known concluding section of *Peri hypsous* (44.1–12), in which Longinus attributes the decline of oratory to the decaying moral character of Roman society, Auerbach argues that the sublime falls into decadence when it comes under the sway of rhetoric in the first century AD:

> Rhetorical excess is very dangerous in treatments of the passions and the sublime; it destroys all immediacy and movement, especially when the

reader has the feeling that the scene did not spring from a single impulse but was carefully pieced together with the help of traditional devices. The leading theorists of ancient eloquence were well aware of this and said as much. Many of their less inspired fellows copied the idea from them, but no remonstrances could prevent the invasion of rhetoric from destroying the sublime style.[24]

Thus, insofar as he endeavors to disengage sublimity from rhetoric, Auerbach can be said to be following Boileau's interpretation of Longinus. For Boileau's diatribe against style is in fact an attack on rhetoric, which had fallen into disrepute in seventeenth-century France.[25]

There are many occasions in *Mimesis* in which Auerbach explicitly distinguishes sublimity not only from rhetoric but also from style. For example, in the famous first chapter, commenting on the Old Testament, Auerbach writes, "The sublime influence of God here reaches so deeply into the everyday that the two realms of the sublime and the everyday are not only actually unseparated but basically inseparable."[26] Here "sublime" refers to a "realm," a domain of being rather than a category of style. And in the section in which he discusses the mixture of styles in the Gospels, Auerbach writes, "These significant passages are concerned with the thing itself, not with its literary treatment. *Sublimitas* and *humilitas* are here wholly ethico-theological categories, not aesthetico-stylistic ones."[27] Discussing Dante, Auerbach observes, "Beside them we find formulations of the highest sublimity, which are also stylistically 'sublime' in the antique sense."[28] And: "Yet there is no denying that Dante's conception of the sublime differs essentially from that of his models, in respect to subject matter no less than to stylistic form."[29] In all of these instances, Auerbach shows that he is aware of a difference—ethical, conceptual, or ontological—between sublimity and the sublime style, even if he does not theorize "the sublime" in an explicit manner.

If we look closely at Boileau's preface, we can discern that behind the separation of style (rhetoric) from sublimity there is a desire to demonstrate a continuity between sacred and secular literature—a procedure that will also be consequential for Auerbach in *Mimesis*. Most famously, Boileau cites Longinus's discussion of the *fiat lux* ("let there be light"—a reference to the Old Testament that was unique in a rhetorical treatise of this era written in Greek) as a prime example of how the sublime style differed from the sublime proper:

> As for Example, *The Sovereign Arbiter of Nature with one Word only form'd the Light*; this is in the sublime style, and yet is far from being Sublime, because there's nothing very marvelous in it, and which might not be easily thought and expressed on that Occasion by any one; but God said, *Let there be Light, and there was Light*, is an extraordinary Turn of expression which so well denotes the Obedience of the Creature

to the Orders of the Creator, that it is truly Sublime, and has something Divine in it.[30]

Boileau's association between divinity and sublimity has the effect of blurring the category distinction between pagan literature and the Christian Bible. Boileau sacralizes literature even as he rhetoricizes scripture. This move would antagonize some members of the clergy, such as Pierre-Daniel Huet, who attacked Boileau in his *Demonstratio evangelica*, published in 1678.[31] What roiled Huet was the implication that the word of God could be subjected to the methodologies of literary analysis; thus, according to Huet, the Bible cannot be considered sublime.[32]

One of Auerbach's main objectives in *Mimesis* is to show how the aesthetic structure of Biblical texts, principally the Gospels, provides a model for realistic representation in secular literature. Hence Auerbach's interest in the early polemics surrounding the *fiat lux* passage in Longinus's treatise. In the context of a discussion of parataxis, Auerbach writes:

> An elevated style operating with paratactic elements is not, in itself, something new in Europe. The style of the Bible has this characteristic. Here we may recall the discussion concerning the sublime character [*erhabenen Charakters*] of the sentence *dixit que Deus: fiat lux, et facta est lux* (Gen. 1.3) which Boileau and Huet carried on in the seventeenth century in connection with the essay *On the Sublime* attributed to Longinus. The sublime [*das Erhabene*] in this sentence from Genesis is not contained in a magnificent display of rolling periods nor in the splendor of abundant figures of speech but in the impressive brevity which is in such contrast to the immense content and which for that very reason has a note of obscurity which fills the listener with a shuddering awe. It is precisely the absence of causal connectives, the naked statement of what happens—the statement which replaces deduction and comprehension by an amazed beholding that does not even seek to comprehend—which gives the sentence its grandeur.[33]

Here Auerbach reinterprets Boileau's distinction between the sublime style and the sublime as a distinction within the elevated style between the paratactic and the nonparatactic, while also gesturing in the direction of the aesthetic conception of sublimity ("fills the listener with a shuddering awe"). Auerbach draws a contrast between "impressive brevity" and the "immense content"; sublimity occurs in the disparity between what is said and what is signified. However, what is this opposition between the paratactic and the nonparatactic if not the difference between the true sublime, the mixture of humility and height that characterizes Biblical writing, particularly the Gospels, and the sublime style of pagan literature that consists in grand rhetoric? Thus the simple style of the Gospels derives from its extensive use of sublime parataxis. The idea that the simple style can be a sort of grand style is typical of Auerbach's dialectical intuitions.

When we come to the notion of the "mixture of styles" (*Stilmischung*), we are confronted with the following problem: In what sense are the high and low styles "mixed"? Does this mean that they are fused with one another to create a level that lies between them? Definitely not. As was remarked above, Auerbach rejects the idea that the mixture of the high and the low will result in a sort of middle or intermediate level of style. Nor does Auerbach mean that the high and low should be mixed in the sense that they are juxtaposed or arranged in the form of antitheses, as they are in Shakespeare's plays or Victor Hugo's novels.[34] Let us examine the following passage: "In antique theory, the sublime and elevated style was called *sermo gravis* or *sublimis*; the low style was *sermo remissus* or *humilis*; the two had to be kept strictly separated. In the world of Christianity, on the other hand, the two are merged, especially in Christ's Incarnation and Passion, which realize and combine *sublimitas* and *humilitas* in overwhelming measure."[35] The two styles were previously "separated" in the sense that one style could not grasp the subject matter that belonged to the other by convention. Thus the mixture of styles is less the mixture of one style with another than a relation between style and content. As René Wellek observes in his review essay of *Mimesis*, the mixture of styles is directed against "the hierarchical view of subject matters for art."[36] What Auerbach means, then, is that the usual correspondence between style and subject matter is broken:

> The styles in which it was presented possessed little if any rhetorical culture in the antique sense; it was *sermo piscatorius* and yet it was extremely moving and much more impressive than the most sublime [*höchste*, highest] rhetorico-tragical literary work. And the most moving account of all was the Passion. That the King of Kings was treated as a low criminal, that he was mocked, spat upon, whipped, and nailed to the cross—that story no sooner comes to dominate the consciousness of the people than it completely destroys the aesthetics of the separation of styles; it engenders a new elevated [*hohen*] style, which does not scorn everyday life and which is ready to absorb the sensorily realistic, even the ugly, the undignified, the physically base. Or—if anyone prefers to have it the other way around—a new *sermo humilis* is born, a low style, such as would probably only be applicable to comedy, but which now reaches out far beyond its original domain, and encroaches upon the deepest and the highest [*Höchste*], the sublime [*Erhabene*] and the eternal.[37]

One could thus say that the mixture of the grand and humble styles creates a new kind of "elevated" style, which is simple (paratactic, for example) instead of ornate and which deals with everyday subjects; or one could say the contrary: that a new "low" style is created, which "encroaches upon the deepest and the highest, the sublime and the eternal." It is clear that

Auerbach cannot conceptualize the mixture of styles except in terms of one of the two opposing poles: a new "elevated" style that comprehends the everyday, or a low style that contains the sublime. The "mixture" is in fact a *dialectic*.[38] The realism of the Gospels is produced by a dynamic tension between opposites, a contamination of elements that had heretofore been considered mutually exclusive: God and man; sovereigns and slaves; religious ideas and the humble milieu.

It is thus as a dialectical entity that the sublime functions as a structural category in Auerbach's scheme. It mediates between the stylistic and the ethical, the aesthetic and the social, the historical and the political. Erected around the two major events of Western history, the birth of Christianity and the French Revolution, Auerbach's *Mimesis* is as much a literary history—a history of literature—as it is a narrative of social evolution. Thus, Hayden White speaks of a "two-fold order of changes" that Auerbach's work addresses:

> The manifest story told by Auerbach is of the twofold order of changes that have taken place in the classical hierarchy of literary (poetic or discursive) styles (high, middle, and low or humble) and genres (tragedy, comedy, epic, romance, novel, history, essay, satire) on the one side, and a social reality in which people are divided into classes and treated as more or less human and consequently considered to be more or less worthy of being represented as the subjects of these styles and genres, on the other.[39]

This is Auerbach's ethico-political narrative of realism. It is the story of the triumph of the notion of equality and the concomitant notion of human dignity. As the average person attains a certain mobility with respect to wealth, power, and social status and becomes more important in terms of receiving equal treatment under the law and the right to political participation, he demands serious representation of himself and his milieu. Literary history and social history interact through a common structural force: dehierarchization. The dehierarchization of styles mirrors the dehierarchization of society. But this dehierarchization is not mere leveling. Just as the realist mixture of styles does not result in a middle or intermediate style, the egalitarian society was not supposed to announce the triumph of mediocrity (e.g., public opinion, the lowest common denominator). Here we begin to perceive the gulf that separates the negative social vision of the nineteenth-century French novelists (Stendhal, Balzac) from the social achievement that made their realistic aesthetic possible. For Auerbach, however, it is not a matter of deciding whether literature is an expression or instigator of social change. What is important to Auerbach is how human reality shows itself at a particular moment and how this particular moment is related to other moments and to the historical whole.

These relations between part and whole—the very essence of structural and hermeneutic analysis—are best described as "figural," as White argues, rather than causal. In his essay (quoted from above) "Auerbach's Literary History: Figural Causation and Modernist Historicism," White takes what for Auerbach was a notion with a very specific application (the figural realism of the Middle Ages) and expands it into a general methodological principle (figural interpretation): "Historical things are related to one another as elements of structures of figuration (*Figuralstrukturen*). This means that things historical can be apprehended in their historicity only insofar as they can be grasped as elements of wholes that, in both their synchronic and diachronic dimensions, are related to their fulfillments."[40] The historical realism of Balzac and Stendhal can thus be seen as the figural fulfillment of the sublime realism of the Gospels. Beyond White's larger point that history is essentially figural in nature (discussed in Chapter 5), the emphasis he places on the "structural" element in figural analysis is instructive. The structure of figures is also a figural structure. The structure is itself a figure that finds its fulfillment in a new context.

Due to its scope and structuring ambition, Auerbach's *Mimesis* can thus be usefully considered alongside recent work in social history and the history of religion. Political philosopher Alain Renaut describes how the Christian idea of equality of all before God first cohered with, but then eventually triumphed over, the principle of hierarchy:

> It can easily be seen that this principle [of equality of all before God] contained the seeds of modern individualism: because the principle of equality operated in relation to God (that is, outside the world), it could thus coexist with a principle of hierarchy (operating within the world). Medieval Christianity carried on this ancient dualism, superimposing an otherworldly value of equality on the worldly, holistic value that structured all social relations. For modern individualism to be born, it was necessary for the individualistic and universalistic element in Christianity to "contaminate" worldly life, so to speak, to the point that the worldly and unworldly came to be gradually unified.[41]

In Auerbach's literary history, this unification is achieved through the notion of the sublime.[42] The "contamination" of which Renaut speaks had occurred in exemplary fashion in the mixture of sublimity and humility in the Gospels. To the extent that this new aesthetic comes to "dominate the consciousness of the people" (as Auerbach remarks in a passage quoted above), it has real, and not merely literary-stylistic, effects.[43] In his early book on Dante, Auerbach remarks, "It is well known though seldom stated in this connection, that the mimetic content of the story of Christ required a very long time, more than a thousand years, to enter into the consciousness of the faithful."[44] Thus, in the case of the Gospels, the efficient-causal and figural-causal become one.

The ur-structure of Auerbach's sublime, the high within the low, traverses all the boundaries that separate the domains of the social, the literary, the ethico-political, and the religious; for, as discussed above, Auerbach is no less concerned with the sociopolitical developments that form the backdrop of his history of realism. For Auerbach, as for Renaut, the Gospels contain "the seeds of modern individualism." "In the Gospels," writes Auerbach, "all social and aesthetic limits have been effaced."[45] The realism of the Gospels was a function of an ethical reconfiguration in the relationship between immanence and transcendence. The common realm of Jesus's milieu is connected to the otherworldly realm of divine transcendence; low-born, anonymous individuals are represented with dignity and nobility, in effect performing aesthetically the ethical-religious ideas expounded in the text: The meek will inherit the earth. Sublimity is democratized; or, put another way, the Gospels become the aesthetic model of the concept of equality.

This aesthetic performative would have profound implications for the development of modern realism. The sublime in the figural realism of the Middle Ages possessed an essential ambiguity that allowed it to coexist with the feudal system—the sublimation of Christian *caritas* into the chivalric romance, for example—while still tending in the direction of social emancipation. Through the notion of the *figura*, Christian thinkers were able to sustain the literal truth of the New Testament. Efforts to allegorize or otherwise de-realize the Gospels were rebuffed. Figural realism was also seen by Christian authors such as Dante as a way to link Biblical figures to mundane events, so that those events or people, taken from the world in which he lived, became themselves figures of Christian ideas (e.g., of conversion and salvation) without negating either their historicity or their reality. Auerbach notes that "many important critics—and indeed whole epochs of classicistic taste—have felt ill at ease with Dante's closeness to the actual in the realm of the sublime."[46] This sublime realism of figures, which had reached perfection in the *Commedia*, was the cultural form best suited for the dissemination of Christian thought: Christian populism mixed with sublime transcendence announced a democratic humanism. Hence the title of Auerbach's first book: *Dante als Dichter der irdischen Welt* (translated as *Dante, Poet of the Secular World*).[47] In *Mimesis*, he makes the dialectical movement explicit: "Dante's work made man's Christian-figural being a reality, and destroyed it in the very process of making it."[48] This is why Auerbach regards Dante's *Commedia* as one of the two summits of the history of realistic representation—the other being the French realist novel of the nineteenth century.

From a modern perspective, the literary impulses that emerged out of the social upheaval of the French Revolution represent the most obvious and spectacular break with the "separation of styles" (*Stiltrennung*) (which had existed in a stricter form under the *Ancien Régime*).[49] Victor Hugo's romantic manifesto, the preface to his drama *Cromwell* (1827), agitated for the mixture of the sublime and the grotesque; Stendhal's *Racine et Shakespeare* (1823) advocated the aesthetic modernity of the latter over the conservatism of the former; and novels such as Stendhal's *The Red and the Black* (1830) and Balzac's *Le père Goriot* (1835) elevated the sentimental novel by lending an existential weight and historical depth to depictions of everyday life. However, it is difficult to read *Mimesis* without concluding that for Auerbach, the real driving force behind the development of realism, up to and including its modern form, is the Gospels. As Auerbach writes in the epilogue to *Mimesis*: "It was the story of Christ, with its ruthless mixture of everyday reality and the highest and most sublime tragedy, which had conquered the classical rule of styles."[50]

But if the historical realism of the nineteenth century is read as the aesthetic and social fulfillment of the Gospels, what becomes of the sublime? Commenting on Hugo's preface, Auerbach writes, "In Hugo's formula there is something too pointedly antithetical; for him it is a matter of mixing the sublime and the grotesque. These are both extremes of style which give no consideration to reality."[51] This judgment may appear somewhat arbitrary, since Auerbach praises Dante's *Commedia* precisely for this mixture of the sublime and the grotesque: "Dante knows no limits in describing with meticulous care and directness things that are humdrum, grotesque, or repulsive. Themes which cannot possibly be considered sublime in the antique sense turn out to be just that by virtue of his way of molding and ordering them."[52] One could argue that such exaggerated dialectics as those found in Dante are realistic within Dante's particular worldview, and that within a worldview based on the contingency of life, in which the role of the transcendental is replaced by the social and the historical, the sublime has less of a place; sharp dialectical contrasts are attenuated; random movements are emphasized.

This solution is not really satisfactory. Auerbach generally tends to underemphasize the extent to which the sublime plays a structuring role in the realist authors he admires. One need look only at, for example, Stendhal's contrast between *amour-passion* and *amour-vanité*, Balzac's rhetoric of sublimity in *Eugénie Grandet* ("Eugénie était sublime, elle était femme") and *Le père Goriot* ("Le père Goriot est sublime").[53] Nevertheless, there are a few passages in which Auerbach does appear to recognize that sublimity plays an integral role in his conception of modern realism. Discussing Zola, Auerbach writes, "There is indeed here, beyond all doubt, great historical tragedy, a mixture of *humile* and *sublime* in which, because of the content, the latter prevails. Statements like Maheu's (*si l'on avait plus d'argent on aurait plus d'aise*—or *ça finit toujours par des hommes soûls et par des filles pleines*), not to mention his wife's, have come to be part of the grand style."[54] The dialectic of the high and the low is still the driving force of realistic representation, even in Zola's grotesque version (naturalism). The sublime "prevails" because Zola has completely internalized the Christian orientation toward the victim or marginal person, calling attention to his or her *innocence* and inherent dignity. In the association between the victim and the sublime, we have come full circle: Realism finds its culmination and ethical fulfillment in the elevation of the humble/humiliated masses that the Gospels first brought to light.

Auerbach's unease with the sublime in modern realism is a function of his desire to see realism as the gradual emergence of a historical sensibility to the exclusion of any transcendental grounding. Contingent, historical being-in-the-world replaces the sublime or otherworldly dimension that had previously supported the existential orientation of realist representation. Society replaces religion; chance replaces fate: "Neither the antique nor the Christian nor the Shakespearian nor the Racinian level of conception and expression could easily be transferred to the new subjects; at first there was some uncertainty in regard to the kind of serious attitude to be assumed."[55] As a critic, Auerbach too is somewhat uncertain as to how the dialectic of the sublime and the humble can inform the new historical sensibility that is modern realism's distinctive marker.

René Wellek—who, at the moment Auerbach was writing, represented the school of "theory" in contradistinction to literary history—sees an irresolvable conflict between Auerbach's simultaneous commitment to the existential and the historical in modern realism. How are we to square, as Auerbach puts it, "the entrance of existential and tragic seriousness into realism, as we observe it in Stendhal and Balzac"[56] with the historical consciousness that distinguishes nineteenth-century French realism from eighteenth-century sentimental realism? Wellek remarks:

> Is there not a contradiction between existence and history? Existence seems to me by definition unhistorical. . . . Historicism, immersion in social and political reality, contradicts existentialism. . . . It is precisely the "historical" realism of the French—with its reliance on milieu, moment, race, and in its later stages in Zola, on a deterministic belief in heredity—which rejects human freedom and the greatness of man's self-assertion in the face of history and its forces. It is not tragic, not existential because it is deterministic and fatalistic.[57]

For all of his acute insights, I think Wellek (and, for that matter, Auerbach) has missed the mediating role that the sublime plays in bridging the gap between the existential and the historical in modern realism. Geoffrey Green has it basically right when he asserts that "the value of the humanistic outlook of Christianity was partially caused by its existential stance: it simultaneously existed in history and outside of it. Auerbach refers to this quality in what he terms the sublimity of Genesis 1.3."[58] The transhistorical or structural element is the mixture of styles itself: the dialectic between *sublimitas* and *humilitas* that underlies all realistic representation in Auerbach's sense. Thus, the sublime forms an essential part of the concept of the human being as a self-transcending entity that can be the subject of history. Just as Hegel's dialectic is the structural principle that underpins his historical methodology, the dialectic of the sublime in the mixture of styles is what allows Auerbach's historicism to reach its ethical fulfillment as both literary history and cultural criticism.

* * *

Reading *Mimesis* as a response to contemporary European realities, Green observes that

> Auerbach was proceeding from certain valued concepts which, far from being detached and relativistic for him, were urgently important and ideologically crucial. . . . Auerbach attempted to outline the path of past history and then to use his version of history as a fortress—an arsenal—from which he could wage a passionate and vehement war against the possible flow of history in his time.[59]

Indeed, Auerbach's account of the development of realistic representation is ethical at bottom, not only in the sense that it was intended to capture a vision of European cultural unity at a time of extreme crisis but also in the more direct sense that his very concepts are, as Green notes, "value-laden." The mixture of *sublimitas* and *humilitas* reveals the *moral superiority* of the Gospels over the hierarchy/separation of styles in pagan antiquity and *Ancien Régime* Europe. Thus, *Mimesis* recounts the titanic struggle between the positively valued *Stilmischung* and the negatively valued *Stiltrennung*, culminating in the ethical victory of the former over the latter in the democratic vision of the nineteenth-century novel.

CHAPTER NINE

The ethics of philology

Erich Auerbach and the fate of humanism

The debate between formalism and historicism that characterized much of twentieth-century criticism has been largely displaced and superseded by a debate about the politicization of literary studies, that is, about the extent to which questions of social justice—including colonialism, group identity, and so on—should be of primary concern in academic disciplines such as literature, where there is no obvious real-world application for the results of its research (unlike, say, in sociology or political science). In a sense, this debate represents a revival of the arguments opposing committed art to aesthetic autonomy. However, identity politics has added a new dimension. While the political turn sounded the death knell for formalism, signaled the resurrection of the author, and emphasized the group identity of the critic, the fate of the classic tomes of literary criticism—Erich Auerbach's *Mimesis*, Northrop Frye's *Anatomy of Criticism*, and Georg Lukács's writings on the novel—remained uncertain. How could these critics find their place in the midst of a paradigm shift that appeared to cast their work as old fashioned and perhaps even irrelevant, as not in tune with the new direction of literary studies?

It was thus a masterstroke to have Edward Said—perhaps the thinker most responsible for and most identified with the politicization of literary studies—compose a new introduction for the fiftieth anniversary edition of *Mimesis*, published by Princeton University Press in 2003 (the same year as Said's death). Of course, Said had been identified with Auerbach since publishing a translation of Auerbach's seminal essay "Philology and *Weltliteratur*" in 1969, but the mere fact that the founder of postcolonial studies considered *Mimesis* worthy of continued attention and study was enough to ensure open-mindedness on the part of the skeptical.[1] (And there is also the magnanimous gesture of an Arab writer closely associated with the Palestinian cause paying tribute to a Jewish scholar.) I shall return to Said's superb introduction a bit later on in this chapter.

While the political turn may have destroyed a certain kind of formalism, namely, a reductive textualism, the more general question of "literariness" remained, and, in the first decade of the 2000s, began to reassert itself. In her 2006 president's address to the Modern Language Association, Marjorie Perloff laments the dearth of formalist approaches to the text, complaining that literary studies had degenerated into what she called "content analysis."[2] In an interview conducted in 2005, Perloff remarks:

> What you get today . . . [are] people using literature as an excuse to talk about the war in Iraq. Literature becomes a symptom of a particular social formation. As soon as literature becomes instrumental in that way, it becomes uninteresting, since you can always use other things instead. That's why there is a kind of malaise [in literary studies].[3]

Perloff fears that the literary domain has lost its specificity, that it has become increasingly indistinguishable from adjacent disciplines such as history, sociology, religious studies, or anthropology, in which literature is a secondary object, a means in the pursuit of some nonliterary end. In this vein, one could also mention Jonathan Culler's 2007 book *The Literary in Theory*, which decries the "neglect of theoretical issues that are particular to literature and the system of the literary."[4] Culler confides that, in the 1990s, busied with notions of "race and gender, identity and agency, distracted by the notoriety of Knapp's and Michaels's now largely forgotten antitheory theory, I inadvertently forgot the theory of literature."[5]

Of course, this "forgetting of literature" or "the literary" was the initial impetus that led to the development of New Criticism and later of structuralist poetics.[6] These formalisms attempted to carve out a proper domain for literary studies, thereby extricating it from its archenemy literary history, which it saw as inordinately focused on extraneous issues such as authorial biography. Have we come full circle? Will a neoformalism rise up and put the political critics in their place?

On one level, the divide is perhaps less extreme now than it was in the 1950s and 1960s. Looking, for example, at the specialties of the editorial board members in the winter 1969 issue of the *Centennial Review* (in which Auerbach's "Philology and *Weltliteratur*" appears), a journal that describes itself as a "publication concerned with the interrelations among the disciplines," one finds the following list of fields: economics, education, history, literary criticism, literary history, mathematics, music, philosophy, and so on. "Literary criticism" and "literary history" appear on this list as two *distinct* and, given their common object, *rival* disciplines within the panoply of academic areas, as opposed to merely two different approaches within literary studies that might complement or complete one another. Needless to say, literary criticism won the day, and thus we now refer to the activity of those in literary studies as "criticism" as opposed to "history" (although one could argue that there is a division between those who do "criticism" and those who do "theory," but this distinction is a bit arbitrary, as the composite "critical theory" demonstrates).[7] Literary history was widely derided and dismissed for ignoring the text, for not being able to grasp the essence of literature. In their classic (but now rarely discussed) *Theory of Literature*, René Wellek and Austin Warren summed up the view of many when they wrote, "Literary history has been so preoccupied with the setting of a work of literature that its attempts at analysis of the works themselves have been slight in comparison with the enormous efforts expended on the study of environment."[8]

So where does all of this leave Auerbach, renowned for his historical approach to the study of literature? How did Auerbach escape the fate of literary history? Of the thousands of volumes of literary history now gathering dust in our university libraries, why does his work survive?

Indeed, with Auerbach we are speaking about a very special type of literary history, which he calls *philology*—although it would perhaps be more precise to say that literary history is a special type of philology, since philology is the more inclusive term. It denotes a methodology that can be applied to the law, religion, and politics, as well as to literature. Auerbach's model in this regard is Giambattista Vico,[9] who applied his historical methodology to all of these areas. This methodology undergoes further development in the late eighteenth century, in Johann Gottfried Herder, and subsequently forges a distinctively German tradition culminating, in the literary field, in the work of the romance philologists: Ernst Curtius, Karl Vossler, Leo Spitzer, and of course Auerbach himself. Traditional literary history, on the other hand, is associated by and large with French scholarship, whose major, and now largely forgotten, figures were Hippolyte Taine (1828–93) and Gustave Lanson (1857–1934).[10]

Auerbach is adamant that German philology not be confused with the (generally positivist) French tradition of literary history. In his introduction to *Literary Language and Its Public* (1958), which remains the most explicit and definitive statement of his critical approach, Auerbach takes pains to distinguish his conception of literary history from what he considers to be an unfortunate stereotype:

> There is a widespread tendency to reject historical perspectivism tacitly or explicitly; particularly in the field of literary criticism, this tendency is related to a distaste for philology of the nineteenth-century type, which is looked upon as the embodiment *par excellence* of historicism. Historicism, many believe, results in antiquarian pedantry, in overestimation of biographical detail, in failure to appreciate a work of art as such. . . . These critics forget, first of all that the historicism of Vico, of Herder

and the Romantics, or of Hegel . . . is not identical with it. It is true that many scholars, including some to whom we owe a great deal, became so absorbed in specialization that they forgot the purpose of their efforts; but this cannot be taken as an argument against a philosophical outlook which unfortunately they have lost. It is true too that preoccupation with biographical details, and above all the endeavor to interpret all literary productions as biographical in the most literal sense, are exceedingly naïve and often absurd. But it seems to me that this brand of scholarship has been sufficiently attacked and ridiculed.[11]

Auerbach thus rejects the main tenets of traditional literary history, namely the importance of authorial biography and the reduction of the text to the status of historical artifact. But what *are* the distinguishing features of Auerbach's historical method that contrast it so sharply with that of scholars such as Taine and Lanson?[12]

What is distinctive about German philology, in addition to its debt to German historicism, is its close relationship with the largely German intellectual tradition of hermeneutics, in particular the work of Friedrich Schleiermacher (1768–1834) and Wilhelm Dilthey (1833–1911). Hermeneutics seeks to uncover the nonapparent meaning of texts, often by studying the historical context out of which the text emerges. Hermeneutics is, however, as ambiguous and as broad a term as philology. There are as many types as there are eminent practitioners. And, like philology, hermeneutics is also cross-disciplinary. It began as a method for understanding scripture and was later applied to the law, philosophy, and history as well as to literary studies. Thus, I think that Edward Said is dead on when he qualifies Auerbach's approach as "philological hermeneutics" in his introduction. In this manner, he highlights the irreducibly interpretive dimension of Auerbach's practice, distinguishing it from philology understood as textual criticism (the methodology used in the critical editions of texts) or as the study of etymologies. Therefore, in my view, Auerbach's success is principally due to his *interpretative* acumen, most spectacularly on display in *Mimesis*.

But how does this hybrid approach fit within the discipline of literary studies, broadly conceived? As I see it, there are four basic approaches that are capable of treating the literary object in its specificity: (1) *poetics*, the study of literary genre, technique (*technê*), and formal structure; (2) *rhetoric*, the study of eloquence, figures, or the general effectiveness of language; (3) *hermeneutics*, the study of meaning, interpretation, and understanding; and (4) *aesthetics*, the study of the psychological responses of the reader/spectator (reception aesthetics) or the study of the creative process (creation aesthetics).[13] Only the first approach, poetics, is exclusively or even particularly "literary" in its purview; being "formalist," it is also the most disengaged from the world. The others see the literary object as merely one object of study among others. Nevertheless, these are all eminently capable of conceiving the literary object as having peculiar qualities that separate it from other objects.¹⁴ This is not the case with disciplines such as history or philology, which, generally speaking, must be associated with one of these approaches or critical modes to treat literature with any specificity. Thus, philology only becomes an effective approach to the literary text when combined with hermeneutics, as in Auerbach, or with rhetoric or poetics. The production of critical editions of texts and the study of etymologies are important scholarly activities, but they do not thereby constitute a critical approach to the literary text. Similarly, history cannot constitute an approach to the literary text simply by taking literature as its object, any more than history becomes political science or philosophy by taking politics or philosophy as its object. For example, a biography of Balzac is not part of literary studies per se, even if it includes extensive discussions of his works. Nor, on the other hand, is history simply the neutral, commonsensical, or nontheoretical basis on which the critic can base his activity. Historiography contains as many presuppositions as any other area of inquiry (as we saw in Chapters 5 and 6).

Although there are few critics as sensitive to the underlying presuppositions of historical inquiry or to the vicissitudes of historical consciousness as Auerbach, he nonetheless appears to perpetuate the dichotomy between a supposedly nontheoretical, intuitive historicism and a criticism oriented toward concepts and theories. As he writes in *Mimesis*, "In the historical forms themselves we gradually learn to find the flexible, always provisional, categories we need."¹⁵ As I argued in the previous chapter, I do not think that this antitheoretical stance is borne out by Auerbach's own practice. Concepts such as representation,¹⁶ the separation of styles (*Stiltrennung*), the mixture of styles (*Stilmischung*), *figura*, the *sermo humilis*, and the sublime (*sublimitas*) are ubiquitous in his work, and they are not found in the historical forms themselves but are rather introduced or imposed by the critic. In his 2003 introduction to the anniversary edition of *Mimesis*, Said decries Auerbach's reluctance to expound on concepts that appear central to his critical project: "From a contemporary standpoint there is something impossibly naive, if not outrageous, that hotly contested terms like 'Western,' 'reality,' and 'representation'—each of which has recently brought forth literally acres of disputatious prose among critics and philosophers—are left to stand on their own, unadorned and unqualified."¹⁷ Said's sentiment echoes that of René Wellek, who writes in his 1954 review of *Mimesis*:

> I cannot help feeling that Mr. Auerbach's extreme reluctance to define his terms and to make his suppositions clear from the outset has impaired the effectiveness of [*Mimesis*]. It certainly has given rise, to judge from the reviews I have seen, to an interminable series of misunderstandings. Mr. Auerbach goes so far as to wish that it had been possible for him not to use "general expressions" at all, that he had been able to suggest his idea purely through the presentation of a series of particulars. But this conception of criticism and scholarship seems an extremely dangerous

one. It certainly would open the door to unlimited idiosyncrasies and would defeat the idea of scholarship as a transmissible, continuous body of knowledge.[18]

Although one might be tempted to chalk this critique up to the difference between literary theory (of which Wellek was the chief exponent at the time) and philology/literary history, I think that this criticism is fair and justified insofar as it addresses Auerbach's stated intentions. Nevertheless, Auerbach's methodological introduction to *Literary Language and Its Public* does offer some insight into his critical presuppositions, despite its claim to a "radical relativism" and its defense of critical intuitionism. And if one takes Auerbach's formidable 1938 essay on "*Figura*," one finds not only an etymological analysis of the word *figura* but a prolegomenon to a theory of interpretation—even if one had to wait for Hayden White and others to fully flesh out its theoretical consequences.[19]

Now if *Mimesis* were merely a history of realistic representation in literature, a narrative of a series of particulars, it would not hold the interest that it does for us today (even if some general readers treat it as just such a history). What Auerbach in fact offers is an *interpretation* of the history of realistic representation *as a whole*, so to establish its particular *meaning*. In "Philology and *Weltliteratur*," Auerbach writes, "History is the only science in which human beings step before us in their totality."[20] Following Vico's *verum-factum* principle—that man only truly knows what he has made—*Mimesis* investigates the ways in which man has given meaning to his world through literary representation (verbal mimesis), insofar as it forms a coherent totality that the historical perspective allows us to grasp as such:

> For there is always going on within us a process of formulation and interpretation whose subject matter is our own self. We are constantly endeavoring to give meaning and order to our lives in the past, the present, and the future, to our surroundings, to the world in which we live; with the result that our lives appear in our own conception as total entities—which to be sure are always changing, more or less radically, more or less rapidly, depending on the extent to which we are obliged, inclined, and able to assimilate the onrush of new experience.[21]

The quasi-Sartrean overtones of this passage from *Mimesis* might lead us to speak of an *existential philology*. It is in this sense that Auerbach's enterprise is profoundly ethical, for it ultimately concerns self-interpretation (self-creation) and social emancipation. As Auerbach notes in "Philology and *Weltliteratur*": "The inner history of the last thousand years is the history of mankind achieving self-expression: this is what philology, a historicist discipline, treats."[22]

Like Hegel's *Phenomenology*,[23] Auerbach's philology is an interpretation of man's self-interpretation, yielding insights into the nature of the human spirit as an immanent process of *becoming*: "Under the rubric of history one is to understand not only the past, but the progression of events in general; history therefore includes the present."²⁴ That is, there is a fundamentally *teleological* aspect to interpreting the past—in addition to the *figural* dimension of which Hayden White speaks (discussed in Chapter 5)—that is contained in the paradoxical conclusion that the historical contingencies lead inexorably and inevitably to the present.

What distinguishes Auerbach's philology, then, from traditional literary history is the way in which the whole relates to the parts—what is generally called the *hermeneutic circle*. The parts should reflect the whole, and the whole should be reflected in each of its constitutive parts. The question is how to jump into the circle, and this is where Auerbach's notion of *Ansatzpunkt* or "point of departure" becomes important.²⁵ The *Ansatzpunkt* is the always-contingent entry point from which the critic can begin his or her work without predetermination. As the particulars are amassed and are related to the point of departure, the overall meaning gradually takes shape. Auerbach writes, "I never approach a text as an isolated phenomenon; I address a question to it, and my question, not the text, is my primary point of departure [*Ansatzpunkt*]."²⁶ In *Mimesis*, the *Ansatz* is the representation of the everyday in a serious manner as it originated in the *sermo humilis*, "the Christian form of the Sublime,"²⁷ as Auerbach describes it. From this simple idea, Auerbach erects a mighty edifice, the ultimate conclusion or meaning of which can be described, alternately, as the idea that *Mimesis* shows how historicity becomes man's particular mode of being in the world, or how human dignity is bound up with a conception of equality based on a dialectic between sublimity and humility, the high and the low.²⁸

Is it possible that Wellek and Said have fundamentally misconstrued Auerbach's method as theoretically naïve, that what they took as a resistance to conceptual thought was simply part of a methodological procedure as well founded and as theoretically sound as their own? Certainly, as noted above, Auerbach's hermeneutics is grounded in the German philosophical tradition of Schleiermacher and Dilthey. But what seems to particularly irk these critics is Auerbach's intuitionism, which appears to give his interpretive attitude an inscrutable character. However, even this seemingly arbitrary element is based on a philosophical concept, namely Dilthey's hermeneutic notion of *Einfühlung* ("feeling into").²⁹ In his essay "The Hermeneutic Significance of Auerbach's *Ansatz*," Wolfgang Holdheim observes that

> [personal intuition] is by no means to be mistaken for an excursion into mysticism of any sort. Intuition is simply the ability to grasp the occasions that come our way. "Learn it by heart," Auerbach once advised me when I complained that I did not understand a certain poem by Mallarmé. In other words: let it come to you, let it act on you; insight may follow at some point.³⁰

This intuitive understanding of literary works and their interconnections is one of the endearing hallmarks of Auerbach's criticism, even if it can be maddening to critics of a more analytical bent. This intuitionalism (*Einfühlung*) is moreover the most intractable element in his work, for it is exceedingly difficult to emulate.

Few scholars in Auerbach's day—and fewer scholars now—possessed the breadth of erudition and knowledge of languages that made such "intuition" possible. Part of the reason for this is the decline of what Auerbach called "bourgeois humanistic culture," which, he laments, "has collapsed nearly everywhere" (and he was speaking about the late 1950s). This bourgeois education required the mastery of Greek, Latin, and the Bible at the secondary level and was part of the academic training of all prewar intellectuals. Vestiges of this education persist in the Italian *liceo classico*,[31] which may account for the survival of philology in Italy, though it has all but disappeared in the United States and in much of Europe, and has resulted in a strong shift in emphasis to modern languages and literature. Philology has thus undergone a series of transformations or permutations, its compass further circumscribed at each successive stage: from a discipline primarily focused on classical Latin and Greek culture to the study of medieval texts; from the history of the national literature to its marginalization in favor of contemporary and modern authors.[32] As a result of this preference for the modern and contemporary, which Auerbach notes with great regret in his "Philology and *Weltliteratur*" essay, the inculcation of historical consciousness that Auerbach saw as the specific task of humanistic education is no longer a priority or even a goal. Indeed, history in the age of the image, and of the cinematic image in particular, has been reduced to mere "costumery" (Lukács's term).[33] The idea that historical periods differ sharply in mental outlook and perspective escapes the average reader entirely.

The increase in social equality has paradoxically coincided with the weakening of humanistic education, and this is the challenge we face today and the challenge that the criticism of the future will face tomorrow. Latin, once a compulsory part of the high school curriculum in the United States, was summarily eliminated (surviving only in elite "prep schools"), as was the teaching of grammar and rhetoric. The reasons for this are complex, but what is clear is that the democratization of education, instead of liberating the middle and working classes, has actually had the opposite effect by offering a heavily watered-down version of humanistic instruction. As Hayden White observes in his essay "The Suppression of Rhetoric in the Nineteenth Century":

> If the relationship among rhetoric, literacy, and social class power is as intimate as the history of that relationship suggests, then the democratization of society in the nineteenth century should have been attended by the extension of training in rhetoric to all classes of society

as a necessary component in their political empowerment to which their training in basic literacy was meant to contribute. The exclusion of rhetoric from such training can thus be seen as an aspect of a more general program of political domestication of the mass of the citizenry by the powerful classes, who never ceased, incidentally, to provide training of a kind in rhetoric for their own children in elite schools and universities.[34]

White is clearly using the term "rhetoric" as a metonymy for humanistic education in general, arguing that "democratization" simply meant the effective removal of this curriculum from the public education system, due to its supposed "elitism." But it was this anti-elitist attitude that was in fact elitist, for it implied that the middle and lower classes were incapable of critical thinking, learning dead languages, and of benefiting from the study of the classics. The current crisis of the humanities in the university is certainly a function of this elitist anti-elitism.

The turn toward the political in literary studies has, I think, been a response to this weakening of humanism rather than its cause. Both poetics and philology were more appropriate to a time when bourgeois culture still reigned in the university, before higher education was vastly expanded in the late 1960s and 1970s. Formalism and historicism appear to us now as the quaint remnants of ivory-tower academics who waxed interminably on the use of the imperfect tense in Flaubert or on variants in medieval manuscripts—while the world burned.

As the humanist presuppositions of historicist endeavors came under broad attack by poststructuralist theory, the response was to throw the historical baby out with the historicist bath water. Historicism of all stripes was dismissed as the baleful and burdensome legacy of a bankrupt humanism. Poststructuralism rightly saw hermeneutics as underpinning this humanism. It thus developed radical interpretive strategies (derived from the German phenomenological tradition) that sought to highlight equivocations in meaning as forestalling any attempt to locate an origin or authority. Separating meaning from intention, word from world, sign from sound, text from work, poststructuralism celebrated the death of "man" in a sort of ritual immolation. The conflagration lasted for quite some time, but when the last embers finally cooled, Auerbach still remained—almost defiant, seemingly unscathed, though perhaps lacking some of his former luster.

Literary history will probably never return. Philology has been dying a slow death, linked to the death of the bourgeois education. Formalist poetics (now often subsumed under the rubric of "narratology") will always reappear periodically,[35] but it will most likely never again attain the preeminent status it enjoyed during the heyday of structuralism, and it will always remain essentially Aristotelian. However, the future looks very different for a banalized hermeneutics, simply because it has become, for better or for worse, the critical norm. Literary studies is by and large seen as being identical with the interpretation of a text. One need only look at *Cliff's Notes*, *Spark Notes*, or any basic guide to literature aimed at the student or the general reader to see that this is the case. In regard to academic criticism, the weakening of humanism has endowed interpretation with a new significance: It has become a political act. The ideal of self-interpretation, of man making himself in and confronting himself with his own image, is now fragmented into competing claims to particular dignities in tension with one another.

Auerbach's hermeneutic philology can, I think, play a role in this new dispensation. Its attention to the particular, to the relation between text and world, and the manner in which it conceives the relation between part and whole as dynamic and relativistic can certainly be attractive to a political criticism searching for a way to reconcile its fragmentary antihumanism with the notion of a shared humanity that must necessarily ground any concept of human rights.

If the attacks of September 11, 2001 have taught us anything, it is that the project of a cultural hermeneutics or a "critical humanism" (to borrow a term from Tzvetan Todorov)[36] is more urgent than ever. Understanding the Other means understanding the Other's history, and it means understanding the intertwining of cultural horizons. As Said notes:

> *Mimesis* itself is not, as it has so frequently been taken to be, only a massive reaffirmation of the Western cultural tradition, but also a work built upon a critically important alienation from it, a work whose conditions and circumstances of existence are not immediately derived from the culture it describes with such extraordinary insight and brilliance but built rather on an agonizing distance from it.[37]

That the slogan of the "clash of civilizations"[38] could claim intellectual validity and even shape US foreign policy in the Middle East (even today)[39] is only the most visible consequence of the loss of historical consciousness. It is only when we have learned to equate, as Auerbach says, the "historical with the human" and realize that "humanism has always been the true purpose of philology"[40] that we will begin to fulfill the promise of Auerbach's *Mimesis*.

CHAPTER TEN

Edward Said, *Orientalism*, and the "political turn" in literary and cultural studies

In a review of Edward Said's *Beginnings: Intention and Method* (1975), published in 1976, thus before the books that would make Said famous, Hayden White begins by declaring, "Among contemporary literary critics writing in English, few are more 'political' than Edward Said."[1] Indeed, perhaps no theorist has contributed more to the "political turn" in literary studies than Said. His relentless critique of Theory in the 1970s and early 1980s as an ideology of "pure textuality and critical noninterference"[2] eventually led to a reassessment that inspired a generation of literary scholars to integrate a real-world and sociopolitical dimension into their critical practice. And yet, and as we saw in the previous chapter, there is also a "conservative" or humanist side to Said's thought that is seemingly at odds with his progressive-activist inclinations.[3] This is the Said who extolls the classics of the Western canon, and who lauds the historicism of Giambattista Vico and Erich Auerbach. The two Saids are not, however, in conflict. Together, they inform his two-pronged attack on Theory in its formative phase (1960–82): (1) From the right, Said attacks Theory for its antihumanism and for its subversion of subjectivity and concomitant undermining of individual agency and responsibility; (2) from the left, he takes Theory to task for its lack of political and social engagement and for its seeming complicity or impotence with regard to structures of power.

The effect of this intellectual pincer movement would, however, not be felt for many years. Thus, Said's polemical and magisterial *Orientalism*, while it attracted considerable attention upon its publication in 1978, initially had relatively little effect on the direction of literary studies, which was just starting to hear the clarion call of Theory. (According to the Harvard Library Hollis Catalog, there was, prior to 1991, only one book published on Said [in 1983]; starting in 1991 and continuing to the present, there are sixty-two titles with Said listed as a subject.)[4] Born into an era dominated by structuralism and poststructuralism—Jonathan Culler's *Structuralist Poetics* had appeared in 1975 (winner of the Modern Languages Association James Russell Lowell Prize) and the English translation of Jacques Derrida's seminal *Of Grammatology* in 1976—*Orientalism* was seen as at best peripheral and at worst reactionary to the current of high formalism then sweeping through literature departments in the United States. Even in the early 1980s, it was clear that the sympathies of most theoretically inclined critics lay more with Culler's 1982 blockbuster *On Deconstruction: Theory and Criticism After Structuralism*,[5] than with the "worldly" criticism Said advocated in his 1983 tome *The World, the Text, and the Critic* (which nevertheless won the René Wellek Prize of the American Comparative Literature Association). Deconstruction would remain the dominant force in literary studies until 1987 when, as I described in the introduction and in Chapter 3, the twin controversies of the de Man Affair and the Heidegger Affair precipitated the decline of textualism and the emergence of an activist and socially committed current in literary studies and other humanistic disciplines.

The newly engaged critic would give voice to the downtrodden, detect patterns of power and authority in artistic forms that were supposedly defined by their aesthetic nature, and affirm the group identity of the critic himself or herself. The principal figure in this shift was Gayatri Spivak, who, paradoxically, was responsible *both* for the inauguration of the high-formalist phase, with her translation of and formidable introduction to Derrida's *Of Grammatology, and* for the subsequent rise of political criticism, with a series of publications initiated by her pivotal 1988 essay "Can the Subaltern Speak."[6] As I noted in the introduction, Spivak helped create the conditions under which Said's magnum opus could achieve iconic status, retrospectively, as the progenitor of postcolonial studies. Indeed, a sudden surge of interest in Said led to a reissue of *Orientalism* in 1995 with a new afterword, in which Said responds to his critics and assesses the impact of his book.

Said's increased visibility during the 1990s, which continued up until his death in 2003, is, however, only partly attributable to the changes in the academy noted above. An Arab born into a small Christian community in Jerusalem, Said strongly identified with the Palestinian cause, as reflected in his 1979 book *The Question of Palestine* and in his decade-long membership on the Palestinian National Council (and one could also mention *Covering Islam*, published in 1981).[7] This identification transformed him from a more or less traditional literary critic (Said's first book was *Joseph Conrad and the Fiction of Autobiography*, 1966) into a true activist-scholar and public intellectual (the same evolution that can be observed in Spivak).[8] In addition, one cannot discount the role of historical events—namely the Iran hostage crisis (November 4, 1979 to January 20, 1981), the first Palestinian Intifada (1987–93), the Gulf War of 1991, and, most spectacularly, the attacks of September 11, 2001—in highlighting the neuralgic relationship between the West and the Arab-Islamic world, a relationship Said famously explores in his *Orientalism*, which in retrospect seems almost prescient. As if to confirm Said's ever-increasing relevance, a twenty-fifth anniversary edition of *Orientalism* was published in 2003 with a new preface by the author.

Said's oeuvre is varied and voluminous, as is the commentary on his thought. In this chapter, I shall limit myself to Said's pioneering work from the late 1970s, in particular *Orientalism*, his most widely read work, with a view toward understanding Said's role in the transformation of Theory from a literary-textualist orientation to a politically attuned, proto-activist critical practice. Thus, I do not aim to treat Said's political theses as such but rather his almost obsessive attention to questions of methodology in literary studies (as first evidenced in his *Beginnings: Intention and Method*),[9] specifically his efforts to integrate the humanist-historicist tradition of Vico and Auerbach with certain elements of Theory, despite the latter's antihumanist and antihistoricist tendencies.

Orientalism, Foucault, and the ethics of theory

Although, as mentioned above, Said was sharply critical of poststructuralist writing, he was nevertheless strongly inspired by the work of Michel Foucault,[10] in particular the nexus the French philosopher drew between discourse, knowledge, and power. Indeed, as one critic notes, *Orientalism* was "one of the first extended applications of Foucault's work in English."[11] Said observes in the introduction to *Orientalism*:

> I have found it useful here to employ Michel Foucault's notion of a discourse, as described by him in *The Archaeology of Knowledge* and in *Discipline and Punish*, to identify Orientalism. My contention is that without examining Orientalism as a discourse one cannot possibly understand the enormously systematic discipline by which European culture was able to manage—and even produce—the Orient politically, sociologically, ideologically, scientifically, and imaginatively during the post-Enlightenment period.[12]

In other words, Said seeks to situate Orientalism in terms of a *discursive structure or system* that shapes, organizes, and even creates the various contents it presents as simply found or existing in the things themselves. Inherent in this structure are the asymmetric power relations that define the oppositional relationship between the West and what goes under the name of the "Orient." This part of Said's theory is orthodox Foucauldianism.[13]

Where Said departs from Foucault is on the question of the *autonomy* of "discursive formations" or of the "author function," as expressed in "What is an Author?" (1969) and *The Archeology of Knowledge* (1971).[14] As Said remarks in *Orientalism*:

> Unlike Michel Foucault, to whose work I am greatly indebted, I do believe in the determining imprint of *individual writers* upon the otherwise anonymous collective body of texts constituting a discursive formation like Orientalism. . . . Foucault believes that in general the individual text or author counts for very little; empirically, in the case of Orientalism (and perhaps nowhere else) I find this not to be so. Accordingly my analyses employ close textual readings whose goal is to reveal the dialectic between individual text or writer and the complex collective formation to which his work is a contribution.[15]

Said here rejects one of the chief tenets of structuralist and poststructuralist thought: that of "discourse" or "text" conceived of as a seemingly *self-contained system of signs* that produces its effects independently of authorial intention and referentiality: "[Foucault] pretty much ignores the whole category of intention."[16] In effect, Said is proposing to literalize and personalize the nexus between discourse and power, thereby refusing the systematic privileging of the "text" (discursive formation) over the "work" (individual text as the volitional-creative and ideological expression of the singular author).[17] Said's unabashedly humanist approach thus represents a sustained attack on formalism,[18] which he associates with the misguided attempt to separate pure from practical knowledge: "No one has ever devised a method for detaching the scholar from the circumstances of life."[19] But his anti-formalism also serves to distance him from many of the antihumanist implications of Foucault's thought of the late 1960s and early 1970s. James Clifford notes in his review of *Orientalism* that while "Said's general attempt to extend Foucault's conception of a discourse into the area of cultural constructions of the exotic is a promising one . . . Said's humanist perspectives do not harmonize with his use of methods derived from Foucault, who is, of course, a radical critic of humanism."[20] However, what Clifford misses, I believe, is the critical influence of Vico in helping to explain how the two tendencies can work in tandem (I discuss this in more detail below). Indeed, Clifford never mentions Vico in his review.

In essence, Said was advocating that literary studies renounce the hard-fought autonomy that formalism (or literary theory)[21] had won for it in its epochal struggle against literary history, as it sought to carve out a specific space within the academy.[22] Said proposed both a fundamental change in the critical methodology of literary scholars as well as a reassessment of the role of literary studies in the university and in society more generally. In this respect, Said's challenge can be said to represent a revival of the old debate between autonomous and engaged literature (such as that between Sartre and Adorno),[23] recasting it as a debate between autonomous and engaged *criticism*. Said's methodological critique of literary criticism thus possesses normative force; for, according to Said, the critic who studies literary texts in isolation from the social world is at best complacent toward discourses of domination and at worst complicit with them: "Too often literature and culture are presumed to be politically, even historically *innocent*; it has regularly seemed otherwise to me, and certainly my study of Orientalism has convinced me (and I hope will convince my literary colleagues) that society and literary culture can only be understood and studied together."[24] It is this "innocence" that Said saw embodied in the New Criticism of the 1940s and 1950s and that he saw as being continued, breathlessly, in the structuralism and poststructuralism of the 1960s and 1970s.[25] In *The World, the Text, and the Critic*, Said observes that "textuality has therefore become the exact antithesis and displacement of what might be called history.... As it is practiced in the American academy today, literary theory has for the most part isolated textuality from the circumstances, the events, the physical senses that made it possible and render it intelligible as the result of human work."[26] Said sees textualism as tantamount to a kind of idolatry, in which the text is venerated as a seemingly self-constituting artifact, a *causa sui* that acts independently of history. Said thus proposes, in what he terms his "secular" criticism, to return in some sense to the perspective of historicism, to an attention to the *human process* of a text's production as a temporal nexus between intention, ideology, and collective forces: "My position is that texts are worldly, to some degree they are events, and, even when they appear to deny it, they are nevertheless part of the social world, human life, and of course the historical moments in which they are located and interpreted."[27] Although the idea of text-as-event is also an element of the poststructuralist approach (inspired by Heidegger's concept of *Ereignis*), Said's understanding is more specifically historical.

There is, however, a fundamental tension in Said's work with regard to the tug of war between history and theory. Although Said strongly opposes the linguistic formalism of Theory, it is not a matter of a simple rejection of Theory and a return to literary history, even if Said appreciates the work of some of its major exponents, such as Auerbach. In essence, Said performs a delicate balancing act: avoiding the metaphysical naïveté of the historicists while remaining resolutely opposed to the ironic perspective (textual quietism)[28]: "Even if we accept (as I in the main do) the arguments put forward by Hayden White—that there is no way to get past texts in order to apprehend 'real' history directly—it is still possible that such a claim need not also eliminate interest in the events and circumstances entailed by and expressed in the texts themselves."[29] That is, Said accepts the basic premise of Theory that there is no unmediated access to historical reality, but at the same time, he insists that this premise need not thereby exclude or in any way devalue the historical perspective. As this passage suggests, Said is in many respects close to Hayden White's thought (Said in fact cites White in the acknowledgments of some of his books) despite White's reputation as a kind of "formalist": They both share a humanistic viewpoint and consider the philological historicism of Vico and Auerbach to be a formative influence on their thought.[30]

Nevertheless, there is perhaps an irreducible ambivalence in Said's attitude toward Theory, which he alternately finds stimulating and tedious, useful and useless. As Said remarks in an interview conducted in 1993:

> This is where I found problems in some of the French theorists: First of all it struck me—and this is absolutely central to what I did in *Beginnings* and to what I have done ever since—that even those theorists like Derrida, who appear to be breaking away from all the structures and the orthodoxies, the logocentrism, phallocentrism, etc., etc., in time became prisoners of their own—I would not call it "system," but I would certainly call it their own "manner." And I became more disillusioned with Foucault because at least in parts of Derrida there is wit; sometimes there is almost an aspect of triviality because there is so much of it. There is a lot of circling around, a lot of meandering, a lot of, finally, dismissal of stuff, with some interesting insights, particularly in his earlier work.[31]

Said thus sees two contradictory forces at work in Theory: On one side there is the (quasi-Protestant) antiauthoritarianism, the break with all systems and dogmas, and a call for a return to the (sacred) text; on the other, there is a kind of circularity, an inability to get beyond their own language games, which become in the end a kind of constraint, resulting (paradoxically) in new orthodoxies.

But, as this passage implies, Said also perceives *the ethics of Theory*; that is, as an intrinsically antiauthoritarian discourse, Theory, whatever its stated intentions, was perfectly calibrated to subvert and contest real-world systems of hegemony and oppression in the name of the aggrieved—as Said himself does in *Orientalism*:

> For readers in the so-called Third World, this study proposes itself as a step towards an understanding not so much of Western politics and of the non-Western world in these politics as of the *strength* of Western cultural discourse, a strength too often mistaken as merely decorative or "superstructural." My hope is to illustrate the formidable structure of cultural domination and, specifically for formerly colonized peoples, the dangers and temptations of employing this structure upon themselves or upon others.[32]

It was Theory that, in fact, enabled Said first to locate, and then to destabilize, the "*structure* of cultural domination" that supports the discourse of Orientalism. It was Theory, and in particular the thought of Foucault, that allowed Said to see the "*strength* of Western cultural discourse" as a function of the power/knowledge nexus: the will to power lurking behind the will to truth, the system of exclusion inherent in Western rationality,[33] as expressed in disparate and seemingly "innocent" scientific, ethnographic, and imaginative writing. Finally, it was Theory—specifically textualism—that allowed Said to vastly expand the scope and orientation of literary studies. Just as the textualist sees his or her domain as textuality itself, the Saidean literary scholar sees it as culture-in-general. If the literary text offers the literary critic a privileged vantage point, it is because literature is textual in the most self-conscious or literal sense. Inherently unlimited with regard to content, the import—and thus the effect—of literature can be at once sociological, political, economic, philosophical, and historical. The critic can lay claim to these disparate areas, per his or her own "involvement (conscious or unconscious) with a class, a set of beliefs, a social position, or [simply] from the activity of being a member of a society,"[34] without thereby asserting any institutionally sanctioned expertise.[35] Thus, it is the expansive perspective of textualism, which knows no generic or disciplinary limits, that inspires Said to effectively "colonize" other disciplines or areas of research, effacing boundaries in the name of an ethico-political imperative.

Reconsiderations: The "Afterword" to *Orientalism*

In his 1994 afterword to the new edition of *Orientalism* (published in 1995), Said expresses his exasperation with what he considers to be blatant misreadings of his book. He is particularly irked by the perception of *Orientalism* "as a surreptitiously anti-Western work" and one that "elevates the image of an innocent and aggrieved Islam."[36] This misprision has two aspects: (1) "the phenomenon of Orientalism is a synecdoche, or a miniature symbol, of the entire West" and "therefore the entire West is an enemy of the Arab . . . and other non-European peoples who suffered Western colonialism and prejudice"; and (2) to criticize Orientalism is tantamount to being "a supporter of Islamism or Muslim fundamentalism,"[37] since such fundamentalists sees their relation vis-à-vis the West in similarly stark terms (oppressor/oppressed).

Although it might be said that Said slightly exaggerates the criticisms leveled against him, denying in the process the suggestiveness of his own language in inspiring such misguided interpretations (many of which are nonetheless sympathetic),[38] what is important is how he defends himself in the afterword:

> One scarcely knows what to make of these caricatured permutations of a book that to its author and in its arguments is explicitly anti-essentialist, radically skeptical about all categorical designations such as Orient

and Occident, and painstakingly careful about *not* "defending" or even discussing the Orient and Islam. Yet *Orientalism* has been read as a systematic defense of Islam and the Arabs, even though I say explicitly in the book that I have no interest in, much less capacity for, showing what the true Orient and Islam really are. Actually I go a great deal further when, very early in the book, I say that words such as "Orient" and "Occident" correspond to no stable reality that exists as a natural fact.[39]

Said thus locates the main source of misunderstanding in the *essentialist* aspirations imputed to him. Although, as we have seen above, Said has a difficult relationship with Theory, one area where he marches in lockstep with French poststructuralist thought is precisely with regard to its virulent antiessentialism: its emphasis on the contingency of all concepts and the constructed nature of identity. Thus, most of those who attack Said in this manner are not doing so under the banner of Theory (the partisans of Theory are predictably more interested in critiquing Said's "residual humanism").[40] On the contrary, they are reading Said without the benefit of Theory. Said had (perhaps naively) presupposed a measure of theoretical sophistication that was no doubt unreasonable for a book with such broad aims.

Of course, "constructivism" is also a feature of Vico's thought, namely his *verum-factum* principle,[41] which Said invokes in the afterword[42]: the idea that humans *make* truth, history, and knowledge rather than discover them. As Said writes in the body of *Orientalism*: "We must take seriously Vico's great observation that men make their own history, that what they can know is what they have made, and extend it to geography: as both geological and cultural entities—to say nothing of historical entities—such locales, regions, geographical sectors as 'Orient' and 'Occident' are man-made."[43] (Let us recall that Said's 1975 book *Beginnings* features a concluding chapter on Vico: "Conclusion: Vico in His Work and in This.") Thus, Said can treat Foucault's (Nietzsche-inspired) power/knowledge thesis as simply a *further development* of the Vichian principle[44]; for if knowledge is perceived as contingent (constructed) rather than necessary (given), so is the power it projects. We must thus recognize that a large part of Theory's attractiveness for Said lay in the fact that many of its bedrock assumptions and attitudes can also be traced to Vico's philosophy—the singular importance of which for Said cannot be underemphasized.

Interestingly, the formulations of the afterword also go beyond the constructivism of Vico and poststructuralist theory to include a specifically Sartrean element, namely the inherently *conflictual* nature of identity (interpersonal relations as reciprocal definition—in the doctrine of "the look" in *Being and Nothingness*).[45] Said seemingly reflects Sartre's dialectical approach to identity, as when he asserts that *Orientalism* should not be construed as arguing that we could ever overcome the impulse to define one's culture or society in contradistinction to another culture or society, that the very process of identity formation is necessarily *agonistic*: "Each age and society re-creates its 'Others.' Far from a static thing then, identity of self or of 'other' is a much worked-over historical, social, intellectual, and political process that takes place as a *contest* involving individuals and institutions in all societies."[46] The key word in this passage, "contest," implies that there is an *irremediable violence* (which could be physical, but not necessarily) involved in identity formation. Moreover, this struggle for self-definition also occurs *within* a culture or unitary social context: "Even the primitive community we belong to natally is not immune from the interpretative contest, and what appears in the West to be the emergence, return to, or resurgence of Islam is in fact a struggle in Islamic societies over the definition of Islam."[47] Thus *Orientalism* cannot be legitimately construed as simply criticizing the idea that Orientalism represents a contest between self-interpretation and other-interpretation, since this is in fact how identities are created, according to Said.

But how, then, do we locate Said's ethical critique vis-à-vis this analytical imperative? Does he not thereby legitimate Orientalism as one possible or perhaps even inevitable way of defining the "West" vis-à-vis the "Orient"? What Said specifically attacks, however, is not the effort *per se* to define the other, but rather the bad-faith nature of the Orientalist project to impose an *essentializing identity* on the Orient, namely as the function of a putatively scientistic (supposedly value-neutral) or merely aesthetic attitude (supposedly non-ideological), when in fact it *produces* the very identity it presents as simply inhering in the things themselves. Revealing what he calls this "uncritically essentialist standpoint"[48] is the crux of Said's ethical critique of Orientalism, which, again, does not thereby claim that every attempt to distinguish one's society from another is ipso facto illegitimate, oppressive, and so on. For this would be akin to saying that the victim position is the only legitimate one, that *any* struggle for identity *necessarily* involves a winner and a loser (or, *à la* Foucault, is defined by "power" in a pejorative sense).[49] Rather than seeking to strip the will to self-interpretation of its conflictual elements (as if this were possible), Said instead seeks to cure the process of identity formation of its essentializing tendencies and objectivist claims.

Said's point is similar to what we observed in Chapter 6 regarding Hayden White's ethical critique of academic historical writing. White criticizes historiography not for the fact that it makes truth claims or seeks to redeem the past (since this is simply what history does), but rather for its assumption that historical reality is something that can be discovered or uncovered, as opposed to being *constructed* with the help of the historian's imagination and informed by his or her ethical disposition. A *recognition* of the ethical (ideological) and aesthetic (emplotment) nature of historical writing thus conduces to a general maximization of human freedom—which does not preclude conflict, but in fact presupposes it in the relativism of interpretation.[50]

The afterword thus shows Said as criticizing those—both on the activist Left and the Islamist Right (those who saw "the virtues" of Orientalism as having "pointed out the malicious dangers of the Orientalists and somehow pried Islam from their clutches")[51]—as self-deceived with regard to the stakes involved in a critique of oppression, as if the alternative were some kind of Edenic world in which identity is revealed and preserved in its native purity without struggle or strife. As Said observes in this strikingly Sartrean passage, "No one finds it easy to live uncomplainingly and fearlessly with the thesis that human reality is constantly being made and unmade, and that anything like a stable essence is constantly under threat."[52] Said's invocation of the Sartrean-existentialist notion of "human reality" (*la realité humaine*, Sartre's translation of Heidegger's notion of *Dasein*), would seem to confirm a specifically Sartrean influence on Said's "secular" criticism. Therefore, according to Said, we must face up to the fact that we are "condemned to be free"; we must relinquish our bad-faith assumptions concerning identity (the bad-faith desire of the "for-itself" to be an "in-itself," a "stable essence")[53] and accept our lot as beings who must choose ourselves in every moment and whose personal, national, and cultural identities are the ever unstable result of struggle, contest, and conflict.

NOTES

Introduction

1 See in particular Jean-Michel Rabaté's fascinating book *Crimes of the Future: Theory and its Global Reproduction* (London: Bloomsbury, 2014).

2 Translated by Jeff Fort (Minneapolis: University of Minnesota Press, 2008). Originally published in French as *French Theory: Foucault, Derrida, Deleuze & Cie et les mutations de la vie intellectuelle aux États-Unis* (Paris: La Découverte, 2003/05). Gary Gutting discusses the ethical turn in some detail in *Thinking the Impossible: French Philosophy Since 1960* (Oxford: Oxford University Press, 2010), 117–48.

3 In this sense, this book is somewhat like Fredric Jameson's *The Ideologies of Theory* (London: Verso, 2009).

4 See, for example, the recent anthology *Deleuze and Ethics*, ed. Nathan Jun and Daniel W. Smith (Edinburgh: Edinburgh University Press, 2011), and *Ethics and Phenomenology*, ed. Mark Sanders and J. Jeremy Wisnewski (Plymouth: Lexington Books, 2012).

5 Jean-Michel Rabaté speaks of the "complex relationship between Theory and philosophy" (*The Future of Theory* [Oxford: Wiley-Blackwell, 2002], 149). While insisting that "Theory should work through philosophy relentlessly, destabilizing it in the name of other discourses," Rabaté nevertheless holds that "literature will provide only one strategy, and not a particularly privileged access" (ibid., 150).

6 For an exhaustive account of this relation, see Jean Bessière, *Dire le littéraire: Points de vue théoriques* (Liège, Brussels: Pierre Mardaga, 1990). See also the recent work by Jonathan Culler, *The Literary in Theory* (Stanford, CA: Stanford University Press, 2007).

7 See, for example, the work of literature professors Paul de Man and J. Hillis Miller.

8 Marxism in such figures as Louis Althusser (philosophy) and Lucien Goldmann (literary studies); psychoanalysis in Jacques Lacan. In the early 1960s, there were, according to a Derrida biographer, three kinds of students: "Marxists, Lacanian, or structuralist" (Benoît Peeters, *Derrida: A Biography*, trans. Andrew Brown [London: Polity, 2012], 146).

9 Quoted in James Miller, *The Passion of Michel Foucault* (New York: Simon and Schuster, 1993), 51.

10 Foucault, *Power/Knowledge: Selected Interviews and Other Writings, 1972-1977*, trans. Colin Gordon (New York: Vintage, 1980), 80–81.

11 Jean-Paul Sartre, "Self-Portrait at Seventy," in Sartre, *Life/Situations: Essays Written and Spoken*, trans. Paul Auster and Lydia Davis (New York: Pantheon, 1977), 18.

12. Sartre continues: "[Foucault's] task is to come up with a new ideology: the latest barrier that the bourgeoisie once again can erect against Marx" ("Replies to Structuralism: An Interview," *Telos* 9 [1971]: 110).

13. Peeters, *Derrida*, 150. Derrida would only turn to Marx relatively late in his career, in his *Spectres de Marx* (Paris: Galilée, 1993), translated by Peggy Kamuf as *Specters of Marx: The State of the Debt, The Work of Mourning & the New International* (New York: Routledge, 1994).

14. Membership in the French Communist Party (PCF) declined precipitously in the 1970s.

15. See, in particular, Peter Starr's *Logics of Failed Revolt: French Theory After May '68* (Stanford, CA: Stanford University Press, 1995) and Kristen Ross's *May '68 and Its Afterlives* (Chicago: Chicago University Press, 2002).

16. Jacques Derrida, "The Ends of Man," in Derrida, *Margins of Philosophy*, trans. Alan Bass (Chicago: University of Chicago Press, 1982), 111.

17. Quoted in Peeters, *Derrida*, 197. Thus, while May 1968 certainly had an effect on French philosophy, it did not thereby transform it into an ethico-political discourse. A Foucault biographer describes his "icy solitude dissolved only by the events of May 68, and his subsequent emergence as a public figure" (Miller, *The Passion of Michel Foucault*, 335). Foucault's efforts in favor of prison reform in the early 1970s are an example of this (as part of the GIP—Groupe d'Informations sur les Prisons). But it was only in his later years, inspired by the gay liberation movement, that Foucault overcame his natural reserve and feeling of isolation (as I explore in Chapter 2).

18. See the first chapter of Jean-Michel Rabaté, *The Future of Theory*, entitled "Genealogy One: Hegel's Plague" (21–46), and Judith Butler's doctoral dissertation, published as *Subjects of Desire: Hegelian Reflections in Twentieth-Century France* (Columbia: Columbia University Press, 2012, reprint edition).

19. See Jacques Lacan, *The Seminar of Jacques Lacan, Book VII: The Ethics of Psychoanalysis 1959-1960*, ed. Jacques Alain-Miller, trans. Dennis Porter (New York: W. W. Norton, 1992).

20. See in particular Terry Eagleton, *Literary Theory* (Minneapolis: University of Minnesota Press, 1983/1996/2008), Jameson, *The Ideologies of Theory*, and Rabaté, *The Future of Theory* and *Crimes of the Future*.

21. But also Sartre's novel *Nausea* (1938) and his plays of the 1940s (*No Exit*, *The Flies*), which popularized the concept of existentialism.

22. We must not forget that phenomenology was first introduced into French philosophy in 1930 via Emmanuel Levinas's *La théorie de l'intuition dans la phénoménologie de Husserl* (*The Theory of Intuition in Husserl's Phenomenology*). As Paul Ricoeur notes in his *À l'école de la phénoménologie* (Paris: Vrin, 1986/2004), 361, this text was foundational for the study of Husserl in France.

23. This is also true of American academics such as Fredric Jameson and Hayden White. In an interview, White notes that "like [Fredric] Jameson, my formation was in existentialism. As a young man I was completely swept into the Jean-Paul Sartre world and Nietzsche" (Angelica Koufou and Miliori Margarita,

"The Ironic Poetics of Late Modernity. An Interview with Hayden White," *Historein* 2 [2000], http://www.historein.gr/vol2_interview.htm, accessed January 28, 2013). Fredric Jameson's doctoral dissertation and first book were on Sartre. See Fredric Jameson, *Sartre: The Origins of a Style* (New Haven, CT: Yale University Press, 1961/84). Arthur Danto, who studied at Wayne State under the same undergraduate history professor as White (William J. Bossenbrook), published *Jean-Paul Sartre* in 1975 (New York: Penguin Books).

24 Quoted in Peeters, *Derrida*, 33 (original source: Derrida, *Sur parole: Instantanés philosophiques* [Paris: Éditions de l'Aube, 2003], 82).

25 Foucault famously dismissed Sartre as "a man of the nineteenth century" who failed to understand the twentieth.

26 Gutting, *Thinking the Impossible*, 82.

27 See especially Thomas Flynn's two-volume *Sartre, Foucault, and Historical Reason* (Chicago: University of Chicago Press, 1997 [vol. 1], 2005 [vol. 2]); Christina Howells's *Derrida: Deconstruction from Phenomenology to Ethics* (Cambridge: Polity Press, 1999); and Gutting's *Thinking the Impossible*, esp. 67–83.

28 The major figures include Roman Jakobson (*Essais de linguistique générale 1 et 2*, 1963), Émile Benveniste (*Problèmes de linguistique générale 1*, 1966; *Le Vocabulaire des institutions indo-européennes 1 et 2*, 1969), and Algirdas Greimas (*Sémantique structurale: recherche de méthode*, 1966).

29 See Lévi-Strauss, *Les structures élémentaires de la parenté* (1949) (trans. *The Elementary Structures of Kinship*) and the essay collection *Anthropologie structurale* (1958) (trans. *Structural Anthropology*). See also Marcel Hénaff's *Claude Lévi-Strauss and the Making of Structural Anthropology*, trans. Mary Baker (Minneapolis: University of Minnesota Press, 1998), especially the concluding chapter "The Moral Issue" (237–44).

30 Although Heidegger aims to neutralize the subject-object dichotomy, there remain vestiges of a subject-centered or humanist philosophy. As Derrida remarks, "*Dasein*, though *not* man, is *nothing other* than man" (*Margins of Philosophy*, 127).

31 Culler, *The Literary in Theory*, 23.

32 Culler notes that "when so many of yesterday's structuralists are today's post-structuralists, doubts arise as to the distinction" (*On Deconstruction: Theory and Criticism after Structuralism* [Ithaca, NY: Cornell University Press, 1982/2007], 25). It is also instructive to consider Fredric Jameson's *The Prison-House of Language: A Critical Account of Structuralism and Russian Formalism* (Princeton, NJ: Princeton University Press, 1972), which contains substantial discussions of Derrida.

33 *The Structuralist Controversy: The Languages of Criticism and the Sciences of Man*, ed. Richard Macksey and Eugene Donato (Baltimore: John Hopkins University Press, 2007 [40th Anniversary Edition]).

34 In 1966, *Yale French Studies* published a double issue entitled "Structuralism." The volume covered the rise and influence of this new movement in the areas of linguistics, anthropology, art, psychoanalysis (the section was actually called "psychiatry"), and literature, and included essays by Lévi-Strauss, Jacques Lacan, Geoffrey Hartman, and Michael Riffaterre.

35 Derrida and Lacan met for the first time at this event (see Peeters, *Derrida*, 166).
36 See Jacques Derrida, "Structure, Sign, and Play in the Discourse of the Human Sciences," in Derrida, *Writing and Difference*, trans. Alan Bass (London: Routledge, 1978), 278–94. Derrida had visited the United States exactly ten years earlier as an exchange student at Harvard University (1956–57).
37 Ibid., 292.
38 Ibid. In his *Of Grammatology*, trans. and intro. Gayatri Spivak (Baltimore: John Hopkins University Press, 1997), Derrida similarly observes that "the ethic of speech is the *delusion* of presence mastered" (139, original emphasis).
39 See Chapter 3.
40 David Carroll, quoted in Peeters, *Derrida*, 167.
41 Jacques Derrida, "Some Statements and Truisms about Neologisms, Newisms, Postisms, Parasitisms, and Other Small Seismisms," in *The States of "Theory": History, Art, and Critical Discourse*, ed. David Carroll (New York: Columbia University Press, 1990), 80.
42 Jacques Derrida, *Speech and Phenomena, and Other Essays on Husserl's Theory of Signs*, trans. David B. Allison (Evanston, IL: Northwestern University Press, 1973).
43 Jürgen Habermas, *The Philosophical Discourse of Modernity*, trans. Frederick G. Lawrence (Cambridge: MIT Press, 1987), 193.
44 Thus, literary theorists generally ignored, for example, the references to "protention" and "retention" in the famous essay "*Différance*" (1968), even if these Husserlian notions were key to understanding what Derrida was talking about in the essay.
45 Jonathan Culler, *On Deconstruction*, 85, n. 1. Habermas in fact uses Culler's version of deconstruction in his critique of Derrida (*The Philosophical Discourse of Modernity*, 194–99).
46 Indeed, when I was a teaching assistant for Richard Rorty's course on Heidegger and Derrida (Stanford University, 1999), I was somewhat shocked to discover a very different Derrida than the "theorist of the text" I had been accustomed to hearing about in my earlier studies.
47 Cusset, *French Theory*, 112.
48 I am leaving aside the debate about whether Derrida should be considered a transcendental philosopher à la Kant, a thesis advanced by Rodolphe Gasché and Christopher Norris and contested by Richard Rorty. For an overview, see Richard Rorty, "Is Derrida a Transcendental Philosopher?" in Rorty, *Essays on Heidegger and Others* (Cambridge: Cambridge University Press, 1991), 119–28.
49 An alternate translation was provided in the "corrected edition" of Derrida's *Of Grammatology* (1997), 158. One can also see this dictum as an updated version of Heidegger's maxim "language is the house of being."
50 Although this did not stop Alain Renaut and Luc Ferry from titling their jeremiad against Theory *La pensée 68: Essai sur l'anti-humanisme contemporain* (Paris: Gallimard, 1985).
51 Karl Löwith's *From Hegel to Nietzsche* (1941) was published by Columbia University Press in 1964.

52 Alan Schrift, *Nietzsche's French Legacy: A Genealogy of Poststructuralism* (New York: Routledge, 1995), 5.
53 Martin Heidegger, *Nietzsche*, vols. 1–4, trans. David Farrell Krell (San Francisco: Harper & Row, 1979 [vol. 1], 1984 [vol. 2], 1987 [vols. 3 and 4]).
54 Foucault, "Le retour de la morale," http://1libertaire.free.fr/MFoucault209.html, my translation.
55 Edward Said, *Orientalism*, 25th Anniversary Edition (New York: Vintage Books, 2003), 23.
56 See the collection *The Death and Resurrection of the Author?* ed. William Irwin (Westport, CT: Greenwood Press, 2002).
57 Thus, Gutting writes that "there was no 'ethical turn' in the work of Levinas or in the later work of Derrida and Foucault, if we use 'ethics' in the standard philosophical sense of a theory (or applications of a theory) about ethical norms" (*Thinking the Impossible*, 147).
58 Unlike Derrida, whose Jewishness was largely passive, Levinas drew on and thematized Judaism in his philosophical works and wrote on specifically Jewish topics. Levinas also published occasional works, such as his short essay "Reflections on the Philosophy of Hitlerism" (1934).
59 Jacques Derrida, *Writing and Difference*, trans. Alan Bass (Chicago: University of Chicago Press, 1980), 111.
60 Jacques Derrida, "En ce moment même dans cet ouvrage me voici," in *Textes pour Emmanuel Levinas*, ed. François Laruelle (Paris: Jean-Michel Place, 1980).
61 Foucault's "turn" toward Nietzsche can be located in his 1971 essay "Nietzsche, Genealogy, History" (collected in *The Foucault Reader*, ed. Paul Rabinow [New York: Pantheon, 1984], 76–100).
62 See Ethan Kleinberg's chapter "Jean Beaufret, the First Heidegger Affair, and the 'Letter on Humanism,'" in his *Generation Existential: Heidegger's Philosophy in France 1927-1961* (Ithaca, NY: Cornell University Press, 2005), 157–206.
63 I discuss these in Chapter 3.
64 An English translation by Jeff Fort is forthcoming.
65 Gayatri Spivak, "Can the Subaltern Speak," in *Marxism and the Interpretation of Culture*, ed. Cary Nelson and Lawrence Grossberg (Urbana and Chicago: University of Illinois Press, 1988), 66–111.
66 Spivak did not coin the term "subaltern." The term apparently originated in Antonio Gramsci and was popularized by the Subaltern Studies Group in the mid-1980s, before being picked up by Spivak.
67 Richard Bernstein writes in 1992: "The 'reception' of deconstruction has been almost totally apolitical. . . . Indeed, I think Edward W. Said is right when he notes that recent literary criticism (in particular, deconstruction) bears its own form of complicity with recent 'neo-conservatism'" (*The New Constellation: The Ethical-Political Horizons of Modernity/Postmodernity* [Cambridge, MA: The MIT Press, 1992], 188). See Chapter 10.
68 Edward Said, *The World, the Text, and the Critic* (Cambridge, MA: Harvard University Press, 1983).

69 Feminists were put on notice in the first chapter of Judith Butler's *Gender Trouble: Feminism and the Subversion of Identity* ([New York: Routledge 1990], 2): "For the most part, feminist theory has assumed that there is some existing identity, understood through the category of women, who not only initiates feminist interests and goals within discourse, but constitutes the subject for whom political representation is pursued."

70 Crusset describes "two castes of literary scholars" designated by the term "deconstruction": "Those who, to echo Marx's eleventh thesis on Feuerbach, have the naïveté to believe that they will transform the world *through* interpretation, and those who, more discretely and with greater exigency, had the imprudence to want to transform the world of interpretation itself" (*French Theory*, 113, original emphasis).

71 One could cite, in this context, the acrimonious "divorce" at the University of California, Irvine (where Derrida was a visiting professor for many years), between the English Department and the Comparative Literature program, which split off and became its own department. Many of the early proponents of Theory (in particular, the Yale group) elected to stay in the English Department, where they felt that the textual approach was still valued, rather than join the Comparative Literature department, where the more political, ethnically diverse, and global aspects of Theory were emphasized.

72 Arthur Danto, *What Art Is* (New Haven, CT: Yale University Press, 2013), 138.

73 See: https://judithbutler.wordpress.com/. Derrida's *Of Grammatology* "only" sold some 80,000.

74 See, for example, Gloria Steinem's attack on deconstruction: http://www.theguardian.com/world/2005/jan/17/gender.melissadenes.

75 Derrida only begins to write about his youth in 1989–90, namely in his "autobiography" contained in Geoffrey Bennington and Jacques Derrida, *Jacques Derrida* (Paris: Seuil, 1991). Derrida's text, "Circonfession," runs at the bottom of the page, while Bennington's "Derridabase" runs at the top. Although Foucault does speak about homosexuality in the *History of Sexuality*, he became a kind of symbol of gay liberation only *after* his death (and let us recall that the fact he died of AIDS was initially covered up by his family).

76 See: https://www.insidehighered.com/news/2015/01/12/mla-members-debate-when-and-how-take-stand-issues-such-israel-boycott.

77 Marjorie Perloff, "It Must Change," *PMLA* 122, no. 3 (2007): 656.

78 Ibid., 658.

79 Ibid., 656.

80 Ian Watt recounts in his *The Rise of the Novel* (Berkeley and Los Angeles: University of California Press, 1957/2001, 304) that during his undergraduate days at Harvard in the early 1950s, the novel was considered a "popular" and "marginal" genre when compared with the aesthetic dignity of lyric poetry.

81 As I note in Chapter 9, this represents a revival of the debate, in the 1940s and 1950s, between literary history and literary theory (New Criticism), in which the latter sought to carve out an autonomous space for literary study by purging it of all extraneous concerns (the life of the author, historical events, sociological theses). René Girard notes that René Wellek's and Austin Warren's *The Theory*

of Literature (1948) was "the old standby of graduate English studies in the Fifties" ("French Theories of Fictions, 1947–1974," *The Bucknell Review* 21, no. 1 [1976]: 118).

82 Jonathan Culler, *Theory of the Lyric* (Cambridge, MA: Harvard University Press, 2015).

83 "Natural attitude" is a key term of phenomenology, especially that of Husserl, in which it refers to our everyday, unreflective view of the world around us.

84 For a sophisticated and spirited defense of critical "common sense," see Antoine Compagnon's 1998 book *Le démon de la théorie*, translated by Carol Cosman as *Literature, Theory, and Common Sense* (Princeton, NJ: Princeton University Press, 2004). To be fair, however, we must note that Compagnon is seeking some kind of middle ground between common sense and high theory. Compagnon was, after all, a student of Roland Barthes.

85 Unlike in the United States, in many European countries philosophy is taught at the high school level; thus, the general public has at least a rudimentary knowledge of some classic philosophical texts.

86 In addition, "poetics" had always been concerned with society, ethics, and cultural critique. For example, even a cursory acquaintance with neoclassical poetics and its concepts, such as verisimilitude and *la bienséance* (decorum), reveals a critical attitude deeply concerned with social and moral attitudes. It is only with the advent, in the nineteenth century, of *l'art pour l'art* aestheticism in the wake of Kant's third *Critique* and the establishment of the art museum that genre criticism came to exalt the autonomy of art and the artist.

87 See Hayden White's essay "Historical Pluralism and Pantextualism," in which he writes, "What the pantextualists are really being accused of is having the wrong 'sense of history,' of viewing history and especially the history of criticism from the wrong perspective, which is to say, of viewing history from a typically modernist (or postmodernist) perspective or at least from a different perspective than that of a humanistic pluralist" (Hayden White, *The Fiction of Narrative: Essays on History, Literature, and Theory, 1957-2007*, ed. Robert Doran [Baltimore: Johns Hopkins University Press, 2010], 225).

88 For an interesting take on this, see Hayden White, "The Limits of the Concept," *PMLA*, forthcoming.

89 White, *The Fiction of Narrative*, 227.

90 Culler, *The Literary in Theory*, 2.

Chapter 1

1 Jean-Paul Sartre, *Critique of Dialectical Reason, Volume One* (London: Verso, 2004), 69.

2 Lévi-Strauss, *The Savage Mind* (Chicago: University of Chicago Press, 1966), xii.

3 Ibid.

4 See the essay by Françoise Lionnet, "Consciousness and Relationality: Sartre, Beauvoir, and Glissant," *Yale French Studies* 123 (2013): 100–17.

5   Annie Cohen-Solal, *Sartre: A Life*, trans. Anna Cancogni, ed. Norman Macafee (New York: Pantheon Books, 1987), 389.

6   The English translation was published in 1976, and the corrected edition, based on the revised French version of 1985, was published in 1991. Needless to say, by 1976 the intellectual world had left both existentialism and structuralism far behind, and thus, apart from being addressed by a few Marxist organs such as *New Left Review*, Sartre's great work was met with virtual silence in the English-speaking world.

7   See Jean-Paul Sartre, *Existentialism and Humanism*, trans. Carol Macomber (New Haven, CT: Yale University Press, 2007 [French 1946]), and Denis Kambouchner, "Lévi-Strauss and the Question of Humanism," in *The Cambridge Companion to Lévi-Strauss*, ed. Boris Wiseman (Cambridge: Cambridge University Press, 2009), 19–38.

8   Thomas Flynn, *Sartre and Marxist Existentialism* (Chicago: Chicago University Press, 1984), 31.

9   Jean-Paul Sartre, *Critique de la raison dialectique II* (Paris: Gallimard, 1985); *Critique of Dialectical Reason, Volume 2*, trans. Alan Sheridan-Smith (London: Verso, 2006).

10 Quoted in Emmanuel Barot, "Le marxisme, philosophie vivante: La leçon de Sartre," in *Lectures de Sartre*, ed. Philippe Cabestan and Jean-Pierre Zarader (Paris: Ellipses, 2011), 165.

11 Sartre, *Critique*, 375 (original emphasis).

12 See Vincent Debaene's article "Lévi-Strauss: What Legacy?" *Yale French Studies* 123 (2013): 14–40. Marcel Hénaff observes in his essay "L'adieu à la structure" (*Esprit*, August–September 2011) that, particularly after 1962, Lévi-Strauss's concept of "structure" evolves away from the traditional structuralist conception of Saussure and Jakobson toward a notion of "transformation." Could this shift have been a response to Sartre's critique?

13 Flynn, *Sartre and Marxist Existentialism*, 100. Thus praxis-parole/practico-inert language form a dialectic of their own: "There can be no doubt that language is *in one sense* an inert totality. But this materiality is *also* a constantly developing organic totalization" (Sartre, *Critique*, 98, original emphasis).

14 Ibid., 262.

15 "The intensity of isolation, as a relation of exteriority between the members of a temporary and contingent gathering, expresses *the degree of massification* of the social ensemble" (ibid., 257, original emphasis).

16 Sartre also speaks of the "interpenetration" of individuals and their environment. See ibid., 253–56.

17 Ibid., 267.

18 Ibid., 268.

19 "Isolation does not remove one from the visual and practical field of the Other" (ibid., 258).

20 Thus there must be a minimal reciprocity, even at the level of seriality: "The ensemble of isolated behavior . . . presupposes a structure of reciprocity at every level. . . . For otherwise the social models in currency (clothes, hair

style, bearing, etc.) would not be adopted by everyone" (ibid., 258). Seriality thus suggests René Girard's notion of "mimetic desire." See Chapter 7 for an overview of this notion.

21 Fredric Jameson, "Foreword," in Sartre, *Critique*, xxviii.
22 Iris Marion Young, "Gender as Seriality: Thinking about Women as a Social Collective," *Signs* 19, no. 3 (1994): 713–38.
23 This goes as well for ethnic groups, such as Jews, which for Sartre are also defined by seriality. See Sartre, *Critique*, 267–68.
24 Ibid., 687, original emphasis. As Thomas Flynn notes, "The true 'subject' of history is the closely knit group, in the sense that only in the group does one overcome the passiveness and exteriority of the practico-inert and achieve a degree of mutual recognition among freedoms that Sartre visualizes as the 'reign of man'" (*Sartre, Foucault, and Historical Reason, Volume One: Toward an Existentialist Theory of History* [Chicago: Chicago University Press, 1997], 126).
25 However, there is no ontological priority for series or groups in terms of one being more fundamental or temporally prior; any such foundationalism would be inimical to Sartre's dialectical method.
26 Martin Heidegger, *Being and Time: A Translation of* Sein und Zeit, trans. Joan Stambaugh (Albany: SUNY Press, 1996), 119. While, according to Heidegger, the authentic and the inauthentic are supposedly two dimensions or levels of a single being, rather than simply an opposition between an exalted self and the inauthentic crowd, Samuel Moyn observes that "this view ignores Heidegger's consistently derogatory rhetoric when speaking of the one [*das Man*]" (*Origins of the Other: Emmanuel Levinas between Revelation and Ethics* [Ithaca, NY: Cornell University Press, 2005], 67–68, n. 25).
27 In Sartre's *Critique*, the contrast between the authentic individual and the crowd is replaced by that between the authentic group and the (serial) crowd.
28 Lévi-Strauss, *The Savage Mind*, 248.
29 In a sense, however, Sartre is also saying that primitive societies lack history "insofar as the relationship between purposeful action and the universe of material and man-made limitations has reached such a state of equilibrium that men simply live out their existence in a sort of ritualistic myth. Only when events pose a contradiction is history made" (Lawrence Rosen, "Language, History, and the Logic of Inquiry in Lévi-Strauss and Sartre," *History and Theory* 10, no. 3 [1971]: 283).
30 Lévi-Strauss, *The Savage Mind*, 479, original emphasis.
31 Ibid., 480, original emphasis.
32 Ibid., 489.
33 Ibid., 483.
34 Joseph S. Catalano, *A Commentary on Jean-Paul Sartre's* Critique of Dialectical Reason (Chicago: University of Chicago Press, 1986), 194.
35 Rosen continues: "[Structure] is that pattern of freedoms and constraints which men have chosen in concert as their own solution to the problems of scarcity and the needs with which they are necessarily confronted" ("Language, History," 282). Similarly, Richard Harvey Brown observes that

Sartre sees individuals "as conscious, intentional actors, whose projects, meanings, and moral decisions are not merely epiphenomenal of deeper unconscious structures that somehow possess a superior ontological status" ("Dialectic and Structure in Jean-Paul Sartre and Claude Lévi-Strauss," *Human Studies* 2 [1979]: 16).

36 Lévi-Strauss, *The Savage Mind*, 253.

37 Claude Lévi-Strauss, "Overture to *le Cru et le cuit*," trans. Joseph H. McMahon, *Yale French Studies* 36–37 "Structuralism" (1966): 53. And in *Tristes tropiques*, trans. John Russell ([New York: Atheneum 1964], 160), Lévi-Strauss remarks, "I am convinced that the number of these systems is not unlimited and that human societies, like individual human beings . . . never create absolutely: all they do is to choose certain combinations from a repertory of ideas which it should be possible to reconstitute."

38 Jean-Paul Sartre, "Itinerary of a Thought," *New Left Review* 58 (1969): 57.

39 Sartre, *Critique*, 486.

40 I am adapting Fredric Jameson's remark in his "Foreword" to Sartre's *Critique* that "the scandal of the existence of other people [is] surely Sartre's central philosophical motif and the most original and durable element of his various systems" (xxii).

41 Claude Lévi-Strauss, *The Elementary Structures of Kinship* (Boston: Beacon Press, 1969), 497.

42 Claude Lévi-Strauss, "Histoire et ethnologie," *Revue de métaphysique et de morale* 54, nos. 3–4 (1949): 363–91.

43 Lévi-Strauss, *Structural Anthropology* (New York: Basic Books, 1963), 18.

44 Ibid., 16.

45 "The French Revolution of 1789 lived through by an aristocrat is not the same phenomenon as the Revolution of 1789 lived through by a *sans-culotte*, and neither would correspond to the Revolution of 1789 as conceived by Michelet or Taine" (ibid., 16–17). Lévi-Strauss repeats this idea in *The Savage Mind*, 258.

46 Ibid., 17.

47 Ibid.

48 Ibid., 18.

49 Michael E. Harkin, "Lévi-Strauss and History," in *The Cambridge Companion to Lévi-Strauss*, 40.

50 "Rather than make the difficult argument that anthropology was *sui generis*, being able to align it with an established prestigious discipline [such as history] was helpful" (ibid.).

51 Quoted in ibid., 41 (Marcello Massenzio, "An Interview with Claude Lévi-Strauss," *Current Anthropology* 42 [2001]: 420).

52 Lévi-Strauss, *The Savage Mind*, 256.

53 Vincent Debaene notes that Lévi-Strauss republished *The Elementary Structures* with "no alterations," even though "ethnographic knowledge had evolved, revealing some errors and confusions" ("Lévi-Strauss: What Legacy?" 38).

54 Lévi-Strauss, *The Elementary Structures*, 108, n. 3.
55 Lévi-Strauss, *The Savage Mind*, 246.
56 Ibid., 248. The phrase "refuse history" is referred to below.
57 Ibid., 253.
58 Ibid., 249, note.
59 Ibid., 249.
60 Ibid.
61 Ibid., 246 (original emphasis).
62 Ibid., 245.
63 Catalano, *A Commentary*, 75, note.
64 Rosen, "Language, History," 274.
65 Marcel Hénaff, *Claude Lévi-Strauss and the Making of Structural Anthropology*, trans. Mary Baker (Minneapolis: University of Minnesota Press, 1998), 235.
66 Lévi-Strauss, *The Savage Mind*, 256.
67 Hénaff notes that "for [Lévi-Strauss] the diachronic is not to be confused with the historical perspective" (*Claude Lévi-Strauss*, 230); this may be true in general; however, in these pages, Lévi-Strauss seems to unnecessarily confuse the issue.
68 Fernand Braudel's article "Histoire et sciences sociales: La longue durée" was published in 1958, and Braudel's most famous work, *The Mediterranean and the Mediterranean World in the Age of Philip II*, had appeared in 1949.
69 Claude Lévi-Strauss, *Structural Anthropology, Volume 2*, trans. Monique Layton (Chicago: University of Chicago Press, 1983), 321–22. Original source: Claude Lévi-Strauss, "Les discontinuités culturelles et le développement économique et social," *Information sur les sciences sociales* 2, no. 2 (1963): 7–15. Hénaff also quotes part of this passage in his analysis. See Hénaff, *Claude Lévi-Strauss*, 225–27.
70 Sartre, *Critique*, 69.
71 Catalano, *A Commentary*, 65.
72 Hénaff, *Claude Lévi-Strauss*, 108 (original emphasis).
73 Lévi-Strauss, *Structural Anthropology*, 279.
74 Lévi-Strauss, *The Savage Mind*, 245.

Chapter 2

1 Michel Foucault, *Ethics: Subjectivity and Truth*, ed. Paul Rabinow (New York: The New Press, 1997), 256.
2 Foucault, *Ethics: Subjectivity and Truth*, 262. Foucault also claims that *Madness and Civilization* combines all three aspects.

3   *The Final Foucault*, ed. James Bernauer and David Rasmussen (Cambridge, MA: MIT Press, 1988).

4   Thus, for example, Wolfgang Detel's *Foucault and Classical Antiquity: Power, Ethics and Knowledge*, trans. David Wigg-Wolf (Cambridge: Cambridge University Press, 2005), was originally published in 1998 (in German), before any of the lecture courses had appeared. Timothy O'Leary's *Foucault and the Art of Ethics* was published in 2002, just as the lecture course that directly addresses the book's topic appears in French (*L'herméneutique du sujet*, 2001; the last entry for Foucault in the book's bibliography is 1997). On the other hand, it is somewhat inexplicable how Gary Gutting, who has published widely on Foucault, could ignore the late lecture courses in his otherwise well-researched book *Thinking the Impossible: French Philosophy Since 1960* (Oxford: Oxford University Press 2010), which includes a section entitled "Foucault and Ethics" (140–47). The crucial 1981–82 course was available as early as 2001 in French and 2005 in English. Similarly, despite including a chapter entitled "The Silence of Ethics," Johanna Oksala's *Foucault on Freedom*, published in 2005 (Cambridge: Cambridge University Press), cites only the course summary of *The Hermeneutics of the Subject*, not the lectures themselves. In his revised article, "Ethics as Ascetics: Foucault, the History of Ethics, and Ancient Thought," for the second edition of *The Cambridge Companion to Foucault*, ed. Gary Gutting (Cambridge: Cambridge University Press, 2003), 123–48, Arnold Davidson also refers only to the course summary of *The Hermeneutics of the Subject*. He does, however, use notes taken during the 1983–84 lecture course, as indicated in endnotes 85–88. The recently founded *Foucault Studies* (2004–present) is one place where Foucault's late lecture courses have been covered extensively (http://rauli.cbs.dk/index.php/foucault-studies/issue/archive). See, for example, Daniel Smith, "Foucault on Ethics and Subjectivity: 'Care of the Self' and 'Aesthetics of Existence,'" *Foucault Studies* 19 (2015): 135–50.

5   The compilation *Ethics: Subjectivity and Truth*, published in 1997, offers some indication of the ethical turn. Thomas Flynn provides an account, based on his own notes, of the 1983–84 lecture course in his contribution to *The Final Foucault*, ed. James Bernauer and David Rasmussen: "Foucault as Parrhesiast: His Last Course at the Collège de France" (102–18).

6   With the publication in May 2015 of the 1971–72 course, *Théories et Institutions Pénales*, all the lecture course have now been published; two have yet to be translated into English.

7   The specific idea of the "ethics of the self" is treated in the short chapter "Morality and the Practice of the Self" in *The Use of Pleasure*: Volume 2 of *The History of Sexuality*, trans. Robert Hurley (New York: Vintage, 1985), 25–32, and in a chapter entitled "The Culture of the Self" in *The Care of the Self*: Volume 3 of *The History of Sexuality*, trans. Robert Hurley (New York: Vintage, 1986), 39–68. The idea is also developed in a quartet of late interviews (available in various volumes): "On the Genealogy of Ethics: An Overview of a Work in Progress" (1983); "The Ethics of the Concern of the Self as a Practice of Freedom" (1984); "Politics and Ethics: An Interview" (1983); and "Polemics, Politics, and Problematizations" (1984).

8   The title of the new book was supposed to be *Technologies of the Self*, according to the editors of the eponymously titled book *Technologies of the Self: A Seminar with Michel Foucault*, ed. Luther H. Martin, Huck Gutman, and Patrick H. Hutton (Amherst: University of Massachusetts Press, 1988), 3.

9   Michel Foucault, *The Hermeneutics of the Subject: Lectures at the Collège de France, 1981-82*, trans. Graham Burchell, ed. Frédéric Gros (New York: Picador, 2005), 515.

10 Foucault, *The Hermeneutics of the Subject*, 395–96.

11 Foucault insisted that there be no posthumous publications; the sole exception to this rule was the course lectures, which had been recorded by others.

12 The very first lecture on the topic appears to have been given outside of France, at the University of California, Berkeley, on October 20, 1980. The lecture was entitled "The Genealogy of the Modern Subject." See James Miller, *The Passion of Michel Foucault* (New York: Simon and Schuster, 1993), 321. In this lecture, Foucault announces a shift from "techniques of domination" to "techniques of the self" (ibid., 321–22).

13 Foucault begins his 1981–82 course by saying "I would like to take up a notion about which I think I said a few words last year. This is the notion of 'care of oneself'" (*The Hermeneutics of the Subject*, 2). The editor remarks in a footnote (20, n. 5) that "in the 1981 lectures there are no analyses explicitly concerned with the care of the self, but there are lengthy analyses dealing with the arts of existence and processes of subjectification (the lectures of 13 January, 25 March, and 1 April)."

14 Frédéric Gros, "Course Context," in Foucault, *The Hermeneutics of the Subject*, 509. Gros notes that the 1981–82 lecture course represents in fact an "expanded and developed version" of this chapter from *The Care of the Self* (ibid., 508).

15 Foucault, *The Hermeneutics of the Subject*, 515. Davidson similarly speaks of the "conceptual and philosophical distinctiveness of Foucault's last works" ("Ethics as Ascetics," in *The Cambridge Companion to Foucault*, 123).

16 Although, as noted in the Introduction, Levinas's ethical philosophy is more of a metaethics, or "Ethics of Ethics," as Jacques Derrida calls it.

17 Pierre Hadot, "Exercices spirituels," *École pratique des hautes études, Section des sciences religieuses. Annuaire* 84 (1974): 25–70.

18 See Arnold Davidson, "Spiritual Exercises and Ancient Philosophy: An Introduction to Pierre Hadot," *Critical Inquiry* 16 (1990): 475–82. For a more recent take, see Thomas Flynn, "Philosophy as a Way of Life: Foucault and Hadot," *Philosophy and Social Criticism* 31, nos. 5–6 (2005): 609–22.

19 Pierre Hadot, *Philosophy as a Way of Life: Spiritual Exercises from Socrates to Foucault*, ed. and intro. Arnold I. Davidson, trans. Michael Chase (Oxford: Blackwell, 1995).

20 Miller, *The Passion of Michel Foucault*, 287.

21 Quoted in ibid. Miller notes that "between 1968 and 1975, [Foucault] had known what he wanted to say; politically, he had known where he wanted to go" (ibid.).

22. Foucault, *Power/Knowledge: Selected Interviews and Other Writings, 1972-1977*, ed. Colin Gordon (New York: Vintage, 1980), 78.
23. Miller, *The Passion of Michel Foucault*, 322.
24. Michel Foucault, *The History of Sexuality I: An Introduction*, trans. Robert Hurley (New York: Vintage Books, 1978), 140–41, 143–44.
25. The first volume of which was published in 1976. The second and third volumes were published just before Foucault's death in 1984. A fourth volume, *Les aveux de la chair* (Confessions of the Flesh), was written but never appeared in print. The manuscript is contained in the Foucault archives, but under the terms of the Foucault estate, it cannot be published.
26. Foucault, *The Use of Pleasure*, 3.
27. Most notably Noam Chomsky, who, as noted in my introduction, remarked: "[Foucault] struck me as completely amoral. I'd never met anyone who was so totally amoral" (quoted in Miller, *The Pasion of Michel Foucault*, 201).
28. Foucault was involved in prison reform efforts in the early 1970s.
29. The beginning of the gay rights movement (now known as lesbian, gay, bisexual, and transgender [LGBT] rights) is usually located in the Stonewall riots in New York in June of 1969. (On June 24, 2016, President Obama designated the Stonewall Inn and surrounding area as a National Monument.) Miller observes that "news of the Stonewall riots was not long in crossing the Atlantic. In March of 1971, a small group of French ultra-leftists announced the formation of the 'Front Homosexuel d'Action Révolutionnaire' (or FHAR), a group explicitly modeled on the American Gay Liberation Front" (*The Passion of Michel Foucault*, 255). The Center for Disease Controls in the United States started using the acronym *AIDS* in 1982 for the condition caused by HIV infection. Foucault appears to not have believed in the linkage between homosexual behavior and AIDS: "Je n'y crois pas" (I don't believe it) (quoted in Miller, *The Passion of Michel Foucault*, 349). In a personal conversation I had in the mid-1990s with John Searle (professor of philosophy at UC Berkeley, which Foucault often visited in the early 1980s), he conveyed his belief that Foucault's philosophical position kept him from recognizing the danger of AIDS.
30. Michel Foucault, *The Government of Self and Others: Lectures at the Collège de France, 1982-83*, trans. Graham Burchell, ed. Frédéric Gros (New York: Picador, 2010), 15.
31. Ibid., 21. In *Discipline and Punish* (30–31).
32. "What is Enlightenment?" is contained in *The Foucault Reader*, ed. Paul Rabinow (New York: Vintage Books, 1984/2010), 32–50. Foucault had also given a lecture on Kant's essay at the Société française de philosophie on May 27, 1978, titled "Qu'est-ce que la critique?" The English translation, "What is Critique?" by Kevin Paul Geiman, was published in *What Is Enlightenment? Eighteenth-Century Answers and Twentieth-Century Questions*, ed. James Schmidt (Berkeley and Los Angeles: University of California Press, 1996), 382–98.
33. Foucault, *The Foucault Reader*, 38.
34. Ibid., 39, my italics on "voluntary choice."

35 Foucault, *The Hermeneutics of the Subject*, 237, 372.
36 Foucault, *Ethics: Subjectivity and Truth*, 286.
37 See Michel Foucault, "The Return of Morality," in *Foucault Live: Collected Interviews, 1961-1984*, ed. Sylvère Lotringer (New York: Semiotext(e), 1989), 465–73.
38 Michel Foucault, *Introduction à l'anthropologie* (Paris: Vrin, 2008). Foucault's translation of Kant's text is included in this edition. English edition: *Introduction to Kant's* Anthropology, ed. with afterword and notes, Roberto Nigro, trans. Roberto Nigro and Kate Briggs (Los Angeles: Semiotext(e), 2007).
39 Foucault, *Introduction to Kant's* Anthropology, 51.
40 Ibid., 53.
41 Ibid., 49. Foucault should have said "*published* in the same year (1798)," since the *Anthropology* collects a great deal of older material.
42 Paul M. Cohen, *Freedom's Moment: An Essay on the French Idea of Liberty from Rousseau to Foucault* (Chicago: University of Chicago Press, 2007), 55.
43 Foucault, *The Use of Pleasure*, 6.
44 Some commentators refuse to accept this idea of a "theoretical shift." Thus, for example, Johanna Oksala sees it as "simply a shift of emphasis" (*Foucault on Freedom*, 164).
45 Foucault, *Ethics: Subjectivity and Truth*, 290, my emphasis. Foucault also puts it thus: "Replacing the history of knowledge with the historical analysis of forms of veridiction, replacing the history of domination with the historical analysis of procedures of governmentality, and replacing the theory of the subject or the history of subjectivity with the historical analysis of the pragmatics of the self and the forms it has taken, are to some degree the possibility of the history of what could be called 'experiences'" (*The Government of Self and Others*, 5).
46 Foucault, *Ethics: Subjectivity and Truth*, 281. Foucault tends, in his later work, to stress continuity and unity even amid shifts and changes of position.
47 The subtitle of Sartre's *Being and Nothingness* reads "A Phenomenological Essay on Ontology" (Essai d'ontologie phénoménologique).
48 Foucault, *The Hermeneutics of the Subject*, 189 (*L'herméneutique de sujet: Cours au Collège de France*, 1981–1982 [Paris: Seuil/Gallimard, 2001], 182). See Hans Sluga, "Foucault's Encounter with Heidegger and Nietzsche," in *The Cambridge Companion to Foucault*, 210–39. As mentioned in the introduction, Foucault remarks that "I tried to read Nietzsche in the 1950s, but Nietzsche by himself said nothing to me. Whereas Nietzsche and Heidegger—that was the philosophical shock!" (*Foucault Live*, 470).
49 In his short text "The Subject and Power," Foucault appears to want to have it both ways. So whereas he begins by stating that "my work has dealt with three modes of objectification which transform human beings into subjects," he nevertheless avers that "finally, I have sought to study—it is my current work—the way a human being turns him- or herself into a subject" (Afterword to Hubert L. Dreyfus and Paul Rabinow, *Michel Foucault: Beyond*

Structuralism and Hermeneutics, 2nd edn [Chicago: University of Chicago Press, 1983], 208).

50 Foucault, *Ethics: Subjectivity and Truth*, 263, my emphasis.

51 Thus, as Gutting notes, "Foucault's historical study of modern sexuality made explicit the central role of the subject or self in the network of social constraints. It was . . . now apparent that constraints on our behavior were not only externally imposed . . . they were also internalized as our own view of our self-identity" (*Thinking the Impossible*, 141).

52 Foucault, "Le retour de la morale," my translation.

53 For example, Gros observes, "A true subject was possible, therefore, no longer in the sense of subjection, but of subjectivation" (Foucault, *The Hermeneutics of the Subject*, 511). I thus disagree with Oksala, who insists that "Foucault's 'ethical turn' does not essentially change his understanding of the subject," which was "always constituted in the power/knowledge networks of a culture" (*Foucault on Freedom*, 4). If this were true, then there would be no way to respond to Richard Bernstein's critique of the "ethics of the self": "[Foucault's] genealogical analyses seem effectively to undermine any talk of agency which is not a precipitate of power/knowledge regimes" (*The New Constellation: The Ethical-Political Horizons of Modernity/Postmodernity* [Cambridge, MA: The MIT Press, 1992], 164). See also Gilles Deleuze, *Foucault* (Paris: Les Editions de Minuit, 1986), in particular the chapter titled "Les plissements, ou le dedans de la pensée (subjectivation)" (101–30).

54 Certainly the advent, in 2015, of gay marriage might be construed as such a compromise. By allowing public recognition of the dignity of gay union within what had been a heterosexual institution, gay marriage has certainly legitimated homosexuality in a far more effective way than antidiscrimination laws. Nevertheless, this achievement of "bourgeois respectability" (or heteronormality) has significant tradeoffs. See, for example, Judith Butler's essay "Competing Universalities" (in *Contingency, Hegemony, Universality: Contemporary Dialogues on the Left*, ed. Judith Butler, Ernesto Laclau, and Slavoj Žižek [London: Verso, 2000], 136–81), in which she points out the danger of "marginalization" as "marriage assumes the status of a normative ideal within the gay rights movement" (181, n. 16).

55 Quoted in Didier Eribon, *Michel Foucault*, trans. Betsey Wing (Cambridge, MA: Harvard University Press, 1991), 280.

56 See in particular Martha Nussbaum's blistering review (*The New York Times*, November 10, 1985) of *The Use of Pleasure* (https://www.nytimes.com/books/00/12/17/specials/foucault-use.html).

57 Foucault, *The Use of Pleasure*, 7, n.

58 See Frédéric Gros, "Situation du cours," in Michel Foucault, *Subjectivité et Verité: Cours au Collège de France, 1980-1981*, ed. Frédéric Gros (Paris: Seuil/Gallimard, 2014), 307. See also Eribon, *Michel Foucault*, in which he notes that Foucault was rated "fourth in Greek" in his secondary studies (23).

59 For the final chapter of his *The Art of Living: Socratic Reflections from Plato to Foucault* (Berkeley and Los Angeles: University of California Press, 1998), "A Fate for Socrates' Reason: Foucault on the Care of the Self" (157–58),

Alexander Nehamas relies on typescripts from the audio tapes of the lectures provided to him by James Miller. Nehamas discusses only two lectures: February 15, 1984 and February 22, 1984 (see *The Art of Living*, 245, note 3).

60 See Chapter 9 for a discussion of the *Ansatzpunkt* (point of departure).
61 Foucault, *The Hermeneutics of the Subject*, 15.
62 Foucault, *Ethics: Subjectivity and Truth*, 279.
63 Foucault, *The Hermeneutics of the Subject*, 294.
64 Richard Rorty, *Contingency, Irony, and Solidarity* (Cambridge: Cambridge University Press, 1989), 63.
65 Pierre Hadot, "Reflections on the notion of the 'Culturation of the Self,'" in *Michel Foucault, Philosopher*, trans. and ed. Timothy J. Armstrong (New York: Routledge, 1992), 226.
66 See especially the third part of Alain Renaut's *Sartre, le dernier philosophe* (Paris: Grasset, 1993), entitled "L'Existentialisme est un individualisme."
67 Foucault, *Ethics: Subjectivity and Truth*, 256.
68 See Foucault, "Polemics, Politics, and Problematizations" (in Foucault, *Ethics: Subjectivity and Truth*); Judith Revel, "La pensée vertical: une éthique de la problématisation," in *Foucault: Le courage et la vérité*, ed. Frédéric Gros (Paris: PUF, 2002/12), esp. 80–86. Gary Gutting sees "problematization" as existing in contrast to "marginalization": "As opposed to the marginalized, those whose lives are merely problematized have a 'social essence' compatible with a significant range of freedom" (*Thinking the Impossible*, 142). Similarly, Gros sees in the 1981–82 course a complete intellectual shift: "It is no longer a genealogy of systems, it is a problematization of the subject" ("Course Context," *The Hermeneutics of the Subject*, 508). Part I of the *The Use of Pleasure* is entitled "The Moral Problematization of Pleasures."
69 See the last section of this chapter.
70 Plato, *Apology*, 30a–30b (trans. Benjamin Jowett, http://www.gutenberg.org/files/1656/1656-h/1656-h.htm).
71 Foucault, *The Hermeneutics of the Subject*, 8.
72 Ibid., 12.
73 Ibid., 525.
74 Clare O'Farrell, "Michel Foucault: The Unconscious of History and Culture," in *The Sage Handbook of Historical Theory*, ed. Nancy Partner and Sarah Foot (London: Sage Publications, 2013), 171.
75 The attribution of the *Alcibiades I* was first challenged by Friedrich Schleiermacher in 1836. Foucault appears to see it as authentically Platonic.
76 "Extension to the individual life, or coextensiveness of care of the self and the art of living (the famous *tekhnê tou biou*), the art of life or art of existence which we know from Plato, and especially in the post-Platonic movements, becomes the fundamental definition of philosophy. Care of the self becomes coextensive with life" (Foucault, *The Hermeneutics of the Subject*, 86).
77 Ibid., 9.
78 In the "Course Summary," Foucault notes that "it would be wrong to think that the care of the self was an invention of philosophical thought and that it

was a precept peculiar to the philosophical life. In actual fact it was a precept of life that, in a general way, was very highly valued in Greece" (ibid., 493).

79 Foucault, *The Government of Self and Others*, 43.
80 Foucault, *The Hermeneutics of the Subject*, 81.
81 Ibid., 11.
82 I thus disagree in part with Richard Bernstein when he observes that "despite what at times has the ring of global claims. . . . Foucault is always drawing our attention to what is local, specific, and historically contingent" (*The New Constellation*, 159). While this is true as far as it goes, it ignores Foucault's systematizing zeal.
83 Gutting observes, "Without taking over any of Braudel's specific results or methods, Foucault tried to effect a parallel change of perspective in the history of thought: a move away from the standpoint of the individual thinker and toward the standpoint of broader but more fundamental categories and structures" (*French Philosophy in the Twentieth Century* [Cambridge: Cambridge University Press, 2001], 260). Nevertheless, Foucault is adamant that works such as *Les mots et les choses* not be construed as "structuralist": "In France certain half-witted 'commentators' persist in labeling me a 'structuralist.' I have been unable to get it into their tiny minds that I have used none of the methods, concepts, or key terms that characterize structural analysis" (quoted in Miller, *The Passion of Michel Foucault*, 161).
84 Foucault, *The Hermeneutics of the Subject*, 10–11.
85 Ibid., 13.
86 Foucault, *Ethics: Subjectivity and Truth*, 287.
87 Nehamas, *The Art of Living*, 181. In his essay "The Connection of the Care for Self and Other in Plato's *Laches*," Will Tilleczek takes Nehamas to task for confusing "an ethic in which the care of the self is ethically prior for one in which the care of the self is wholly sufficient." Tilleczek avers that for Plato's Socrates, "the care of the self is bound to the care of others" (*Pseudo Dionysius* 16 [2014], https://ojs.library.dal.ca/PseudoDio/article/view/4866/4383).
88 Foucault says in an interview, "What makes [the care of the self] ethical for the Greeks is not that it is care for others. The care of the self is ethical in itself; but it implies complex relationships with others insofar as this *êthos* of freedom is also a way of caring for others" (*Ethics: Subjectivity and Truth*, 287).
89 Foucault, *The Hermeneutics of the Subject*, 177.
90 Ibid.
91 Ibid.
92 Ibid., 112.
93 Ibid.
94 Ibid., 113.
95 Nevertheless, in the *Alcibiades*, Socrates remarks, "And the next step will be to take care of the soul, and look to that? . . . Leaving the care of our bodies and of our properties to others?" (http://www.gutenberg.org/files/1676/1676-h/1676-h.htm). This suggests that one would require servants in order to properly care for oneself.

96 Foucault, *The Hermeneutics of the Subject*, 119. This effectively prefigures the Christian idea that all are called but only a few are saved: "This rare salvation from which no one is excluded *a priori*" (ibid., 120).

97 Ibid., 75.

98 "Extensive work by the self on the self is required for this practice of freedom to take shape in an *êthos* that is good, beautiful, honorable, estimable, memorable, and exemplary" (Foucault, *Ethics: Subjectivity and Truth*, 286). For a fascinating discussion of self-construction in terms of self-disentanglement, see Razvan Amironesei, "La déprise de soi chez Michel Foucault comme pratique d'écriture et enjeu de l'identité subjective" (*Symposium: The Canadian Journal of Continental Philosophy* 15, no. 1 [2011]: 146–69).

99 See Michel Foucault, "Le retour de la morale" (interview with G. Barbedette and A. Scala on May 29, 1984), *Les Nouvelles littéraires* 2937 (June 28–July 1984), 36–41 (http://1libertaire.free.fr/MFoucault209.html).

100 Pierre Hadot, *What is Ancient Philosophy?* trans. Michael Chase (Cambridge, MA: Belknap Press, 2002), 3.

101 Sartre in fact uses the term "conversion" in his *Notebooks for an Ethics*. See Chapter 7.

102 Foucault, *The Hermeneutics of the Subject*, 28.

103 Ibid., 15.

104 Ibid., 28.

105 Foucault, *Ethics: Subjectivity and Truth*, 208.

106 Ibid., 210.

107 Foucault, *The Hermeneutics of the Subject*, 120. The Hadot text to which Foucault refers is "*Epistrophê* and *Metanoia*" in *Actes du XIe congrès international de philosophie, Bruxelles, 20-26 août 1953* (Louvain-Amsterdam: Nauwelaerts, 1953), vol. XII, 31–36.

108 Foucault, *The Hermeneutics of the Subject*, 215.

109 Ibid., 214.

110 Ibid., 211.

111 Ibid., 296. Similar ideas about conversion can also be found in Foucault, *The Care of the Self*, 64–66.

112 Foucault, *The Hermeneutics of the Subject*, 213.

113 Ibid., 214. Foucault here (p. 214) recaps what he stated on pp. 85–86.

114 Ibid., 85–86.

115 Ibid., 190.

116 Ibid., 178.

117 This essay marks Foucault's shift to the "genealogical" method of analysis.

118 Foucault, "The Return of Morality," 468.

119 Foucault, *The Hermeneutics of the Subject*, 252.

120 Foucault, *Ethics: Subjectivity and Truth*, 255–56.

121 Foucault, *The Hermeneutics of the Subject*, 251.

122 "Ethical self-creation of one's life as a work of art extends Nietzsche's concept that life has value as an aesthetic achievement and that one must give style to one's life by integrating the diffuse nature of oneself into a coherent whole" (Mark Olssen, *Michel Foucault: Materialism and Education* [Westport, CT: Bergin & Garvey, 1999], 143).

123 Foucault, *Ethics: Subjectivity and Truth*, 262.

124 Ibid. In *The Gay Science* ([New York: Vintage Books, 1974], 232, original italics), Friedrich Nietzsche writes, "*One thing is needful.*—To 'give style' to one's character—a great and rare art! It is practiced by those who survey all the strengths and weaknesses of their nature and then fit them into an artistic plan until every one of them appears as art and reason, and even weaknesses delight the eye . . . through long practice and daily work." See note 122.

125 "Foucault's comments on Sartre betray a clear anxiety of influence" (Gutting, *Thinking the Impossible*, 72).

126 Ibid.

127 Ibid.

128 Jean-Paul Sartre, "Existentialism Is a Humanism" (https://www.marxists.org/reference/archive/sartre/works/exist/sartre.htm).

129 Sartre himself did not outline an ethics in his published writings. The *Cahiers pour une morale* (*Notebooks for an Ethics*) appeared posthumously in 1983.

130 Foucault, *The Hermeneutics of the Subject*, 252.

131 Ibid.

132 This concept was first outlined in the 1977–78 course, *Security, Territory and Population*, and was applied to state apparatuses.

133 Foucault, *Ethics: Subjectivity and Truth*, 292.

134 In a lecture series given at the Catholic University of Louvain in 1981, published under the title *Mal dire, dire vrai: Fonction de l'aveu en justice* (Louvain: Presses Universitaires de Louvain, 2012), Foucault defined "government" as "the way of forming, of transforming and directing the behavior of individuals" (12, my translation).

135 Gros, "Course Context," in *The Hermeneutics of the Subject*, 512.

136 Richard Rorty, *Essays on Heidegger and Others* (Cambridge: Cambridge University Press, 1991), 194.

137 Olssen, *Materialism and Education*, 156.

138 Rorty, *Essays on Heidegger and Others*, 196.

139 Foucault, "Le retour de la morale," my translation.

140 Ibid.

141 Foucault, *Foucault Live*, 386, original emphasis.

142 Foucault, *Ethics: Subjectivity and Truth*, 256.

143 See Charles Taylor, "Foucault on Freedom and Truth," in *Foucault: A Critical Reader*, ed. David Hoy (Oxford: Blackwell, 1986), 69–102.

144 Gutting, *Thinking the Impossible*, 141. Even Gros, arguably the commentator most sympathetic to Foucault's own position, has recourse to existentialist

language, as when he observes, "The subject and the truth are not bound together here externally, as in Christianity, as if in the grip of a higher power, but as the result of an irreducible *choice of existence*" (in Foucault, *The Hermeneutics of the Subject*, 511, my emphasis).

145 Foucault, *Ethics: Subjectivity and Truth*, 282. Derrida expresses a similar sentiment apropos of May 1968: "What bothered me [about May 1968] was not so much the apparent spontaneity, which I do not believe in, but the spontaneist political eloquence, the call for transparency, for communication without relay or delay, the liberation from every sort of apparatus, party or union" (quoted in Benoît Peeters, *Derrida: A Biography*, trans. Andrew Brown [Cambridge: Polity Press, 2012], 68).

146 See James D. Marshall, "Michel Foucault: Marxism, Liberation, and Freedom," in *Dangerous Coagulations? The Uses of Foucault in the Study of Education*, ed. Bernadette M. Baker and Katharina E. Heyning (New York: Peter Lang, 2004), 265–78.

147 Foucault, *Ethics: Subjectivity and Truth*, 131.

148 Foucault, *The Hermeneutics of the Subject*, 117.

149 Michel Foucault, "Power, Moral Values, and the Intellectual," *History of the Present* 4 (1988): 1.

150 See Chapter 1 for an explanation of these Sartrean terms.

151 See Chapter 6 for a discussion of Sartre's idea of maximizing freedom.

152 Foucault is quoted in Didier Eribon's biography as having said in the 1960s that he was a left-wing anarchist.

153 From an interview in 1980: "It's actually in that moment that power ceases to be power and becomes mere physical force. . . . It's clear that power should not be defined as a constraining act of violence that represses individuals, forcing them to do something or preventing them from doing some other thing" ("Power, Moral Values, and the Intellectual," 2). This is very different in tone and substance from the views Foucault expressed in his televised debate with Noam Chomsky in 1971.

154 Foucault, "Power, Moral Values, and the Intellectual," 11 (the parenthetical interpretations are my own).

155 French scholarship on Foucault has made greater strides in this direction.

156 Foucault, *Foucault Live*, 386. The interview from which this quotation is taken was conducted in 1982.

Chapter 3

1 Jacques Derrida, Hans-Georg Gadamer, and Philippe Lacoue-Labarthe, *La conférence de Heidelberg (1988): Heidegger, portée philosophique et politique de sa pensée*, ed. Mireille Calle-Gruber (Paris: Lignes, 2014). The conference was held in French, at the French Institute of Heidelberg. An English translation, by Jeff Fort, is forthcoming under the title: *Heidegger, Philosophy, and Politics: The Heidelberg Conference* (Fordham University Press).

2 Victor Farias, *Heidegger et le nazisme* (Paris: Verdier, 1987). English edition: *Heidegger and Nazism,* ed. and fwd. Joseph Margolis and Tom Rockmore, trans. Paul Burrell and Gabriel R. Ricci (Philadelphia: Temple University Press, 1989). See also Tom Rockmore, *On Heidegger's Nazism and Philosophy* (Berkeley: University of California Press, 1992).

3 See the *New York Times* article by James Atlas, "The Case of Paul De Man," which appeared on August 28, 1988 (http://www.nytimes.com/1988/08/28/magazine/the-case-of-paul-de-man.html). See also the new biography by Evelyn Barish, *The Double Life of Paul de Man* (New York: W.W. Norton, 2014).

4 Benoît Peeters, *Derrida: A Biography*, trans. Andrew Brown (Cambridge: Polity Press, 2012), 401. The chapter in question is titled "From the Heidegger Affair to the de Man Affair *1987–1988.*"

5 The relevant publications by Derrida are *Specters of Marx: The State of the Debt, The Work of Mourning & the New International*, trans. Peggy Kamuf (New York: Routledge, 1994/2006); *Force de loi* (Paris: Galilée, 1994/2005); *The Politics of Friendship*, trans. George Collins (London: Verso, 2006); *Monolingualism of the Other, or, The Prosthesis of Origin*, trans. Patrick Mensah (Stanford, CA: Stanford University Press, 1998); *Adieu to Emmanuel Levinas*, trans. Michael Naas (Stanford, CA: Stanford University Press); *Pardonner: L'impardonnable et l'imprescriptible* (Paris: Galilee, 2012). In addition, there are the late seminars, some of which have recently been published, such as *Séminaire: La peine de mort, Volume I (1999–2000)* (Paris: Galilée, 2012), translated by Peggy Kamuf as *The Death Penalty, Volume I* (Chicago: University of Chicago Press, 2013). I presented a paper ("La peine de mort comme théâtre de la vie") in this seminar, with Derrida presiding and commenting, held at the École des hautes études en sciences sociales (EHESS) on March 22, 2000 (see Derrida, *Séminaire: La peine de mort, Volume I*, 365).

6 The great exception is Derrida's essay on Emmanuel Levinas, "Violence and Metaphysics" (1964), collected in *Writing and Difference*, trans. Alan Bass (Chicago: University of Chicago Press, 1978), 79–153.

7 As I noted in the introduction, one of Derrida's earliest texts, "Structure, Sign, and Play in the Discourse of the Human Sciences" (1966), raises the question of ethics as being of central concern: "One no less perceives in [Lévi-Strauss's] work a sort of ethic of presence, an ethic of nostalgia for origins, an ethic of archaic and natural innocence, of a purity of presence and self-presence in speech—an ethic, nostalgia, and even remorse which he often presents as the motivation of the ethnological project when he moves toward archaic societies—exemplary societies in his eyes" (Derrida, *Writing and Difference*, 292).

8 David Bates, "Crisis Between the Wars: Derrida and the Origins of Undecidability," *Representations* 90, no. 1 (2005): 1.

9 Most notably in Simon Critchley's *The Ethics of Deconstruction: Derrida and Levinas* (Edinburgh: Edinburgh University Press, 2014, third edition), originally published in 1992. Also from the 1990s, Geoffrey Bennington's *Legislations: The Politics of Deconstruction* (London: Verso, 1994) is interesting in this context, although it has broader aims. More recently, one can cite Christina Howells, *Derrida: Deconstruction from Phenomenology*

to Ethics (Cambridge: Polity Press, 1999); Peter Pericles, *The Ethics of Writing: Derrida, Deconstruction, and Pedagogy* (Lanham, MD: Rowman & Littlefield, 2000); Marko Zlomislić, *Jacques Derrida's Aporetic Ethics* (Plymouth: Lexington Books, 2007); and Susanne Lüdemann, *Politics of Deconstruction: A New Introduction to Jacques Derrida* (Stanford, CA: Stanford University Press, 2014). See also the following articles: Jacques Rancière, "Should democracy come? Ethics and Politics in Derrida," in *Derrida and the Time of the Political*, ed. Pheng Cheah and Suzanne Guerlac (Durham, NC: Duke University Press, 2009); Edward McGushin, "The Care of the Self and the Gift of Death: Foucault and Derrida on Learning How to Live," in *The Science, Politics, and Ontology of Life-Philosophy*, ed. Scott M. Campbell and Paul W. Bruno (London: Bloomsbury, 2013), 171–84.
10 Marko Zlomislić, *Jacques Derrida's Aporetic Ethics*, 3. It is certainly uncommon to find a phrase such as "evaluation of the objective evidence" in a book on Derrida!
11 *Jacques Derrida and the Humanities: A Critical Reader*, ed. Tom Cohen (Cambridge: Cambridge University Press, 2001), ix.
12 See Chapter 10.
13 Given the prominent role Spivak played in the reception of Derrida's thought, namely her influential introduction to and translation of Derrida's *Of Grammatology*, her words carry additional weight.
14 Gayatri Chakravorty Spivak, *In Other Worlds: Essays in Cultural Politics* (New York: Methuen, 1987), 113.
15 Ibid.
16 Derrida, *La conférence de Heidelberg*, 80.
17 Jacques Derrida, "Force of Law," in *Acts of Religion*, ed. Gil Anidjar (New York: Routledge, 2001), 235, original emphasis.
18 We see this dynamic of interpretation already in Sartre ("choosing the past"), as will be discussed in Chapter 5.
19 Personal conversation, Stanford University, 1999.
20 Despite the euphony, one must not confuse a "philosophy of the present" with a "philosophy of presence," that is, the "metaphysics of presence" that Derrida seeks to deconstruct.
21 See Martin Hagglund, "The Necessity of Discrimination: Disjoining Derrida and Levinas," *Diacritics* 34, no. 1 (2004): 40: "During the last fifteen years, a standard way of defending deconstruction has been to endow it with an 'ethical motivation.' According to this line of argument, Derrida's undermining of metaphysical presuppositions and totalizing systems emanates from an ethical concern to respect 'the Other.' The most prominent advocates for such a perspective are Robert Bernasconi, Drucilla Cornell, and Simon Critchley. . . . What these readings have in common is that they attempt to assimilate Derrida's thinking of alterity to Emmanuel Levinas's ethical metaphysics."
22 That Derrida was concerned with Heidegger in his earliest work is attested by the recently published seminar at the École Normale Supérieure: Jacques

Derrida, *Heidegger: La question de l'être et l'histoire: Cours à l'ENS-Ulm 1964–1965* (Paris: Galilée, 2013). An English translation by Geoffrey Bennington, *Heidegger: The Question of Being and History*, is due to be published in 2016 by the University of Chicago Press.

23 *The Gadamer Reader: A Bouquet of the Later Writings*, ed. Richard Palmer (Evanston, IL: Northwestern University Press, 2007), 372.

24 Derrida, *Of Spirit: Heidegger and the Question*, trans. Geoffrey Bennington and Rachel Bowlby (Chicago: Chicago University Press, 1991).

25 Although Derrida did offer a direct riposte to Farias in the form of an interview published in the French news weekly *Le Nouvel Observateur* (November 6, 1987), the Heidelberg conference can nevertheless be considered his first extended response to the controversy.

26 Gadamer briefly studied with Heidegger and served as his assistant from 1923 to 1928. Their relationship was strained during the Nazi period, but they drew close again after the war. See Richard Palmer, *The Gadamer Reader*, 356.

27 Peeters, *Derrida*, 384. Peeters is referring to the encounter that took place at the conference "Text and Interpretation," held at the Goethe Institute in Paris on April 25, 1981, which was published in the 1989 compilation *Dialogue and Deconstruction: The Gadamer-Derrida Encounter*, ed. Diane P. Michelfelder and Richard E. Palmer (Albany: SUNY Press, 1989). This book also includes later reflections on the event.

28 See Richard J. Bernstein, "The Conversation That Never Happened (Gadamer/Derrida)," *The Review of Metaphysics* 61, no. 3 (2008): 577–603.

29 Derrida, *La conférence de Heidelberg*, 90.

30 "Among the remarkable range of thinkers to have come under the influence of Martin Heidegger, the figure perhaps most deserving to be regarded as Heidegger's proper and faithful 'heir' has been Hans-Georg Gadamer. Gadamer himself has always been quick to acknowledge the intellectual debt to his predecessor. Although the two men were only eleven years apart in age, their relationship to all appearances was very much one of master and pupil; never does Gadamer seem to take umbrage at being described as a 'Heideggerian.' Indeed, he has characterized himself as a 'student of Heidegger' who has 'learned the craft of classical philology'" (Walter Lammi, "Hans-Georg Gadamer's 'Correction' of Heidegger," *Journal of the History of Ideas* 52, no. 3 [1991]: 487). Nevertheless, during the conference, Gadamer states, "This is also why there are no 'Heideggerians.' Heidegger said it himself several times, and I think he wasn't wrong: the work of those who imitate Heidegger has no philosophical value" (*La conférence de Heidelberg*, 46).

31 See Peeters, *Derrida*, 184–85.

32 Most notably by Alain Renaut and Luc Ferry in their *La pensée 68: Essai sur l'anti-humanisme contemporain* (Paris: Gallimard, 1985), in which they state that "French Heideggerianism can be defined by the formula Derrida = Heidegger + Derrida's style" (*French Philosophy of the Sixties: An Essay on Antihumanism*, trans. Mary H. S. Cattani [Amherst: University of Massachusetts Press, 1990], 123, italics in the original). Derrida makes an oblique reference to this characterization at the conference: "Certaines

'lectures' (ne polémiquons pas trop) qui me présentaient comme heideggérien— à la différence de style, disait-on" (*La conférence de Heidelberg*, 77).

33 Ibid., 76.
34 Ibid., 77, original emphasis. In Heidegger's *Being and Time* (trans. Joan Stambaugh [Albany: SUNY Press, 1996], 176–77), *unheimlich* denotes the angst that befalls *Dasein* when it is jolted out of its normal, everyday mode of social being (or in Heidegger's jargon, jolted out of its "entangled absorption" in the world and its "lostness" in the "they"). Richard Bernstein writes that Derrida "has an uncanny (*unheimlich*) ability to show us that at the heart of what we take to be familiar, native, at home . . . lurks (is concealed and repressed) what is unfamiliar, strange, and uncanny" (*The New Constellation: The Ethical-Political Horizons of Modernity/Postmodernity* [Cambridge, MA: The MIT Press, 1992], 174). See also Samuel Weber, *Inquiétantes singularités* (Paris: Hermann, 2014).
35 Derrida, *La conférence de Heidelberg*, 76–77.
36 Michel Foucault, "The Return of Morality," in *Foucault Live: Collected Interviews, 1961–1984*, ed. Sylvère Lotringer (New York: Semiotext(e), 1989), 470.
37 Derrida, *La conférence de Heidelberg*, 55.
38 See Ethan Kleinberg, *Generation Existential: Heidegger's Philosophy in France 1927–1961* (Ithaca, NY: Cornell University Press, 2005), 157–206.
39 Derrida, *La conférence de Heidelberg*, 65.
40 Ibid.
41 Ibid., 78.
42 Ibid., 66.
43 Ibid.
44 Ibid., 59.
45 Derrida also suffered from anti-Semitic policies during WWII: As a boy, he was expelled from school in Algeria for being Jewish.
46 Ibid., 81, original emphasis. In Derrida's EHESS seminar on hospitality (1996–97), which I attended, he noted the paradoxical nature of the concept of forgiveness: What is forgivable does not require forgiveness; what is unforgivable requires forgiveness, but forgiveness in this case is impossible.
47 Ibid., 52, original emphasis.
48 Most notably, the publication of Heidegger's personal "notebooks." See in particular the forthcoming translation: Martin Heidegger, *Ponderings II-VI: Black Notebooks 1931-1938*, trans. Richard Rojcewicz (Bloomington: Indiana University Press, 2016). Laurence Hemming observes Heidegger's "appalling and reprehensible use, both personally and philosophically, of the language and attitude of anti-Semitism, up to at least the year 1946" (*Notre Dame Philosophical Reviews*, June 2015, review of Thomas Sheehan, *Making Sense of Heidegger: A Paradigm Shift*. On this topic, see also Jean-Luc Nancy's recent book *Banalité de Heidegger* (Paris: Galilée, 2015).
49 Imagine, for example, that the Nazis had tried to attack France in, say, 1935, instead of 1939, before it was ready, and was defeated. A new regime would

have taken over by 1936 and there would have been no Auschwitz. Now, the Nazis would still have been considered thugs and aggressors, and Heidegger would have been criticized for his opportunistic association with them, but in this hypothetical case, he could have easily expressed regret.

50 Derrida, *La conférence de Heidelberg*, 81.
51 Ibid., 81.
52 Ibid., 82, original emphasis. Here Derrida seemingly anticipates his analyses of *héritage* in *Specters of Marx*.
53 Derrida, *La conférence de Heidelberg*, 82.
54 Ibid., 83.
55 See Lyotard, *The Differend: Phrases in Dispute*, trans. Georges Van Den Abbeele (Minneapolis: University of Minnesota Press, 1988).
56 See Robert Doran, *The Theory of the Sublime from Longinus to Kant* (Cambridge: Cambridge University Press, 2015), 213, 218, 226 n.7, 269.
57 Hemming, review of Thomas Sheehan, *Making Sense of Heidegger*.
58 Quoted in Bernstein, *The New Constellation*, 130.
59 Gadamer, *La conférence de Heidelberg*, 49, 51.
60 Richard Rorty, "Taking Philosophy Seriously," a review of Victor Farias's *Heidegger et le nazisme*, *The New Republic* (April 11, 1988).
61 Ibid.
62 Ibid.
63 Ibid.
64 Ibid. At the Heidelberg conference, Gadamer notes that "Heidegger was without doubt a religious thinker" (*La conférence de Heidelberg*, 47).
65 Richard Rorty, "Taking Philosophy Seriously."
66 See Chapter 2.
67 This point is developed by Santiago Zabala in his article "What to Make of Heidegger in 2015?" (https://lareviewofbooks.org/essay/what-to-make-of-heidegger-in-2015).
68 Jean-François Lyotard, *Heidegger and the Jews*, trans. Andreas Michel and Mark Roberts (Minneapolis: University of Minnesota Press, 1990), 59.
69 Rockmore, *On Heidegger's Nazism and Philosophy*, 283. This view is also taken by Emmanuel Faye in his *Heidegger, l'introduction du nazisme dans la philosophie: Autour des séminaires inédits de 1933–1935* (Paris: Le Livre de Poche, 2005/2007).
70 Rockmore, *On Heidegger's Nazism and Philosophy*, 49.
71 Thomas Sheehan contends, for example, that "there's no ethics in Heidegger, and no meaningful political philosophy" (http://news.stanford.edu/news/2015/july/paradigm-heidegger-sheehan-070815.html).
72 Julian Young, *Heidegger, Philosophy, Nazism* (Cambridge: Cambridge University Press, 1997), 214, original emphasis.
73 Ibid, 214–15. One of these texts is certainly the *Introduction to Metaphysics* (1935), in which Heidegger refers to Nazism's "inner truth and greatness"

(see the "Revised and Expanded Translation" by Gregory Fried and Richard Polt [New Haven, CT: Yale University Press, 2014], xx).

74 Rockmore talks about Derrida's "defense of Heidegger," which he finds "unconvincing," since it "trivializes Heidegger's commitment to Nazism" (*On Heidegger's Nazism and Philosophy*, 274): "According to Derrida, in his still metaphysical phase Heidegger turned to Nazism, which he renounced in his later move away from metaphysics and beyond philosophy" (ibid., 273).

75 Derrida, *La conférence de Heidelberg*, 63.

76 Ibid.

77 Ibid.

78 See Alfred Bäumler, *Nietzsche, der Philosoph und Politiker* (Leipzig: Reclam, 1931).

79 Derrida, *La conférence de Heidelberg*, 82.

80 See Rockmore, *On Heidegger's Nazism and Philosophy*, 47–48.

81 In a personal e-mail dated November 29, 2015, Hayden White noted (in reaction to this chapter) that "I think that the one thing that has not been done is to treat Nazism's 'philosophical base,' as discerned by Heidegger, as a defensible position. Anti-Semitism and certainly the Holocaust are not necessarily connected to this base, are they?"

82 Derrida, *La conférence de Heidelberg*, 83.

83 Ibid., 102–03.

84 Howells, *Derrida*, 126.

85 Derrida, *La conférence de Heidelberg*, 67.

86 Ibid., 126. Derrida will repeat this formula in "Force of Law": "A decision that would not go through the test and ordeal of the undecidable would not be a free decision; it would only be a programmable application or continuous unfolding of a calculable process" (252).

87 Derrida, "Force of Law," 242, italics in the original.

88 "Nietzsche and the Machine: Interview with Jacques Derrida," *Journal of Nietzsche Studies* 7 (1994): 37.

89 Jean-Paul Sartre, "Existentialism Is a Humanism" (https://www.marxists.org/reference/archive/sartre/works/exist/sartre.htm).

90 Derrida notes at the conference that "I became interested in Heidegger through Sartre and Merleau-Ponty" (*La conférence de Heidelberg*, 61).

91 Derrida, *La conférence de Heidelberg*, 103.

92 Ibid.

93 Ibid., 67–68.

94 Ibid., 125.

95 However, in his 1964–65 lecture course on Heidegger (published in 2013), Derrida makes a distinction between "the question of being" and "ontology": "I say *la question de l'être* and not *ontologie*, since the word *ontologie* will reveal itself to be more and more inadequate as we advance further on the path to Heidegger, to designate what is in question in Heidegger when it is a question of being" (*Heidegger: La question de l'être et l'histoire*, 23, my translation).

96 Derrida, *La conférence de Heidelberg*, 112.

97 Derrida remarks, "Heidegger spoke constantly about responsibility, about responding to the call of being" (ibid., 124).

98 Ibid., 111–12.

99 "How to reconcile the act of justice that must always concern singularity, individuals, groups, irreplaceable existences, or myself *as* other, in a unique situation, with rule, norm, value, or the imperative of justice that necessarily have a general form?" (Derrida, "Force of Law," 245, original emphasis).

100 "In *Being and Time*, [Heidegger] passes from a chapter where he was dealing with being-toward-death to a chapter on conscience (*Gewissen*), the call (*Ruf*), responsibility in the face of the call, and even responsibility as originary guilt (*Schuldigsein*)" (Derrida, *The Gift of Death*, 41). David Wills notes that "in spite of the seeming new or 'ethical' turn in Derrida's work of the last decade or so, the concerns of a text like *The Gift of Death* can be seen to inform, as promise if nothing else, much he has written since the second half of the 1970s" (*Matchbook: Essays in Deconstruction* [Stanford, CA: Stanford University Press, 2005], 114).

101 Derrida, *La conférence de Heidelberg*, 112 ("Je crois que la question est celle de la responsabilité, je crois que le passage par la médiation heideggerienne sur la responsabilité est un passage obligé, c'est un passage dans lequel je n'ai pas cru pouvoir m'arrêter, et donc la question de la responsabilité reste ouverte").

102 Derrida made this statement at a conference (which I attended) held at La Maison Heinrich Heine in Paris in the late 1990s.

103 Howells says as much when she writes that "Derrida is careful in these later works to spell out that deconstruction is not in any way a nihilistic undermining of truth, but rather an exploration of the prejudices and preconceptions that underlie much of what we generally accept without question" (*Derrida*, 154). However, this statement could apply equally well (and perhaps better) to Foucault.

104 Bernstein, *The New Constellation*, 187, original emphasis.

105 Derrida, *Writing and Difference*, 111.

Chapter 4

1 Richard Rorty, *Contingency, Irony, and Solidarity* (Cambridge: Cambridge University Press, 1989), 96.

2 Ibid., 83.

3 Ibid., xiv.

4 Ibid., 84.

5 As far as I can tell, Hayden White seems to have coined the term *cultural politics* in his review of Edward Said's *Beginnings: Intention and Method*. See White, "Criticism as Cultural Politics," *Diacritics* 6, no. 3 (1976): 8–13.

6   See David L. Hall's chapter "Holding One's Time in Thought" in his *Richard Rorty: Prophet and Poet of the New Pragmatism* (Albany: SUNY Press, 1994), 11–64.
7   G. W. F. Hegel, *Elements of the Philosophy of Right*, ed. Allen Wood (Cambridge: Cambridge University Press, 1991), 21, original emphasis.
8   Richard Rorty, *Philosophy as Cultural Politics* (Cambridge: Cambridge University Press, 2007), ix.
9   Richard Rorty, *Philosophy and the Mirror of Nature* (Princeton, NJ: Princeton University Press, 1979), 389–94. The book was republished in a thirtieth-anniversary edition in 2009.
10 Rorty, *Philosophy as Cultural Politics*, x.
11 Rorty, *Contingency, Irony, and Solidarity*, 125. In the 1980s, Rorty liked to contrast the more academic Derrida of the 1960s with the "later" Derrida of *Glas* (1974) and *The Post Card* (1980): "The later Derrida privatizes his philosophical thinking, and thereby breaks down the tension between ironism and theorizing. He simply drops theory" (Rorty, *Contingency, Irony, and Solidarity*, 125). But then, of course, as I explore in Chapter 3, Derrida undergoes an "ethical turn" of sorts, as he focuses on ethical themes such as law, justice, and forgiveness in the 1990s.
12 Rorty, *Philosophy as Cultural Politics*, 129.
13 Collected in Rorty, *Philosophy as Cultural Politics*, 89–104.
14 Collected in *The Rorty Reader*, ed. Christopher J. Voparil and Richard J. Bernstein (Oxford: Wiley-Blackwell, 2010), 389–406.
15 See Ulf Schulenberg, *Romanticism and Pragmatism: Richard Rorty and the Idea of a Poeticized Culture* (Basingstoke: Palgrave Macmillan, 2015), 31–41.
16 Rorty, *Contingency, Irony, and Solidarity*, 40.
17 See C. P. Snow, *The Two Cultures* (Cambridge: Cambridge University Press, 1959/2012).
18 Rorty, *Philosophy as Cultural Politics*, 94.
19 See the interview "Toward a Postmetaphysical Culture," in *Take Care of Freedom and Truth Will Take Care of Itself: Interviews with Richard Rorty*, ed. Eduardo Mendicta (Stanford, CA: Stanford University Press, 2006), 46–55.
20 Rorty, *Philosophy as Cultural Politics*, 91.
21 Ibid., 90.
22 Martin Heidegger, *Being and Time: A Translation of* Sein und Zeit, trans. Joan Stambaugh (Albany: SUNY Press, 1996), 119, original emphasis.
23 Heidegger often insists that his concept of *das Man* is value neutral; it is what we all are on the most basic, everyday level. Thus even the most authentic person (including Heidegger himself!) possesses a they-self that is ineluctable.
24 Ibid., 177.
25 Rorty, *Contingency, Irony, and Solidarity*, 142–43, original emphasis.
26 Schulenberg, *Romanticism and Pragmatism*, 38.
27 See Chapter 2.

28 Martin Heidegger, *Introduction to Metaphysics*, trans. Ralph Manheim (New Haven, CT: Yale University Press, 1959), 45. Rorty, in fact, cites and comments on this passage in his *Consequences of Pragmatism* (Minneapolis: University of Minnesota Press, 1982), 47–48.

29 "For people who work for the minimum wage, which is going to be more and more of America, there is no future. Sooner or later there will be a populist upheaval, probably from the fascist right" (Rorty, "There is a Crisis Coming," in *Take Care of Freedom and Truth Will Take Care of Itself*, 62).

30 From the manuscript version of "Philosophy as a Transitional Genre," although the last sentence does appear in Rorty, *Philosophy as Cultural Politics*, 95.

31 Ibid., 90.

32 Richard Rorty, *Essays on Heidegger and Others: Philosophical Papers Volume 2* (Cambridge: Cambridge University Press, 1991), 85.

33 See Chapter 10 on Said.

34 Ibid.

35 Richard Rorty, "On Philosophy and Politics," in *Take Care of Freedom and Truth Will Take Care of Itself*, 98.

36 See Chapter 7 on Girard and Sartre. Although Girard's notion of "novelistic conversion," with its overtly Christian-religious overtones, is quite different from what Rorty has in mind, at least one commentator has written about a convergence between the two thinkers. See Andrew J. McKenna, "Rorty, Girard, and the Novel," *Renascence* 55, no. 4 (2003): 293–313.

37 Rorty, *Philosophy as Cultural Politics*, 102.

38 Ibid., 89.

39 Richard Rorty, "There Is a Crisis Coming," in *Take Care of Freedom and Truth Will Take Care of Itself*, 64.

40 I think Rorty is using the term "genre" in the way that, for example, ancient rhetorical treatises understood the categories of philosophy, history, oratory, poetry, and so on, namely as different types of artistic writing (which in turn include various subgenres, e.g., lyric poetry, epic poetry). But with the advent of the modern term "literature," which can indeed encompass the writings of Plato, Herodotus, Demosthenes, Homer, and so on, things get a bit muddy. "Literature" can mean artistic writing on any topic or only imaginative writing (poetry, fiction).

41 Rorty, *Philosophy as Cultural Politics*, 91.

42 See the introduction and Chapter 10.

43 Rorty, *Contingency, Irony, and Solidarity*, 141.

44 Ibid., 146.

45 Ibid., 141.

46 Ibid., 144.

47 As in Nietzsche's famous Untimely Meditation "On the Use and Disadvantage of History for Life" ("Vom Nutzen und Nachteil der Historie für das Leben," 1874). See Robert Doran, "Nietzsche: Utility, Aesthetics, History," *Comparative Literature Studies* 37, no. 3 (2000): 321–43 (which was actually originally written as a seminar paper for Rorty's class "Romantic Utilitarianism: Nietzsche and James," which I took in fall 1998 at Stanford University).

48 Rorty, *Contingency, Irony, and Solidarity*, 143–44.

49 Ibid., 144.

50 Ibid., 141.

51 Bloom was at Yale University when deconstruction first burst on the scene. See the recently published book by Marc Redfield: *Theory at Yale: The Strange Case of Deconstruction in America* (New York: Fordham University Press, 2016).

52 Rorty, "Redemption from Egotism," in *The Rorty Reader*, 389.

53 Ibid., 396.

54 Ibid., 393.

55 Ibid.

56 Ibid., 403.

57 See Chapter 8.

58 Aristotle, *Poetics*, trans. Stephen Halliwell, in *Aristotle* Poetics, *Longinus* On the Sublime, *Demetrius* On Style (Cambridge, MA: Harvard University Press, 1995, Loeb Classical Library), 59.

59 See Chapters 8 and 9 of this volume.

60 Rorty, "Redemption from Egotism," in *The Rorty Reader*, 394–95.

61 Jean-Paul Sartre, "Existentialism Is a Humanism" (https://www.marxists.org/reference/archive/sartre/works/exist/sartre.htm).

62 Tzvetan Todorov, "What Is Literature For?" *New Literary History* 38, no. 1 (2007): 27.

63 Rorty, "Redemption from Egotism" in *The Rorty Reader*, 395.

64 See Chapter 8.

65 "The person who hopes to render more confident moral judgments as a result of the study of religious or philosophical treatises is usually hoping to find a principle that will permit of application to concrete cases, for an algorithm that will resolve moral dilemmas. But the person who hopes for greater sensitivity just wants to develop the know-how that will let him make the best of what is always likely to be a pretty bad job—a situation in which people are likely to get hurt, no matter what decision is taken" (ibid.).

66 Ibid., 405.

67 See Chapter 2.

68 Friedrich Nietzsche, *The Gay Science* (New York: Vintage Books, 1974), 232, original italics.

69 Friedrich Nietzsche, *Twilight of the Idols/The Anti-Christ*, trans. R. J. Hollingdale (New York: Penguin Books, 1990), 163.

70 Rorty, "Redemption from Egotism," in *The Rorty Reader*, 390.
71 See Chapter 2.
72 See Chapter 1.
73 "A further reason why my cultural politics, and therefore my account of the relation between philosophy and the novel . . ." (ibid., 402).
74 Schulenberg, *Romanticism and Pragmatism*, 163.
75 Ibid.
76 Rorty, *Contingency, Irony, Solidarity*, 83.
77 "Everything Sartre wrote, up to *Critique of Dialectical Reason*, is full of interesting ideas" (Rorty, "On Philosophy and Politics," in *Take Care of Freedom and Truth Will Take Care of Itself*, 94).
78 Rorty, "There Is a Crisis Coming," in ibid., 61.
79 Colin Koopman, "Challenging Philosophy: Rorty's Positive Conception of Philosophy as Cultural Criticism," in *Richard Rorty: From Pragmatist Philosophy to Cultural Politics*, ed. Alexander Groeschner, Colin Koopman, and Mike Sandbothe (London: Bloomsbury, 2013), 81.
80 Ibid., 80–81.
81 Ibid., 99.
82 Rorty, *Contingency, Irony, Solidarity*, 120–21.
83 Richard Shusterman, *Pragmatist Aesthetics: Living Beauty, Rethinking Art*, 2nd edn (Lanham, MD: Rowman & Littlefield, 2000), 253.
84 Ibid., 254.
85 Ibid., 257.
86 Ibid., 259.
87 Personal e-mail of January 11, 2016.
88 Schulenberg, *Romanticism and Pragmatism*, 33.
89 Rorty, "On Philosophy and Politics," in *Take Care of Freedom and Truth Will Take Care of Itself*, 96. Unfortunately, there is no date given for this interview, but the editor, Eduardo Mendieta, wrote me the following: "[It] was unpublished when I printed it in my book. . . . I think this interview was conducted during the Spring and Summer of 2000, when the presidential campaign is raging" (personal email of June 13, 2016).
90 See Michel Foucault, "The Ethics of the Concern of the Self as a Practice of Freedom" (1984), in Foucault, *Ethics: Subjectivity and Truth*, ed. Paul Rabinow (New York: The New Press, 1997), 281–301.
91 See Pierre Hadot, *Philosophy as a Way of Life: Spiritual Exercises from Socrates to Foucault*, ed. and intro. Arnold I. Davidson, trans. Michael Chase (Oxford: Blackwell, 1995). Rorty was probably more directly inspired by his friend Alexander Nehamas, in particular his *The Art of Living: Socratic Reflections from Plato to Foucault* (Berkeley and Los Angeles: University of California Press, 1998). (Rorty assigned Nehamas's book *Nietzsche: Life as Literature* [Cambridge, MA: Harvard University Press, 1985] as recommended reading in the aforementioned seminar [note 47] at Stanford University in 1998.)
92 See the conclusion to Chapter 2.

Chapter 5

1. Hayden White, *The Fiction of Narrative: Essays on History, Literature, and Theory, 1957–2007*, ed. Robert Doran (Baltimore: Johns Hopkins University Press, 2010), 135.
2. Herman Paul's book, *Hayden White: The Historical Imagination* (Cambridge: Polity Press, 2011), does examine somewhat the role of existentialism in White's thought. However, there is no analysis of how Sartre's philosophy specifically relates to White.
3. Hayden White, *Metahistory: The Historical Imagination in Nineteenth-Century Europe* (Baltimore: Johns Hopkins University Press, 1973). *Metahistory* is now available in a fiftieth anniversary edition (2014) with a new preface by Hayden White and a foreword by Michael Roth.
4. F. R. Ankersmit, "A Plea for a Cognitivist Approach to White's Tropology," in *Philosophy of History After Hayden White*, ed. Robert Doran (London: Bloomsbury: 2013/15), 48.
5. "The Burden of History" is collected in *Tropics of Discourse: Essays in Cultural Criticism* (Baltimore: Johns Hopkins University Press, 1978), 27–50. "What Is a Historical System?" is collected in *The Fiction of Narrative*, 126–35.
6. "The Burden of History," *History and Theory* 5, no. 2 (1966): 111–34.
7. However, we must keep in mind that White's essay was written a few years *before* the poststructuralist explosion with which White, rightly or wrongly, would come to be identified (and before Roland Barthes's seminal essay "Le discours de l'histoire," published in *Social Science Information* 6 [1967]: 63–75). Thus White's examples of avant-garde, antihistoricist French thought in this essay are Camus and Sartre rather than Foucault, Barthes, and Derrida.
8. The essay also attracted attention in literary studies: It was anthologized in the popular textbook collection *Critical Theory Since 1965*, published in 1986, in effect canonizing White as one of the progenitors of the Theory movement in the United States.
9. The essay first appeared in *Biology, History, and Natural Philosophy*, ed. Allen D. Breck and Wolfgang Yourgrau (New York: Plenum Press, 1972), 233–42.
10. In an interview, White notes that "Like [Fredric] Jameson, my formation was in existentialism. As a young man I was completely swept into the Jean-Paul Sartre world and Nietzsche" (Angelica Koufou and Miliori Margarita, "The Ironic Poetics of Late Modernity. An Interview with Hayden White," *Historein* 2 [2000], http://www.historein.gr/vol2_interview.htm, accessed January 28, 2013). Fredric Jameson's doctoral dissertation and first book were on Sartre (*Sartre: The Origins of a Style*, 1961). Arthur Danto, who studied with the same undergraduate history professor as White at Wayne State (William J. Bossenbrook), published *Jean-Paul Sartre* in 1975.
11. Jean-Paul Sartre, *Being and Nothingness: A Phenomenological Essay on Ontology*, trans. Hazel Barnes (New York: Washington Square Press, 1956), 621.
12. See Robert Doran, editor's introduction to White, *The Fiction of Narrative*, xxv–xxxii.

13 Sartre, *Being and Nothingness*, 643.
14 Ibid.
15 Ibid.
16 Ibid.
17 White observes that "what Andreas Hillgruber and Ernst Nolte called 'the pleasures of narration' was advanced in the cause of redeeming a 'portion' of the German past deemed worthy of being narrated and narrated as a drama of fulfillment rather than of degradation and degeneracy" ("History as Fulfillment," in *Philosophy of History After Hayden White*, 42–43).
18 Sartre, *Being and Nothingness*, 640, original emphasis.
19 See Robert Doran, "The Work of Hayden White I: Mimesis, Figuration, and the Writing of History," in *The Sage Handbook of Historical Theory*, ed. Nancy Partner and Sarah Foot (London: Sage Publications, 2013), 106–18.
20 Sartre, *Being and Nothingness*, 643, original emphasis.
21 White says as much when he writes, "I fail to see how the operations of the ordinary historian differ in principle from those of the speculative philosopher of history, even with respect to the matter of the attempt to predict the future. It seems just as questionable to me to maintain, even implicitly, as the 'ordinary historian' characteristically does, that the forces at work in the past or the present will be different in the future as it is to assume a uniformitarian posture and to seek, by reflection on past and present historical processes, to discern the general form that the future will assume" (*The Fiction of Narrative*, 145).
22 White, *Tropics of Discourse*, 39.
23 See Hayden White, *The Practical Past* (Evanston, IL: Northwestern University Press, 2014).
24 See White's essay "Postmodernism and Textual Anxieties," in *The Fiction of Narrative*, 304–17.
25 White, *Tropics of Discourse*, 41.
26 White, *The Fiction of Narrative*, 132, original emphasis.
27 Ibid., original emphasis.
28 Ibid., original emphasis.
29 Ibid., 135.
30 Martin Heidegger, *Being and Time: A Translation of* Sein und Zeit, trans. Joan Stambaugh (Albany: SUNY Press, 1996), 352–53, original emphasis.
31 Richard Rorty, *Philosophy as Cultural Politics* (Cambridge: Cambridge University Press, 2007), 90, original emphasis. See Chapter 4.
32 Gianni Vattimo, "From the Problem of Evil to Hermeneutic Philosophy of History: For Hayden White," in *Philosophy of History After Hayden White*, 207.
33 Ibid., 204. Thus Vattimo's contention that "the past is not an immutable datum ... but a call, a message that always addresses itself to the projectural capacity [*capacità progettuale*] of the one who receives it and who actively interprets it" (ibid., 206) is certainly redolent of White's figural hermeneutics, and particularly of its existentialist dimension in the language of the "project."

34 See Gianni Vattimo and Santiago Zabala, *Hermeneutic Communism: From Heidegger to Marx* (New York: Columbia University Press, 2011).
35 See Hayden White, "The Practical Past," in *The Practical Past*, 3–24.
36 Ibid., 9.
37 White, "The Practical Past," manuscript version (this passage does not appear in the published version).
38 White, "The Practical Past," in *The Practical Past*, 16–17.
39 *The Uses of History: Essays in Intellectual and Social History. Presented to William J. Bossenbrook*, ed. Hayden V. White (Detroit: Wayne State University Press, 1968), 11.
40 In his essay "History as Fulfillment" (*Philosophy of History After Hayden White*, 41), White criticizes the idea of historians as "the passive receivers and forwarders of [historical] messages."
41 White, *Metahistory*, 281.
42 It should be said that there is nothing exclusively or particularly tropological about historical discourse; tropology is a theory of discourse *tout court*.
43 White, *Metahistory*, xi.
44 Or, in David Carr's felicitous phrase, "metaphilosophy of history": "This project, it seems to me, deserves to be called something other than 'metahistory,' which many people now use as a generic term for the analysis of works of history; I suggest metaphilosophy of history, or the philosophy of the philosophy of history" ("Metaphilosophy of History," in *Re-figuring Hayden White*, ed. F. R. Ankersmit, Ewa Domanska, and Hans Kellner [Stanford, CA: Stanford University Press, 2009], 17).
45 Harry Harootunian, "Uneven Temporalities/Untimely Pasts: Hayden White and the Question of Temporal Form," *Philosophy of History After Hayden White*, 120.
46 White, *Metahistory*, xi.
47 Ibid., 427–28.
48 Christopher Dawson, *The Dynamics of World History*, ed. John J. Mulloy (New York: Sheed & Ward, 1956), 289.
49 Leopold von Ranke (1795–1886) sought to professionalize the study of history by grounding it in a rigorous, empirical approach to the past, that is, one based on primary sources and archival research. As Ranke famously stated, the historian should aspire to present the past "as it really was," which meant restricting oneself as much as possible to the particulars, to the "facts," while purging historical writing of all fictional, dilettantish, and extrinsic elements.
50 Ibid., 282.
51 Ibid., 283.
52 Ibid.
53 White, *The Fiction of Narrative*, 144.
54 White, *Metahistory*, xii, original emphasis.

55 Our knowledge of Sartre's ethical thought largely derives from his posthumously published *Notebooks for an Ethics*, which appeared well after White's groundbreaking work of the 1970s.

56 White, "History as Fulfillment," in *Philosophy of History After Hayden White*, 39.

57 Hayden White, *The Content of the Form: Narrative Discourse and Historical Representation* (Baltimore: Johns Hopkins University Press, 1987).

58 Nancy Partner makes the point that "formal fiction" should be distinguished from "fictional invention": "Only the *formal fictions*—for example, significant event, plot, narrative structure, closure, all the artifacts of intelligibility created by language and imposed on the formless seriatim of experience—fill the category of 'the fictions of history' in modern lit. crit. discourse, the area Hayden White brought forward so strongly in *Metahistory*" ("Historicity in an Age of Reality-Fictions," in *A New Philosophy of History*, ed. F. R. Ankersmit and Hans Kellner [Chicago: Chicago University Press, 1995], 24, original emphasis).

59 Hayden White, *Figural Realism: Studies in the Mimesis Effect* (Baltimore: Johns Hopkins University Press, 1999), 9.

60 See Chapters 8 and 9 of this volume.

61 Quoted in White, *The Fiction of Narrative*, 270.

62 White, "History as Fulfillment," in *Philosophy of History After Hayden White*, 42.

63 Søren Kierkegaard, *Fear and Trembling/Repetition*, trans. Howard V. Hong and Edna H. Hong (Princeton, NJ: Princeton University Press, 1983), 149.

64 White, *The Fiction of Narrative*, 270–71.

65 Gabrielle Spiegel, "Rhetorical Theory/Theoretical Rhetoric: Some Ambiguities in the Reception of Hayden White's Work," in *Philosophy of History After Hayden White*, 182.

66 White, *Tropics of Discourse*, 23.

Chapter 6

1 Gabrielle M. Spiegel, "Above, About and Beyond the Writing of History: A Retrospective View of Hayden White's *Metahistory* on the 40th Anniversary of its Publication," *Rethinking History* 17, no. 4 (2013): 497.

2 "The new interpretations of White's *Metahistory*, in particular that of Doran (2010, 2013), Moses (2005), and especially Herman Paul in his recently published intellectual biography *Hayden White: The Historical Imagination* (London: Polity Press, 2011), stress the ways in which 'tropes' . . . were directed at liberating historical consciousness from 'the paralyzing effects of bourgeois modes of realism' characteristic of traditional historical writing in order to endow the historian with the freedom to choose a desired, and morally desirable, future" (ibid., 495). The works of mine Spiegel refers to are Robert Doran, "Humanism, Formalism, and the Discourse of History," editor's introduction to Hayden White,

The Fiction of Narrative: Essays on History, Literature, and Theory, 1957–2007 (Baltimore and London: Johns Hopkins University Press, 2010), xiii–xxxii; and Robert Doran, "Choosing the Past: Hayden White and the Philosophy of History," editor's introduction to *Philosophy of History after Hayden White* (London: Bloomsbury, 2013), 1–33 (Chapter 5 is an adapted version of this introduction). See also the valuable anthology *The Ethics of History*, ed. David Carr, Thomas R. Flynn, and Rudolf A. Makkreel (Evanston, IL: Northwestern University Press, 2004).

3. Hayden White, *Metahistory: The Historical Imagination in Nineteenth-Century Europe* (Baltimore: Johns Hopkins University Press, 1973), 427. *Metahistory* is now available in a fiftieth anniversary edition (2014), with a new preface by Hayden White and a foreword by Michael Roth.

4. See White, *Figural Realism: Studies in the Mimesis Effect* (Baltimore: Johns Hopkins University Press, 1999).

5. I prefer the term *objectivism* instead of *realism*, since part of White's project is precisely to redefine what realism means in historiography (which is something quite different than in philosophy), thereby effecting a rapprochement with literary realism.

6. In short, White contends that narrative form imposes a conceptual form on historical discourse.

7. White, *Metahistory*, xii, original emphasis. As I point out in Chapter 5, this phrase is really a restatement of Sartre's dictum "man is condemned to be free," which raises the question of historiological "bad faith" to which I alluded earlier.

8. Hayden White, *The Practical Past* (Evanston, IL: Northwestern University Press, 2014), 102. This (existential) combination of the ethical and the aesthetic recalls Foucault's "ethics of the self," analyzed in Chapter 2.

9. White, *Metahistory*, xii.

10. Ibid., 433.

11. Hans Kellner, "Hopeful Monsters or, The Unfulfilled Figure in Hayden White's Conceptual System," in *Philosophy of History after Hayden White*, 157.

12. This point is confirmed rather than denied by Gianni Vattimo's recent redefinition of nihilism, which seemingly aligns it with White's metahistorical irony. On the back flap of his book *Nihilism and Emancipation: Ethics, Politics, & Law* (New York: Columbia University Press, 2004), one finds: "Nihilism is not the absence of meaning but a recognition of a plurality of meanings; it is not the end of civilization but the beginning of new social paradigms." As such, nihilism is an "ethical doctrine," according to Vattimo.

13. White, *Metahistory*, 433–34.

14. Nevertheless, metahistorical formalism embraces contingency, whereas objectivism seeks to eliminate it.

15. Ibid., 376.

16. Ibid.

17. See Bernard Reginster, *The Affirmation of Life: Nietzsche on Overcoming Nihilism* (Cambridge, MA: Harvard University Press, 2006).

18 White, *The Practical Past*, 20.

19 Dirk Moses, "The Public Relevance of Historical Studies: A Rejoinder to Hayden White," *History and Theory* 44, no. 3 (2005): 339.

20 Personal e-mail sent to me on July 16, 2012. Spiegel also notes in her essay "Above, About and Beyond the Writing of History" (34) that "Kalle Pihlainen has recently argued that 'White's thinking does not lead to a moral relativism, even if similar positions are held to do so. . . . Placing responsibility for choices at the door of each individual can be an effective way of achieving social responsibility, even if it involves risk'"—to which Spiegel responds, "But is this a risk we are or should be willing to take?"

21 "Conversations with Jean-Paul Sartre," in Simone de Beauvoir, *Adieux* (New York: Pantheon, 1984), 439.

22 See Chapter 10 on Said, especially the last few paragraphs.

23 The conference proceedings were published under the title *Probing the Limits of Representation: Nazism and the "Final Solution,"* ed. Saul Friedlander (Cambridge, MA: Harvard University Press, 1992).

24 The essay, originally published in *Critical Inquiry* 9, no. 1 (1982): 113–37, is collected in *The Content of the Form: Narrative Discourse and Historical Representation* (Baltimore: Johns Hopkins University Press, 1987), 58–82.

25 Cited in Ginzburg, "Just One Witness," in *Probing the Limits of Representation*, 92.

26 Ibid.

27 Ginzburg speaks of the "moral dilemma involved in White's approach" (ibid.).

28 White, *Figural Realism*, 70.

29 As cited in Ginzburg, "Just One Witness," 93.

30 White, *Figural Realism*, 9.

31 Of course, one could accuse White of collapsing the distinction between history and mythology, and in some sense he does (as does Roland Barthes, for example). The distinction for White is rooted in the factual verifiability and professional norms that lend modern historiography its current prestige.

32 As cited in Ginzburg, "Just One Witness," 93, original emphasis.

33 In the same way, a work of fiction can appear true, even if it contains few actual or historical events. Thus, as Balzac announces famously at the beginning of his 1835 novel *Le père Goriot* (Paris: Larousse, 2007), 22: "Ce drame n'est ni une fiction, ni un roman. *All is true*, il est si véritable, que chacun peut en reconnaitre les éléments chez soi, dans son coeur peut-être" (This drama is neither a fiction nor a romance! *All is true*,—so true, that everyone can discern the elements of the tragedy in his own house, perhaps in his own heart [http://www.gutenberg.org/files/1237/1237-h/1237-h.htm, accessed April 2, 2014]).

34 Ginzburg, "Just One Witness," 93.

35 The liberal-capitalist metanarrative is thus more effective to the extent that it accepts science, scholarly consensus, democratic processes, and so on. The debate over climate change is the exception that proves the rule, since even the detractors ostensibly appeal to science ("it's unsettled!") for the justification of their views.

36 See White's *Metahistory*, introduction.
37 Martin Jay, in his contribution to the Holocaust volume ("Of Plots, Witnesses, and Judgments," in *Probing the Limits of Representation*, 97–107), wonders why White does not simply "follow Nietzsche and boldly deny the very existence of an ontological realm of events or facts prior to their reconstruction, thus frankly embracing the radical relativism that haunts White's project and which he wants to exorcise" (97).
38 White, *The Fiction of Narrative*, 232. White derives his notion of "singular existential statements" from the philosopher Arthur Danto.
39 F. R. Ankersmit, *Meaning, Truth, and Reference in Historical Representation* (Ithaca, NY: Cornell University Press, 2012), 69. See as well the wide-ranging discussion of White in the context of the fact/fiction debate in Françoise Lavacot, *Fait et fiction: Pour une frontière* (Paris: Seuil, 2016), 64–90.
40 Ginzburg, "Just One Witness," 93.
41 Martin Heidegger, *Being and Time*, trans. J. Stambaugh (Albany: SUNY Press, 2010), 197, original emphasis.

Chapter 7

1 Wolfgang Palaver devotes two short sections to Sartre's influence in his magisterial *René Girard's Mimetic Theory*, trans. Gabriel Borrud (East Lansing: Michigan State University Press, 2013), 73–78, 82–88. However, while Sartre's name or concepts are mentioned fourteen times in *Deceit, Desire, and the Novel*, no one, to my knowledge, has ever written an essay on Girard and Sartre. Chris Fleming's otherwise excellent study of Girard's oeuvre (*René Girard: Violence and Mimesis* [Cambridge: Polity Press, 2004]), refers only once to Sartre, and only to his early novel *Nausea*. Sartre is completely absent from Michael Kirwan's *Discovering Girard* (Cambridge, MA: Cowley Press, 2005) and is mentioned twice in passing in Kirwin's *Girard and Theology* (London: T & T Clark, 2009). Some even dismiss Sartre's influence: "After the completion of his doctorate, Girard began to take interest in Jean-Paul Sartre's work. Although on a personal level Girard is still very much interested in Sartre's philosophy, it has had little influence on his thought" (Gabriel Andrade, "René Girard [1923-2015]," *Internet Encyclopedia of Philosophy*, http://www.iep.utm.edu/girard/). Nothing could be further from the truth!
2 Personal conversation with Girard.
3 See, in particular, the following essays by Girard: "Existentialism and Criticism," *Yale French Studies* 16 (1956): 45–52; "Où va le roman?" *French Review* 30 (1957): 201–06 (translated by Robert Doran as "The Future of the Novel," *Contagion* 19 [2012]: 1–8); "L'anti-héros et les salauds," *Mercure de France* 353 (1965): 422–49 (translated by Robert Doran as "Bastards and the Antihero in Sartre," in René Girard, *Mimesis and Theory: Essays on Literature and Criticism, 1953–2005*, ed. Robert Doran [Stanford, CA: Stanford University Press, 2008], 134–59); "À propos de Jean-Paul Sartre: Rupture et création littéraire," in *Chemins actuels de la critique*, ed. G. Poulet (Paris: Plon, 1967), 223–41 (translated by Robert Doran as "Rupture and Literary Creation in Jean-Paul Sartre," *Contagion* 22 [2015]: 1–15).

4 René Girard, *Mensonge romantique et vérité romanesque* (Paris: Grasset, 1961), translated by Yvonne Freccero as *Deceit, Desire, and the Novel: Self and Other in Literary Structure* (Baltimore: Johns Hopkins University Press, 1965). The title can be literally rendered as *Romantic Lie and Novelistic Truth*, "romantic lie" referring to the interpretation of desire as having its origin in the individual, "novelistic truth" to the unmasking of this self-deception by the great modern writers.

5 René Girard, *La conversion de l'art* (Paris: Carnets Nord, 2008 [Paris : Flammarion, 2010]), 19, my translation.

6 See my editor's introduction, "Literature as Theory," in Girard, *Mimesis and Theory*, xi–xxvi.

7 Girard also refers to imitative desire as *acquisitive mimesis*, which he opposes to the good, nonacquisitive form of mimesis, of which the paradigmatic example is the *imitatio Christi*—the imitation of Christ. See "Violence Renounced: A Response by René Girard," in *Violence Renounced: René Girard, Biblical Studies, and Peacemaking*, ed. Willard M. Swartley (Telford, PA: Pandora Press, 2000), chapter 14.

8 See the first chapter of *Deceit, Desire, and the Novel*.

9 See Robert Doran, "Imitation and Originality: Creative Mimesis in Longinus, Kant, and Girard," in *René Girard and Creative Mimesis*, ed. Vern Neufeld Redekop and Thomas Ryba (Plymouth: Lexington Books, 2014), 111–22.

10 The preceding paragraph was adapted from my editor's introduction to René Girard, *Mimesis and Theory*.

11 René Girard, *La Conversion de l'art*, 19, my translation.

12 Jean-Paul Sartre, *Being and Nothingness: A Phenomenological Essay on Ontology*, trans. Hazel Barnes (New York: Washington Square Press, 1956), 101–02, original emphasis.

13 Ibid., 353.

14 See Chapter 5 for an application of this idea to history.

15 René Girard, "Marivaudage, Hypocrisy, and Bad Faith," in *Mimesis and Theory*, 75.

16 I analyzed bad faith in Chapter 5 of this volume.

17 Sartre, *Being and Nothingness*, 137.

18 Girard, *Deceit, Desire, and the Novel*, 53, original emphasis.

19 René Girard, *When These Things Begin: Conversations with Michel Treguer*, trans. Trevor Cribben Merrill (East Lansing: Michigan State University Press, 2014), 12.

20 Sartre, *Being and Nothingness*, 140.

21 Ibid.

22 Jean-Paul Sartre, *Notebooks for an Ethics*, trans. David Pellauer (Chicago: University of Chicago Press, 1992), 472.

23 Girard, *Deceit, Desire, and the Novel*, 158.

24 Girard, *Mimesis and Theory*, 57, my emphasis, except for "metaphysical."

25 Girard was inspired by Max Scheler's 1915 book *Ressentiment* (trans. Lewis B. Coser and William W. Holdheim [Milwaukee, WI: Marquette University Press, 1961/94]), using a quotation from the book as the epigraph for the original French version of *Deceit, Desire, and the Novel*: "L'homme possède ou un Dieu ou une idole" (Man possesses either a God or an idol).
26 Girard, *La Conversion de l'art*, 19–20, my translation.
27 See Sartre, *Being and Nothingness*, 301–03.
28 Girard, *Deceit, Desire, and the Novel*, 77.
29 Girard, "Racine, Poet of Glory," in *Mimesis and Theory*, 96.
30 Ibid., 122–23.
31 Michael Kirwan observes that "on several occasions Girard has spoken with some openness about his conversion while working on his first book: this was at first an intellectual conversion, then more properly religious, leading to his return to Christianity at Easter 1959" (*Discovering Girard*, 11).
32 Girard, "Conversion in Literature and Christianity," in *Mimesis and Theory*, 263–64.
33 Girard, *Deceit, Desire, and the Novel*, 294.
34 As the first sentence of the conclusion reads, "The ultimate meaning of desire is death, but death is not the novel's ultimate meaning" (ibid., 290).
35 Ibid., 59, translation modified.
36 Ibid., 294, brackets added to indicate a more literal translation.
37 Ibid., 295, my emphasis, translation modified.
38 Ibid., 308.
39 Ibid., 312.
40 Sartre, *Notebooks for an Ethics*, 472, my emphasis. Commenting on the *Notebooks for an Ethics*, Thomas Flynn writes that "[conversion] denotes a radical shift of the fundamental project to abandon the desire to be God (in-itself-for-itself) and authentically to live one's selfness (ipseity) spontaneously and 'without an ego'" (*Sartre: A Philosophical Biography* [Cambridge: Cambridge University Press, 2014], 272–73).
41 Michel Foucault, *The Care of the Self*: Volume 3 of *The History of Sexuality*, trans. Robert Hurley (New York: Vintage, 1986), 65.
42 David Detmer, *Sartre Explained: From Bad Faith to Authenticity* (Chicago: Open Court, 2008), 138.

Chapter 8

1 It would be instructive here to compare the way in which verbal artifacts are treated with respect to the visual and plastic arts. There are departments of "Art History" in every major university, and this appellation is ostensibly designed to distinguish the contextual study of actual works of art from the practice of creating them. But no literature department is called "Literary

History," even though it must in many cases be separated from "creative writing."

2. As Auerbach notes, Romance philology finds its inspiration in the German historicist tradition inaugurated by Herder, reaching its zenith in Hegel (see note 23 of Chapter 9). Auerbach also finds an inspiration in Vico. See Auerbach's essay "Vico and Aesthetic Historicism," in *Scenes from the Drama of European Literature* (Minneapolis: University of Minnesota Press, 1984), 183–98.

3. Erich Auerbach, *Literary Language and Its Public in Late Latin Antiquity and in the Middle Ages*, trans. Ralph Manheim (Princeton, NJ: Princeton University Press, 1993), 6.

4. Erich Auerbach, *Mimesis: The Representation of Reality in Western Literature*, trans. Willard R. Trask (Princeton, NJ: Princeton University Press, 1953). All page numbers refer to this edition unless otherwise indicated. German original: *Mimesis: Dargestellte Wirlichkeit in der abenländischen Literatur* (Tübingen and Basel: A. Franke Verlag, 1946). A fiftieth anniversary edition of the English translation was published by Princeton University Press in 2003 (reprinted in 2013), with an introduction by Edward Said.

5. Until fairly recently, Ernst Curtius's *European Literature and the Latin Middle Ages* (1948) was one of the most cited books in humanistic studies, but his magnum opus has largely been eclipsed by Auerbach's *Mimesis*.

6. On Auerbach's importance and place in literary studies, see, in particular, Geoffrey Green, *Literary Criticism and the Structures of History: Erich Auerbach and Leo Spitzer* (Lincoln: University of Nebraska Press, 1982). See also *Literary History and the Challenge of Philology: The Legacy of Erich Auerbach*, ed. Seth Lerer (Stanford, CA: Stanford University Press, 1996); David Damrosch, "Auerbach in Exile," *Comparative Literature* 47, no. 2 (1995): 97–117; Emily Apter, "Global Translatio: The 'Invention' of Comparative Literature, Istanbul, 1933," *Critical Inquiry* 29, no. 2 (2003): 253–81. More recently, Auerbach's work has become part of the debate around postcolonial theory. See Paul Reitter, "Comparative Literature in Exile: Said and Auerbach," in *Exile and Otherness: New Approaches to the Experience of the Nazi Refugees*, ed. Alexander Stephen (Bern: Peter Lang, 2005), 21–30.

7. Offering a tribute to Vico's influence in his methodological introduction to *Literary Language and Its Public* (13), Auerbach remarks that Vico's work "remains an irreplaceable prototype" for his own and that "what remains significant in [Vico's thought] is his idea of the structure of history." Thus, Vico's historical methodology in the *Scienza nuova* is at the origin of the tension between the structural and the historical that permeates—and perhaps even haunts—Auerbach's work in general and *Mimesis* in particular, as I endeavor to show in this chapter. The new anthology *Time, History, and Literature: Selected Essays of Erich Auerbach*, ed. James I. Porter, trans. Jane O. Newman (Princeton, NJ: Princeton University Press, 2014), collects several essays on Vico, in addition to the one mentioned above (see note 2).

8. I should note, however, that the ontological conception of mimesis is not completely absent from Auerbach's thinking. In the epilogue, which appeared in a subsequent edition of *Mimesis*, Auerbach confides that his "original starting point was Plato's discussion in book 10 of the *Republic*—mimesis

ranking third after truth—in conjunction with Dante's assertion that in the *Commedia* he presented true reality" (*Mimesis*, 554). The relation between this "starting point" and where he ended up is not adequately explained.

9 Thus, I think that Frank Ankersmit takes Auerbach too much at his word when he writes that "realism only exists for him in the many variants in which it has shown itself in the course of the long history investigated in this book; all that we can meaningfully do is tell the narrative of its history" (*Historical Representation* [Stanford, CA: Stanford University Press, 2002], 198).

10 Indeed, it is difficult to square Auerbach's self-understanding of his methodology with his critical practice, as when he writes the following: "The starting point should not be a category which we ourselves impose on the material, to which the material must be fitted, but a characteristic found in the subject itself, essential to its history, which, when stressed and developed, clarifies the subject matter in its particularity and other topics in relation to it" (*Literary Language*, 19).

11 Auerbach appears to admit as much when he writes in his 1953 article responding to his critics, "Epilegomena to *Mimesis*" (in *Mimesis*, 2003/13, 563), that "the conceptual pair 'stylistic differentiation/stylistic mixing' is one of themes of my book and has always had the same significance throughout the twenty chapters, from Genesis all the way to Virginia Woolf."

12 This is the way in which Auerbach distinguishes between eighteenth- and nineteenth-century realism. Cf. Auerbach, *Mimesis*, 1953, 410–11.

13 In fact, when one looks up the term "sublime" in the index of the German or English edition of *Mimesis*, no page references are provided. Instead one is referred elsewhere: "*See* style, *humilitas*" (*Mimesis*, 562). In the German edition, one is referred to *Stilmischung*, the mixture of styles. However, in the 2014 collection *Time, History, and Literature: Selected Essays of Erich Auerbach*, "sublime" does appear in the index.

14 An exception is Philip Shaw's *The Sublime* (New York: Routledge, 2005), which discusses Auerbach in some detail (19–23).

15 In an intriguing essay on Auerbach's reading of Boccaccio, Albert Ascoli notes how Auerbach's concept of style often becomes fused with content: "For Auerbach, who begins by insisting that Boccaccio's realism is primarily a rhetorical and stylistic effect, in the end there is little that separates the 'realism' of style from the natural and eroticized realities of a newly secular world" ("Boccaccio's Auerbach: Holding the Mirror Up to *Mimesis*," *Studi sul Boccaccio* 20 [1991–92]: 390).

16 Interestingly, Auerbach places a quotation from Longinus (9.2) at the head of his chapter: "Sublimity is the echo of elevation of thought" (*Literary Language*, 181).

17 Ibid., 22.

18 Ibid., 194.

19 In the late seventeenth and early eighteenth centuries, Boileau commanded great respect and attention among European literati. He was considered an unimpeachable authority on matters literary, and thus his endorsement of Longinus was enough to propel the unknown Greek critic into instant notoriety.

20 Boileau would add several paragraphs to his preface in 1683 and 1701. See Robert Doran, *The Theory of the Sublime from Longinus to Kant* (Cambridge: Cambridge University Press, 2015), chapter 4 (on Boileau).

21 *Works of Monsieur Boileau*, 2 vol., ed. and trans. John Ozell and Pierre Desmaizeaux (London, 1712), II, 7.

22 Auerbach, *Literary Language*, 193.

23 Longinus, *On the Sublime*, 17.1 (trans. D. A. Russell, *Ancient Literary Criticism: The Principal Texts in New Translations* [Oxford: Oxford University Press, 1972], 460–503).

24 Auerbach, *Literary Language*, 193.

25 The rejection of ornate (*la préciosité*) or bombastic rhetoric cohered with the stated ideal of *simplicity* in neoclassical poetics. Longinus's preference for Atticism (the classical style) over Asianism (the ornate style) is thus transformed in seventeenth-century France into the quarrel between the ancients and the moderns. Auerbach in fact writes of the "artificial rhetorical style of Asianism" (Erich Auerbach, *Dante, Poet of the Secular World*, trans. Ralph Manheim, intro. Michael Dirda [New York: New York Review of Books, 2007], 19).

26 Auerbach, *Mimesis*, 22–23.

27 Ibid., 153.

28 Ibid., 184.

29 Ibid. Auerbach sees the *Divine Comedy* as representing a "revival of ancient sublimity in a new creation" (*Literary Language*, 232). However, he also observes that the "sublime style of antiquity was not revived by pure imitation, but sprang anew from a new world of which the ancient masters knew nothing" (ibid., 233).

30 *Works of Monsieur Boileau*, II, 7.

31 For a discussion of this debate, see Gilles Declercq, "Boileau-Huet: la Querelle du *Fiat lux*," *Biblio 17* 83 (1994): 237–62, as well as Doran, *The Theory of the Sublime from Longinus to Kant*, 115–20.

32 Huet later reversed himself somewhat, creating a new category, the "sublimity of things," which could properly be said to apply to the Bible. See the previous note.

33 Auerbach, *Mimesis*, 110. Note that Auerbach uses the term *sublime* in much the same way that Boileau does: "The sublime in this sentence." The word *sublime* is here a substantive rather than an adjective referring to the sentence itself or to its style.

34 In Shakespeare's *Macbeth*, for instance, the murder of King Duncan is followed immediately by the comic scene with the porter. I will return to Hugo's aesthetics at the end of this chapter.

35 Auerbach, *Mimesis*, 151.

36 René Wellek, "Auerbach's Special Realism," *The Kenyon Review* 16, no. 2 (1954): 301.

37 Auerbach, *Mimesis*, 72.

38 Auerbach qualifies his historical methodology as "dialectical" but not in terms of the mixture of styles: "Romantic historicism created a dialectical conception of man, dialectical because it was based on a diversity of national individualities; it was profounder and more realistic than the concept of man put forward by the pure Enlightenment with its unhistorical and undialectical approach" (*Literary Language*, 5).
39 Hayden White, *Figural Realism: Studies in the Mimesis Effect* (Baltimore: Johns Hopkins University Press, 1999), 98.
40 White, *Figural Realism*, 99.
41 Alain Renaut, *The Era of the Individual: A Contribution to a History of Subjectivity*, trans. M. B. Debevoise and Franklin Philip (Princeton, NJ: Princeton University Press, 1997), 34.
42 As I argue in *The Theory of the Sublime from Longinus to Kant*, the sublime, understood as *sublimity of mind* (aesthetically realized high-mindedness), represents an appropriation of the aristocratic mind-set by the emergent bourgeoisie.
43 See also Marcel Gauchet's *The Disenchantment of the World: A Political History of Religion* (trans. Oscar Burge, fwd. Charles Taylor [Princeton, NJ: Princeton University Press, 1999]), which examines the persistence of religious structures in a secular context (hence Gauchet's famous dictum "Christianity is the religion of the end of religion" [*le christianisme est la religion de la sortie de la religion*]). See also Gauchet's more recent *La révolution modern: L'avènement de la démocratie I* (Paris: Gallimard, 2007), in which he observes, "It is certainly true that religion no longer orders our being-together; nevertheless, this does not thereby mean that the form that religion had given to it has disappeared. It continues to exercise a subterranean influence over the collective mechanism" (11–12, my translation).
44 Auerbach, *Dante*, 15.
45 Ibid., 14.
46 Auerbach, *Mimesis*, 185.
47 More literally, Auerbach's title would be rendered *Dante, Poet of the Earthly World*.
48 Auerbach, *Mimesis*, 202.
49 Commenting on Auerbach, Ian Watt notes in *The Rise of the Novel* ([Berkeley and Los Angeles: University of California Press, 2001], 79) that "in Protestant countries, however, the *Stiltrennung* never achieved such authority," presumably because they were less hierarchical than the Latin-Catholic countries, such as France.
50 Auerbach, *Mimesis*, 555.
51 Ibid., 468.
52 Ibid., 184.
53 Honoré de Balzac, *Eugénie Grandet*, ed. Eléonore Roy-Reverzy (Paris: Flammarion, 2000), 137, and *Le père Goriot*, ed. Pierre-Georges Castex (Paris: Garnier Frères, 1963), 92.

54 Auerbach, *Mimesis*, 515, Auerbach's italics.
55 Ibid., 481.
56 Ibid.
57 Wellek, "Auerbach's Special Realism," 306–07.
58 Green, *Literary Criticism and the Structures of History*, 48.
59 Ibid., 14–15.

Chapter 9

1 Taking a different tack, one could also argue, as does Michael Holquist, that it is possible to see "the rise of cultural studies in general, and the work of Edward Said in particular, as powerful aspects of Auerbach's legacy" (Holquist, "Auerbach and the Fate of Philology," *Poetics Today* 20, no. 1 [Spring 1999]: 86). See also Holquist's article "The Last European: Erich Auerbach as a Precursor in the History of Cultural Criticism," *Modern Language Quarterly* 54 (1993): 371–91.
2 Marjorie Perloff, "It Must Change," *PMLA* 122, no. 3 (May 2007): 652–62.
3 Quoted by Scott McLemee, "The Grand Dame of Poetry Criticism," *The Chronicle of Higher Education*, January 28, 2005, http://chronicle.com/free/v51/i21/21a01401.htm.
4 Jonathan Culler, *The Literary in Theory* (Stanford, CA: Stanford University Press, 2007), 5.
5 Ibid.
6 See Jonathan Culler's eponymous tome, *Structuralist Poetics: Structuralism, Linguistics, and the Study of Literature* (Ithaca, NY: Cornell University Press, 1975), which was awarded the James Russell Lowell Prize from the Modern Languages Association.
7 In music, interestingly, a bifurcation persists between the disciplines of musicology (history of music) and music theory (harmonic analysis and formal structure), which are separate departments in many universities.
8 René Wellek and Austin Warren, *Theory of Literature*, 3rd ed. (New York: Harcourt Brace, 1956), 127.
9 See Erich Auerbach, "Vico and Aesthetic Historicism," in Erich Auerbach, *Scenes from the Drama of European Literature* (Minneapolis: University of Minnesota Press, 1984), 183–98. On this relation see Luiz Costa Lima, "Erich Auerbach: History and Metahistory," *New Literary History* 19, no. 3 (1988): 467–99.
10 As part of the Modern Language Association's project of translating classic texts of criticism, an essay by Lanson was published in 1995 in the association's journal: "Literary History and Sociology," trans. Nicholas T. Rand and Roberta Hatcher, *PMLA* 110, no. 2 (March 1995): 220–35.

11 Erich Auerbach, *Literary Language and Its Public in Late Antiquity and in the Middle Ages*, trans. Ralph Manheim (Princeton, NJ: Princeton University Press, 1993), 14–15.

12 In the previous chapter, I offered a partial answer to this question, namely Auerbach's structural approach to literary history.

13 One could add that aesthetics is also the study of the concept of beauty, but this understanding is more pertinent to the philosophy of art than to literary studies. Most recently, Jacques Rancière has sought to expand the concept of aesthetics. See Rancière's *Aisthesis: Scenes from the Aesthetic Regime of Art*, trans. Zakir Paul (London: Verso, 2013).

14 I think that we need not get too caught up in the inevitable objection that there is no definable essence of literature, a term that comes into regular use only in the early nineteenth century through the influence of Germaine de Staël's *De la littérature* (1800).

15 Auerbach, *Literary Language and Its Public*, 13.

16 We should note that it is *Darstellung* rather than *Vorstellung* that appears in the subtitle of *Mimesis*, a literal translation of which might read *The Presentation of Reality in Western Literature* (*Dargestellte Wirklichkeit in der abendländischen Literatur*).

17 Edward Said, "Introduction to the Fiftieth Anniversary Edition" in *Mimesis: The Representation of Reality in Western Literature*, trans. Willard Trask, ed. Erich Auerbach (Princeton, NJ: Princeton University Press, 2003/13), xxxii.

18 René Wellek, "Auerbach's Special Realism," *Kenyon Review* 16, no. 2 (1954): 304–05. Wellek is actually responding to Auerbach's 1953 article "Epilegomena to *Mimesis*" (in Auerbach, *Mimesis*, 2003, 572), in which Auerbach explains that "were it possible, I would not have used any generalizing expressions at all, but instead I would have suggested the thought to the reader purely by presenting a sequence of particulars. That is not possible; accordingly I used some much-used terms, like realism and moralism, and, compelled by my subject, I even introduced two little-used ones: stylistic differentiation and stylistic mixing."

19 See especially, Hayden White, "Auerbach's Literary History: Figural Causation and Modernist Historicism," collected in White's *Figural Realism: Studies in the Mimesis Effect* (Baltimore: Johns Hopkins Press, 1999), 87–100, but originally published in *Literary History and the Challenge of Philology*, ed. Seth Lerer (Stanford, CA: Stanford University Press, 1996), 124–42. I discuss this essay in Chapter 5.

20 Erich Auerbach, "Philology and *Weltliteratur*," trans. Edward Said, *Centennial Review* 13 (1969): 5. Originally published as "Philologie und Weltliteratur," in *Weltliteratur: Festgabe für Fritz Strich zum 70. Geburtstag*, ed. Walter Muschg and Emil Staiger (Bern: A. Francke, 1952), 39–50.

21 Auerbach, *Mimesis*, 2003, 549.

22 Auerbach, "Philology and *Weltliteratur*," 5.

23 Indeed, Auerbach has acknowledged his debt to Hegel: "[*Mimesis*] arose from the themes and methods of German intellectual history and philology; it would

be conceivable in no other tradition than in that of German Romanticism and Hegel" ("Epilegomena to *Mimesis*" in Auerbach, *Mimesis*, 2003, 572).

24 Ibid.

25 This idea was also important to Said, who discusses Auerbach's *Ansatzpunkt* in his book *Beginnings: Invention and Method* (New York: Columbia University Press, 1975/85).

26 Auerbach, *Literary Language and Its Public*, 20. Said is convinced that "the extraordinary success of *Mimesis* is considerably the result of the questions Auerbach asks of his text" (*Beginnings*, 69).

27 Auerbach, *Literary Language and Its Public*, 22.

28 See Chapter 8.

29 See the historical reconstruction of this notion by Magdalena Nowak in her article "The Complicated History of *Einfühlung*," *Argument* 1, no. 2 (2011): 301–26.

30 Wolfgang Holdheim, "The Hermeneutic Significance of Auerbach's *Ansatz*," *New Literary History* 16, no. 3 (1985): 628.

31 Auerbach himself was educated in an elite high school, the Berlin Französisches Gymnasium.

32 In the French department at Middlebury College (where I taught for three years), an elite liberal arts college well known for its emphasis on the study of languages, there were no courses offered in French literature prior to 1800—due to lack of student interest.

33 Georg Lukács, *The Historical Novel*, trans. Hannah and Stanley Mitchell, intro. Fredric Jameson (Lincoln: University of Nebraska Press, 1983). In his definition of the genre of the historical novel, Lukács contrasts "mere costumery" with "an artistically faithful image of a concrete historical epoch" (19).

34 Hayden White, "The Suppression of Rhetoric in the Nineteenth Century," in White, *The Fiction of Narrative: Essays on History, Literature, and Theory 1957-2007*, ed. Robert Doran (Baltimore: Johns Hopkins University Press, 2010), 300.

35 See Jonathan Culler, *Theory of the Lyric* (Cambridge, MA: Harvard University Press, 2015).

36 See Tzvetan Todorov's exploration of this notion in his fascinating book *On Human Diversity: Nationalism, Racism, and Exoticism in French Thought* (Cambridge, MA: Harvard University Press, 1993).

37 Edward Said, *The World, the Text, and the Critic* (Cambridge, MA: Harvard University Press, 1983), 8.

38 See Samuel P. Huntington, *The Clash of Civilizations and the Remaking of World Order* (New York: Simon & Schuster, 1996).

39 In response to the terrorist attacks in Paris on November 13, 2015, GOP senator and presidential candidate Marco Rubio invoked the idea of a "clash of civilizations." See the article "Rubio sees a 'clash of civilizations'" (*Politico*, November 15, 2015, http://www.politico.com/story/2015/11/marco-rubio-paris-attacks-isil-215905).

40 Auerbach, "Philology and *Weltliteratur*," 8.

Chapter 10

1. Hayden White, "Criticism as Cultural Politics," *Diacritics* 6, no. 3 (1976): 8.
2. "It is no accident that the emergence of so narrowly defined a philosophy of pure textuality and critical noninterference has coincided with the ascendancy of Reaganism" (Edward Said, *The World, the Text, and the Critic* [Cambridge, MA: Harvard University Press, 1983], 4).
3. "In such matters as culture and scholarship I am often in reasonable sympathy with conservative attitudes, and what I might object to in what I have been describing does not have much to do with the activity of conserving the past, or with reading great literature, or with doing serious and perhaps utterly conservative scholarship as such" (Said, *The World, the Text, and the Critic*, 22).
4. As noted in the introduction and in Chapter 3, one can observe a similar phenomenon regarding Jacques Derrida and the topics of ethics and politics.
5. Jonathan Culler, *On Deconstruction: Theory and Criticism after Structuralism* [Ithaca, NY: Cornell University Press, 1982/2007]. In his influential book *The Philosophical Discourse of Modernity*, trans. Frederick G. Lawrence (Cambridge: MIT Press, 1987), Jürgen Habermas takes Culler's text as representative of the American interpretation of Derrida.
6. Gayatri Spivak, "Can the Subaltern Speak," in *Marxism and the Interpretation of Culture*, ed. Cary Nelson and Lawrence Grossberg (Urbana and Chicago: University of Illinois Press, 1988), 66–111.
7. Edward Said, *Covering Islam* (New York: Vintage Books, 1981/97).
8. Spivak's first book was *Myself, I Must Remake: The Life and Poetry of W.B. Yeats* (1974).
9. Edward Said, *Beginnings: Intention and Method* (New York: Columbia University Press, 1975/85).
10. Said discusses Foucault at length in *Beginnings: Intention and Method*, 279–315.
11. See Clare O'Farrell, "Michel Foucault: The Unconscious of History and Culture," in *The Sage Handbook of Historical Theory*, ed. Nancy Partner and Sarah Foot (London: Sage Publications, 2013), 163.
12. Edward Said, *Orientalism: 25th Anniversary Edition* (New York: Vintage Books, 1978/95/2003), 3.
13. Although Paul Reitter claims that "Said never really frames his work as Foucauldian"(!) ("Comparative Literature in Exile: Said and Auerbach," in *Exile and Otherness: New Approaches to the Experience of the Nazi Refugees*, ed. Alexander Stephen [Bern: Peter Lang, 2005]: 24).
14. Michel Foucault, "What Is an Author?" in *The Foucault Reader*, ed. Paul Rabinow (New York: Vintage Books, 1984/2010), 101–20; Michel Foucault, *The Archaeology of Knowledge and The Discourse on Language* (New York: Vintage Books, 2010).
15. Said, *Orientalism*, 23, my emphasis.

16 Said, *The World, the Text, and the Critic*, 186.
17 "I study Orientalism as a dynamic exchange between individual authors and the large political concerns shaped by the three great empires—British, French, American—in whose intellectual and imaginative territory the writing was produced" (Said, *Orientalism*, 14–15).
18 In an interview, Said states that "there is nothing I disagree with in the broad, humanistic tradition" (*Power, Politics, and Culture: Interviews with Edward W. Said*, ed. Gauri Viswanathan [New York: Vintage Books, 2001], 174).
19 Said, *Orientalism*, 10.
20 James Clifford, review of *Orientalism*, *History and Theory* 19, no. 2 (1980): 212, 213.
21 See the classic text by René Wellek and Austin Warren, *Theory of Literature*, 3rd ed. (New York: Harcourt Brace, 1956).
22 See Chapter 9. René Girard observes in his 1989 essay "Theory and Its Terrors": "With nationalism on the rise, history, and especially the national history of each country, became the dominant discipline of the humanities, and literary studies were first conceived as adjuncts to the study of that national history. Until the Second World War, the professors of literature who dedicated their careers either to critical editions or to literary history were in the majority. 'Criticism' or 'literary interpretation' in our sense did not exist" (*Mimesis and Theory: Essays on Literature and Criticism, 1953-2005*, ed. Robert Doran [Stanford, CA: Stanford University Press, 2008], 195).
23 See Jean-Paul Sartre, *"What is Literature?" and Other Essays* (Cambridge, MA: Harvard University Press, 1988), and Theodor W. Adorno, "Commitment" (1962), *New Left Review* I/87–88 (September–December 1974).
24 Said, *Orientalism*, 27, my emphasis.
25 On this count, Said seconds René Girard's critique of poststructuralism as an updated version of New Criticism. Girard writes, "If we look at deconstruction as the child of New Criticism, we will understand that it entered a literary world from which content had already been expelled. I think we must return to content. We must not be intimidated by linguistic terrorism. Linguistic terrorism makes all reference impossible to reach" (*Mimesis and Theory*, 212).
26 Said, *The World, the Text, and the Critic*, 4.
27 Ibid.
28 On the problem of irony, see Chapters 4 (on Richard Rorty) and 6 (on Hayden White) of this volume.
29 Said, *The World, the Text, and the Critic*, 4.
30 See Robert Doran, "Humanism, Formalism, and the Discourse of History," editor's introduction to Hayden White, *The Fiction of Narrative: Essays on History, Literature, and Theory, 1957-2007* (Baltimore: Johns Hopkins University Press, 2010), xiii–xxxii.
31 Said, *Power, Politics, and Culture*, 166.

32 Said, *Orientalism*, 25, original emphasis.

33 By one account (see O'Farrell, "Michel Foucault: The Unconscious of History and Culture," 163), Said's Orientalist thesis was inspired by the following paragraph from Foucault's *Madness and Civilization*: "In the universality of the Western *ratio*, there is this division which is the Orient: the Orient, thought of as the origin, dreamt of as the vertiginous point from which nostalgia and promises of return are born, the Orient offered to the colonizing reason of the Occident, but indefinitely inaccessible, for it always remains the limit: the night of the beginning, in which the Occident was formed, but in which it traced a dividing line, the Orient is for the Occident everything that it is not, while remaining the place in which its primitive truth must be sought. What is required is a history of this great divide" (Michel Foucault, *Madness and Civilization* [New York: Routledge, 2006], xxx). This 2006 edition is the first unabridged edition of Foucault's classic tome.

34 Said, *Orientalism*, 10.

35 "There will always remain the perennial escape mechanism of saying that a literary scholar and a philosopher, for example, are trained in literature and philosophy respectively, not in politics or ideological analysis. In other words, the specialist argument can work quite effectively to block the larger and, in my opinion, the more intellectually serious perspective" (Said, *Orientalism*, 14).

36 Ibid., 334.

37 Ibid.

38 Such as, for example, when Said notes that the "Orient-versus-Occident opposition was both misleading and highly undesirable" (ibid., 336). It would be difficult to hold that such an opposition was not at least implied in the text.

39 Ibid., 333.

40 Said notes that "among American and British academics of a decidedly rigorous and unyielding stripe, *Orientalism*, and indeed all of my other work, has come in for disapproving attacks because of its 'residual' humanism, its theoretical inconsistencies, its insufficient, perhaps even sentimental, treatment of agency. I am glad that it has! *Orientalism* is a partisan book, not a theoretical machine" (ibid., 339). In his new preface (2003), Said similarly remarks that "I have called what I try to do 'humanism,' a word I continue to use stubbornly despite the scornful dismissal of the term by sophisticated postmodern critics" (ibid., xxiii).

41 Vico's principle was first expounded in his book *De antiquissima Italorum sapientia, ex linguae latinae originibus eruenda* (1710). It has been translated into English by L. M. Palmer as *On the Most Ancient Wisdom of the Italians Unearthed from the Origins of the Latin Language* (Ithaca, NY: Cornell University Press, 1988).

42 "The central point in all this is, however, as Vico taught us, that human history is made by human beings" (Said, *Orientalism*, 331).

43 Ibid., 5.

44 See Hayden White's essay "Vico and Structuralist/Poststructuralist Thought" in White, *The Fiction of Narrative*, 203–07.

45 See Jean-Paul Sartre, *Being and Nothingness: A Phenomenological Essay on Ontology*, trans. Hazel Barnes (New York: Washington Square Press, 1956), "Part Three: Being for Others." In his *Edward Said: Criticism and Society* ([London: Verso, 2004], 31, 39–40), Abdirahman A. Hussein discusses Said's relation to Sartre with respect to Said's first book on Conrad (*Joseph Conrad and the Fiction of Autobiography*), but not in regard to *Orientalism*.

46 Ibid., 332, my emphasis.

47 Ibid. This is of course the struggle we are witnessing in the Arab-Islamic world today, with the rise of the (so-called) Islamic State (ISIS) and global jihadism.

48 Ibid., 333.

49 In his review of *Orientalism*, James Clifford remarks that "Said makes frequent appeals to an old-fashioned existential realism" (207–08). See my discussion of Foucault in Chapter 2, in particular the concluding paragraphs.

50 Said in fact invokes White's notion of "emplotment": "Once we begin to think of Orientalism as a kind of Western projection onto and will to govern the Orient, we encounter few surprises. For if it is true that historians like Michelet, Ranke, Tocqueville, and Burckhardt *emplot* their narratives 'as a story of a particular kind' [Hayden White, *Metahistory: The Historical Imagination in Nineteenth-Century Europe* (Baltimore: Johns Hopkins University Press 1973), 12], the same is also true of Orientalists who plotted Oriental history, character, and destiny for hundreds of years" (ibid., 95, original emphasis).

51 Ibid., 333.

52 Ibid.

53 See Chapter 7.

INDEX

Adorno, Theodor   3, 13, 84, 163, 218
aestheticism   3, 14, 87, 89, 118, 175.
    See also l'art pour l'art
aesthetics   3, 10, 174, 175
    in Auerbach   137–8, 140–6, 149, 152, 210, 212, 215
    in Derrida   69
    in Foucault   52, 54–5, 180, 188
    in Rorty   85, 88–91, 93–5, 200
    in Said   160, 167
    in Sartre   48
    in White   109–12, 116–20, 205
Althusser, Louis   4, 169
Amironesei, Razvan   187
Analytic (Anglo-American) philosophy   30–1, 39, 44, 92
anarchism   58, 189
Ancien Régime   101, 145
Anderson, Perry   120
Ankersmit, F. R.   99, 122, 201, 203, 204, 207, 211
Annales school   32, 46
Ansatzpunkt (point of departure)   43, 78, 155, 185, 216. *See also* Auerbach, Erich
antiquity   38, 137, 212
anti-Semitism   11, 68–9, 71–2, 75, 193, 195
Apter, Emily   210
Aristotle   16, 72, 89–90, 109, 199
art of living (*tekhnê tou biou*)   37, 43, 93, 185
Ascoli, Albert   211
Auerbach, Erich   2, 16, 136–58, 210–16
    Dante, Poet of the Secular World   145, 212
    Literary Language and Its Public   136, 138–9, 151, 154, 210, 211, 212, 213, 215, 216

Mimesis   110–11, 137–46, 148, 149, 152–5, 158, 210–16
    mixture of styles (*Stilmischung*)   89, 137–8, 140, 142–3, 147–8, 153, 211, 213
    and Rorty   89–90
    and Said   159, 161, 163–4, 217
    separation of styles (*Stiltrennung*)   137, 142, 145, 148, 153, 213
    sermo humilis   137, 142, 153, 155
    sublimitas/humilitas   138, 140, 142, 147–8
    and White   110–11, 113
Augustine, Saint   43, 108, 133
Aurelius, Marcus   46, 49
Auschwitz   68–9, 77, 194
authenticity (existentialist concept of)   6
    in Foucault   45, 48, 51–3, 55, 57
    in Girard   127–8, 132, 134–5
    in Heidegger   72–3, 177, 197
    in Rorty   82–5, 89
    in Sartre   21, 24–5, 177, 209
    in White   103–5

Badiou, Alain   4
Balibar, Étienne   4
Balzac, Honoré de   143–4, 146–7, 153, 206, 213
Barthes, Roland   6, 8–9, 175, 201, 206
Baudelaire, Charles   3, 52
Baudrillard, Jean   4
Bäumler, Alfred   73–4, 195
Beaufret, Jean   8, 173
Beauvoir, Simone de   10, 20, 119, 175, 206
Benjamin, Walter   3, 13
Bennington, Geoffrey   174, 190, 192

Benveniste, Émile 171
Bernstein, Richard 65, 78, 173, 184, 186, 192, 193, 196
Bessière, Jean 169
Bible, the 111, 141, 145, 156, 212
Blanchot, Maurice 68
Bloom, Harold 88, 199
Boas, Franz 28–9
Boccaccio, Giovanni 211
Boileau, Nicolas 139–41, 211, 212
Bossenbrook, William J. 106, 171, 201, 203
Bourdieu, Pierre 11, 64
Braudel, Fernand 46, 179, 186
Brown, Richard Harvey 177–8
Butler, Judith 4, 12–13, 15, 174, 184

Calle-Gruber, Mireille 64, 189
Carr, David 203
Catalano, Joseph 26, 31, 33, 177, 179
Catholicism/Catholic Church 27, 103, 213
Cerisy-la-Salle 4, 8
Cervantes, Miguel de 128, 133
Chomsky, Noam 182, 189
Christ, Jesus 88, 90, 134, 142, 144, 146, 208
Christianity 10
  in Auerbach 141–8, 155
  in Foucault 38, 43–4, 46–50, 187, 189
  in Girard 128, 133–5, 209
  in Rorty 88–9, 91, 198
  in Said 160, 213
  in White 103, 111–12
Clifford, James 162, 218, 220
Cohen, Tom 62, 191
Collège de France 20, 35, 37–8, 43, 46, 180–4
colonialism 25, 86, 149, 165
Compagnon, Antoine 175
Continental Philosophy 2–3, 7, 13, 30–1, 39–40, 71, 92
conversion
  as *epistrophê* 49–50, 135, 187
  in Foucault 44, 46, 48–50
  in Girard 85, 127–8, 133–5, 187, 198, 208–9

  as *metanoia* 49–50, 187
  in Sartre 101, 187
Costa Lima, Luiz 214
Critchley, Simon 190, 191
Critical race theory/studies 1, 13
Croce, Benedetto 108, 118
Culler, Jonathan 6–7, 14, 16, 150, 160, 169, 171, 172, 175, 214, 216, 217
  On Deconstruction 7, 160, 171, 172, 217
  The Literary in Theory 14, 150, 169, 171, 175, 214
  Structuralist Poetics 7, 150, 160, 214
  Theory of the Lyric 14, 175, 216
Curtius, Ernst 136, 151, 210
Cusset, François 1, 8, 172

Damrosch, David 210
Dante 14, 133, 140, 144–6, 211
Danto, Arthur 12, 106, 171, 174, 201, 207
Davidson, Arnold 37, 180, 181, 200
Davidson, Donald 94
Dawson, Christopher 108, 203
Debaene, Vincent 176, 178
Declercq, Gilles 212
deconstruction 6, 8, 12, 15, 61–3, 67, 75–8, 84, 107, 160, 172–4, 191, 196, 199, 218. *See also* Derrida, Jacques
Deleuze, Gilles 8, 37, 65, 184
de Man, Paul 8, 11–12, 61, 169, 190
de Man Affair 11, 61, 160, 190
democracy, democratic, democratization
  in Auerbach 145, 148, 156–7
  in Derrida 76
  in Foucault 44, 48, 51, 54, 58
  in Rorty 79, 85, 92
  in Said 206
Derrida, Jacques 2, 4–13, 15–16, 60–78, 170–4, 181, 190–6, 217
  Adieu to Emmanuel Levinas 190
  The Death Penalty, Volume I 190
  "Force of Law" 63, 76, 78, 191, 195, 196
  and Foucault 189

The Gift of Death 78, 196
Of Grammatology 7–8, 11, 160, 172, 174, 191
Heidegger: La question de l'être et l'histoire 192, 195
Monolingualism of the Other 190
The Politics of Friendship 190
and Rorty 79–81, 84–5, 94, 197
and Said 160, 164
and Sartre 20, 65, 76–7, 191, 195
Specters of Marx 170, 190, 194
On Spirit: Heidegger and the Question 64, 67, 75
"Structure, Sign, and Play in the Discourse of the Human Sciences" 6, 172, 190
and White 107, 117, 119, 201
Writing and Difference 8, 172, 173, 190, 196
Descartes, René 6, 41, 43–4, 50
Detel, Wolfgang 180
Detmer, David 135, 209
Dilthey, Wilhelm 152, 155
Donato, Eugene 6, 171
Dostoevsky, Fyodor 133
Dupuy, Jean-Pierre 127
Durkheim, Émile 21, 29

Eagleton, Terry 5, 170
École des hautes études en sciences sociales (EHESS) 190, 193
École Normale Supérieure (rue d'Ulm) 4, 191
École pratique des hautes études 20, 181
Egalitarianism 48, 84–5, 89–90, 94, 128, 143
Enlightenment (*Aufklärung*) 39, 79, 86, 161, 182, 213
Eribon, Didier 184, 189
existentialism, existentialist 1, 5–6, 8–9, 13, 170, 176, 201
  in Auerbach 146–7, 154
  in Derrida 77
  in Foucault 39, 41, 43, 45, 48–9, 51–2, 55, 59, 188
  in Girard 127–8, 130–2, 135
  in Lévi-Strauss 33–4
  in Rorty 82, 84–9, 91–2, 94–5

in Said 166–8, 220
in Sartre 21, 24
in White 99–114, 116, 118, 119, 122, 201–2, 205

Farias, Victor 11, 60, 64, 66–7, 70, 72, 190, 192, 194
  Heidegger et le nazisme 11, 60, 194
Faurisson, Robert 120–2
feminist, feminism 1, 10, 12–13, 15, 23, 62–3, 174
Ferry, Luc 64, 172, 192
Fichte, Johann Gottlieb 75
figura 111–12, 145, 153–4
Flaubert, Gustave 52, 133, 157
Fleming, Chris 207
Flynn, Thomas 21–2, 171, 176, 177, 180, 181, 209
formalism 8, 12, 16. *See also* Russian formalism
  in Auerbach 136, 149–50, 152, 157
  in Rorty 84, 88
  in Said 160, 162–4
  in White 99, 114, 117, 204
Foucault, Michel 2, 4–5, 8–13, 16, 35–59, 169–71, 173–4, 179–89
  The Archeology of Knowledge 162
  biopower 38
  The Birth of the Clinic 35
  The Care of the Self 135, 180, 181, 187, 209
  the care of the self (*le souci de soi*) 37, 45–8, 50–1, 53–4, 56, 181, 184, 185, 186, 191
  The Courage of Truth 36, 53
  and Derrida 60, 63, 65, 71, 75, 77, 191, 193, 196
  Discipline and Punish 11, 35, 37, 42, 161, 182
  egotism 46–7, 58
  epimeleia heautou (the care of the self) 45–7
  and Girard 135
  The Government of Self and Others 36, 53, 182, 183, 186
  governmentality 37, 53, 183

The Hermeneutics of the Subject 36–7, 45–50, 180–1, 183–9
The History of Sexuality 35–8, 56, 174, 180, 182
Introduction to Kant's Anthropology 40, 183
Madness and Civilization 8, 42, 179, 219
The Order of Things (Les mots et les choses) 4, 35, 186
power 9–12, 41–2, 46, 51, 53–5, 57–9, 75, 117, 119, 161–2, 165–7, 184, 189
the relation to oneself (*le rapport à soi*) 37, 45, 52, 55, 135
resistance 53–8, 75, 117
and Rorty 79–81, 83–4, 88, 91–2, 94–5, 200
and Said 161–7, 217, 219, 220
and Sartre 20
Subjectivity and Truth 36–7
techniques/technologies of the self 37, 46–7, 181
The Use of Pleasure 38, 40, 43, 180, 182, 183, 184, 185
"What is an Author?" 9, 162, 217
"What is Enlightenment?" 39, 182
and White 117, 119, 201, 205
foundationalism 33, 78–80, 93, 177
Frank, Manfred 66
Frankfurt school 3
Frege, Friedrich Ludwig Gottlob 71–2
French Revolution 39, 100–1, 143, 145, 178
Freud, Sigmund 3, 13, 131
Friedlander, Saul 120, 206
Frye, Northrop 109, 111, 149

Gadamer, Hans-Georg 11, 60, 65, 68, 70, 192, 194
Gasché, Rodolphe 8, 172
Gauchet, Marcel 213
gay rights 38, 42, 182, 184
Genet, Jean 3
Genette, Gérard 6
Ginzburg, Carlo 120–3, 206–7
Girard, René 2, 6, 85, 127–35, 174, 177, 198, 207–9, 218
Deceit, Desire, and the Novel 85, 127–35, 177, 207–9

internal/external mediation 128, 130
La conversion de l'art 208–9
metaphysical desire 127, 130–5
Mimesis and Theory 207–9, 218
mimetic desire/mediated desire 128–30, 133–4, 177
gnôthi seauton (know thyself) 45
Goldmann, Lucien 20, 169
The Gospels 90, 103, 137–8, 140–1, 143–8
Gramsci, Antonio 173
Greek morality 51
Green, Geoffrey 147, 210
Greimas, Algirdas 171
Gros, Frédéric 36–7, 43, 53, 181, 184, 185, 188–9
Groupe d'Informations sur les Prisons (GIP) 170
Gutting, Gary 5, 52, 55, 169, 171, 173, 180, 184, 185, 186, 188

Hadot, Pierre 37, 40, 44, 49, 95, 181, 185, 187, 200
Hagglund, Martin 191
Hall, David L. 197
Harkin, Michael 29, 178
Harootunian, Harry 106, 107, 203
Hartman, Geoffrey 120, 171
Hegel, Georg Wilhelm Friedrich 4, 8, 13, 170, 172
and Auerbach 147, 152, 154, 210, 215–16
and Girard 127, 131
and Rorty 79–80, 85, 197
and Sartre 21
and White 108
Heidegger, Martin 3–11, 171–3
Being and Time 6, 65, 74, 78, 82, 103–4, 121, 177, 193, 196, 197, 202, 207
Dasein 7, 24, 77, 82, 103–4, 117, 129, 168, 171, 193
das Man (the they) 24, 82–3, 94, 197
and Derrida 60–78, 189–96
and Foucault 41–3, 45, 183
Geschick (destiny) 75
Introduction to Metaphysics 83, 194, 198

Kehre (turn)   74
  and Nazism   64–75
  ontological difference   30
  Rectorship Address   64, 67
  and Rorty   80–5, 90, 94–5, 197–8
  and Said   160, 163, 168
  and Sartre   24, 30, 129, 177
  Schicksal (fate)   75
  Vorhandenheit (objective
    presence)   104–5
  and White   103–6, 117, 121, 123,
    202, 207
  Zuhandenheit (handiness)   104–5
Heidegger Affair   11, 60–3, 160,
  173, 190
Heidelberg Conference   11, 60–78,
  189–96
Hemming, Laurence   70, 193, 194
Hénaff, Marcel   32, 171, 176, 179
Herder, Johann Gottfried   151, 210
hermeneutic circle   155
hermeneutics   30, 117, 152–3, 155,
  157–8, 202
Hillgruber, Andreas   202
Holdheim, Wolfgang   155, 209, 216
The Holocaust   68–9, 83, 101, 114,
  120–3, 195, 207
Holquist, Michael   214
Holy Roman Empire   103
homosexuality   10, 13, 38, 42, 58–9,
  174, 182, 184
Horkheimer, Max   3
Howells, Christina   75, 78, 171,
  190–1, 195, 196
Huet, Pierre-Daniel   141, 212
Hugo, Victor   87, 142, 145–6, 212
Huntington, Samuel, P.   216
Hussein, Abdirahman A.   220
Husserl, Edmund   4–8, 41, 44, 170,
  172, 175

International Psychoanalytical
  Association   3
irony   9
  in Derrida   79, 81, 92
  in Rorty   54, 218
  in White   107, 114, 116–19, 123,
    205, 218
Islam   160–1, 165–8, 220
Israel   13, 120–1, 174

Jakobson, Roman   171, 176
James, Henry   87, 89
Jameson, Fredric   5, 23–4, 169,
  170–1, 177, 178, 201, 216
Jay, Martin   120, 207
Jews   177
Joyce, James   3

Kaes, Anton   120
Kamuf, Peggy   170, 190
Kant, Immanuel   6, 10, 172, 175
  *Anthropology from a Pragmatic
    Point of View*   40
  The Conflict of the Faculties   39–40
  Critique of Judgment (third
    Critique)   69, 175
  Critique of Pure Reason   39–40,
    86, 119
  and Derrida   69, 72, 77, 194
  and Foucault   37, 39–41, 44,
    182, 183
  and Rorty   79, 82, 85, 86, 87
  and White   105, 119, 123
Kellner, Hans   116–17, 203, 204
Kierkegaard, Søren   16, 103, 112, 204
Kleinberg, Ethan   173, 193
Klossowski, Pierre   8
Koopman, Colin   92, 200
Kristeva, Julia   13

Lacan, Jacques   4–5, 6, 13, 15, 41,
  169, 170–2
LaCapra, Dominick   120
Lacoue-Labarthe, Philippe   8, 60,
  64–5, 68, 189
Lammi, Walter   192
Lang, Berel   120
La Nouvelle Critique   1
Lanson, Gustave   151–2, 214
l'art pour l'art   175
Lavacot, Françoise   207
Levinas, Emmanuel   4, 9, 10–11, 20,
  37, 132, 170, 177, 181
  and Derrida   63, 65, 78, 173,
    190, 191
Lévi-Strauss, Claude   2, 5–6, 16,
  19–34, 171, 175–9, 190
  *The Elementary Structures of
    Kinship*   19–20, 26, 28, 34,
    171, 178–9

The Savage Mind   19, 26, 28–34, 175, 177–9
Structural Anthropology   20, 28, 171, 178, 179
Tristes tropiques   20, 178
Lionnet, Françoise   175
literary history   6, 16, 111, 174
    and Auerbach   136–48, 150–2, 154–5, 157, 214–15
    and Said   162–3, 218
literary studies   1–2, 11–16, 84, 169, 201
    and Auerbach   149–58, 210, 215
    and Said   159–65, 218
Longinus   138–41, 208, 211–13
Löwith, Karl   8, 172
Lüdemann, Susanne   191
Lukács, Georg   24, 149, 216
Lynch, Kathryn   14–15
Lyotard, Jean-François   4, 8, 11, 64, 69, 72–4, 194

McGushin, Edward   191
McKenna, Andrew J.   198
Macksey, Richard   6, 171
Malinowski, Bronisław   28–9, 31
Mallarmé, Stéphane   3, 155
Marcel, Gabriel   8
Marshall, James D.   56, 189
Marx, Karl   3–4, 13, 21, 104, 107, 170, 174
Marxism   3–5, 56, 58, 62, 169, 189
Mauss, Marcel   29
May 1968   4, 8, 160
Mendicta, Eduardo   197, 200
Merleau-Ponty, Maurice   5, 195
Middle Ages   137, 144–5
Miller, James   38, 170, 181–2, 185, 186
Miller, J. Hillis   169
Modern Language Association (MLA)   12–14, 150, 214
Moses, Dirk   119, 204, 206
Moyn, Samuel   177

Nabokov, Vladimir   87
Nancy, Jean-Luc   8, 65, 193
Napoleonic Empire   101
Nazism   66–75, 77, 101, 120, 194–5
Nehamas, Alexander   43, 47, 185–6, 200

neoclassicism (French)   138
New Criticism   8, 14, 136, 150, 163, 174, 218
New Historicism   136
New Testament   111, 145
Nietzsche, Friedrich   2–3, 8–11, 16, 172–3
    and Derrida   65, 74–5, 195
    and Foucault   37, 41, 43, 45, 50–2, 54–5, 166, 183, 188
    and Rorty   79, 82–3, 85, 87–9, 91, 94–5, 199, 200
    and White   105, 117–19, 170, 201, 205, 207
nihilism   12, 62, 114, 117–18
Nolte, Ernst   202
Nowak, Magdalena   216
Nussbaum, Martha   184

Oakeshott, Michael   105
Objectivism   115, 123, 205
O'Farrell, Clare   185, 217
Oksala, Johanna   180, 183, 184
Old Testament   111, 140
O'Leary, Timothy   180
Olssen, Mark   188
Orientalism   10–11, 161–8, 218, 220. *See also* Said, Edward
Orwell, George   87
Ovid   139

Palaver, Wolfgang   207
Palestine, Palestinians   13, 120–1, 150, 160–1
Palmer, Richard E.   64, 192
Paris Psychoanalytical Society   3
Parti Communiste Français   3
Partner, Nancy   185, 202, 204, 217
Paul, Herman   114, 201, 204
Peeters, Benoît   61, 64, 169–72, 189, 190, 192
Pericles, Peter   191
Perloff, Marjorie   13–15, 150, 174, 214
phenomenology   1, 4–8, 10, 19, 30, 41, 157, 166, 170, 175, 183
philology   5, 9, 16, 43, 136–7, 149–58, 192, 210, 214, 215
philosophy of history   16, 19, 21, 25, 99–113, 115, 118, 202, 203, 205

philosophy of the present   39–40, 63, 70, 72, 80, 104, 106, 191
Pihlainen, Kalle   206
Plato, Platonic   16, 45–7, 49–50, 85, 89, 185–6, 198, 210
poetics   14, 16, 88–9, 114, 150, 152–3, 157, 171, 175, 201, 212
point of departure (*Ansatzpunkt*)   43, 78, 155, 185, 216
political turn   1, 10–16, 61, 149–50, 159–68
politics, the political   1, 3–5, 9–16, 174
  in Auerbach   143–5, 149, 151, 153, 157–8
  cultural politics   79–95, 196
  in Derrida   60–4, 67, 71–4, 76, 78, 191, 194
  in Foucault   38, 48, 50–8, 180, 181, 185, 189
  identity politics   149
  political philosophy   38
  in Rorty   80–1, 84–6, 91–5, 198, 200
  in Said   159–68, 217–19
  in Sartre   22
  in White   108, 115, 120–1
postcolonial studies   1–2, 11–13, 149, 160–8
postcolonial theory   10, 210
postcolonialism   11, 16
postmodernism   1, 93, 114, 116, 122, 175, 202, 219
poststructuralism   1, 3, 6–9, 13, 31, 60–78, 136, 157, 160–3, 166, 173, 201, 218
Pouillon, Jean   20
Proust, Marcel   16, 81, 85, 87–8, 90, 92, 128–9, 131, 133
  Remembrance of Things Past   85, 87, 128
psychoanalysis   3–6, 56, 169, 170, 171

queer theory   1, 10, 13, 15, 63

Rabaté, Jean-Michel   5, 169, 170
Racine, Jean   133, 145, 209
Rancière, Jacques   4, 191, 215
Ranke, Leopold von   105, 108–9, 203, 210, 220
Redfield, Marc   199

Reginster, Bernard   205
Reitter, Paul   210, 217
relativism   1, 12
  in Auerbach   137, 148, 154, 158
  in Derrida   62
  in Rorty   86
  in Said   167
  in White   100, 114, 119–23, 206, 207
religion
  in Auerbach   144, 147, 151, 213
  in Foucault   49, 51, 53, 57
  in Girard   131–5, 209
  in Rorty   81–3, 85–7, 199
Renaissance, the   15–16, 82
Renaut, Alain   64, 144–5, 172, 185, 192, 213
Revel, Judith   185
rhetoric   7, 177
  and Auerbach   138–42, 146, 152–3, 156–7, 211, 212, 216
  and Girard   133
  Nazism and   63, 74
  and Rorty   198, 204
  and White   121
Ricoeur, Paul   170
Riffaterre, Michael   171
Rockmore, Tom   72–4, 190, 194–5
Rorty, Richard   2, 9, 79–95, 117, 172, 196–200, 218
  Contingency, Irony, Solidarity   79, 81, 83, 88, 90, 94, 200
  and Derrida   172
  egotism   90, 92
  Essays on Heidegger and Others   172, 188, 198
  and Foucault   44, 54, 56, 57–8, 185, 188
  and Heidegger   70–2, 74, 104, 194, 202
  literary culture (post-metaphysical culture)   9, 81–7, 91, 94
  Philosophy and the Mirror of Nature   80, 197
  Philosophy as Cultural Politics   80, 92–3, 197–8
  progress   83, 94, 104
  public versus private   54, 79–81, 85–7, 92–4, 117
  social hope   82–3, 92

Rosen, Lawrence 26, 31, 177, 179
Ross, Kristen 170
Roth, Michael 201, 205
Rousseau, Jean-Jacques 16, 205
Russian formalism 136, 171

Said, Edward 2, 10–16, 62, 84, 159–68, 173, 196, 198, 206, 217–20
  and Auerbach 149–50, 152–3, 155, 158, 210, 214–16
  Beginnings: Intention and Method 159, 161, 196, 217
  Joseph Conrad and the Fiction of Autobiography 12, 160, 220
  Orientalism 11, 159–68, 173, 217–20
  The World, the Text, and the Critic 62, 160, 173, 216–18
Santner, Eric 220
Sartre, Jean-Paul 2, 4–10, 16, 169–75
  analytical reason 27, 30–1
  and Auerbach 154
  bad faith (*la mauvaise foi*) 21, 90, 100–3, 115, 119, 122, 127, 129–30, 132, 134–5, 168
  Being and Nothingness 5, 20–1, 28, 54, 57, 92, 100, 110, 127, 129, 132, 166, 183, 201–2, 208, 209, 220
  being-for-itself (*être-pour-soi*) 100, 130–2, 135, 168, 209
  being-in-itself (*être-en-soi*) 100, 102, 129–32, 135, 168, 209
  Critique of Dialectical Reason 4, 7, 9, 16, 19–34, 57, 92, 109, 175–9, 200
  and Derrida 65, 76–7, 191, 195
  dialectical reason 25, 27, 30–1, 33
  "Existentialism Is a Humanism" 52, 77, 185, 188, 195, 199
  The Flies 20, 170
  and Foucault 41, 43, 52–3, 55, 57–9, 183, 185, 187–9
  and Girard 127–35, 207–9
  group-in-fusion 26
  group praxis 21–2, 24–7, 29, 31, 33, 57, 59, 92, 109, 176
  and Lévi-Strauss 19–34
  Nausea 20, 101, 170, 207
  No Exit 20, 28, 170
  Notebooks for an Ethics 135, 187, 188, 204, 208, 209
  pledged group 26
  practico-inert 22–4, 26–7, 29, 31, 33, 57, 92, 109, 176, 177
  and Rorty 91–2, 94–5, 198, 199, 200
  and Said 162–3, 166, 168, 175–9, 218, 220
  seriality 21–6, 57, 176, 177
  and White 99–103, 105, 109–10, 112–13, 118–19, 201–2, 204–6
Saussure, Ferdinand de 5, 22, 176
  langue/parole 5, 22
Scheler, Max 132, 209
Schleiermacher, Friedrich 152, 155, 185
Schmitt, Carl 73
Schulenberg, Ulf 92, 94, 197, 200
Second World War (WWII) 68, 83, 136, 193, 218
semiology 5, 7–8, 14
Seneca, Lucius Annaeus 139
Shakespeare, William 14–15, 84, 88, 142
Shaw, Philip 211
Sheehan, Thomas 193–4
Shrift, Alan 8
Shusterman, Richard 93–4, 200
Sluga, Hans 183
Smith, Daniel 169, 180
Snow, C. P. 81, 197
social sciences 1–2
Socrates 45, 47, 49, 184, 186
Spengler, Oswald 75
Spiegel, Gabrielle M. 112, 114, 119, 204, 206
Spitzer, Leo 136, 151, 210
Spivak, Gayatri 10–13, 62, 160, 172, 173, 191, 217
Staël, Germaine de 215
Stanford University 47, 90, 191, 200
Starr, Peter 170
Steinem, Gloria 174
Stendhal 128–129, 133, 143–7
stoicism 44, 46
Stonewall riots/monument 182

Stowe, Harriet Beecher   87
structural anthropology   5, 22, 25, 30–3. *See also* Lévi-Strauss, Claude
structural linguistics   4–6. *See also* Saussure, Ferdinand de
structuralism, structure   1, 4–9, 169, 171
  in Auerbach   137, 143–4, 147, 157, 210, 215
  in Foucault   46–7, 49–50, 63, 186
  in Girard   128
  in Rorty   82
  in Said   160, 162–4, 219
  in Sartre and Lévi-Strauss   19–34, 170, 176, 178
subjectivism, anti-subjectivism   1, 9, 41, 43, 77–8
sublime, the   137–48, 153, 155, 211–12

Taine, Hippolyte   151–2
Taylor, Charles   188
Tel Quel   8
textualism   1, 12, 15, 174
  and Auerbach   150, 152
  Rorty's view of   84
  and Said   159–60, 162–3, 165, 217
  and White   175, 202
theoretical knowledge   3, 50, 91, 95
Tilleczek, Will   186
Todorov, Tzvetan   6, 90, 158, 199, 216
transcendental ego   6, 41

uncanny, the   65, 67, 110, 193
University of California, Berkeley   42, 181, 182
University of California, Irvine   174

Vattimo, Gianni   8, 104, 117, 202–3, 205
Vico, Giambattista
  and Auerbach   151, 154, 210, 214
  and Said   159, 161–2, 164, 166, 219
  verum-factum principle   154, 166
  and White   107
Virgil   133

voluntarism   39, 48, 113
Vossler, Karl   136, 151

Wahl, Jean   8
Warren, Austin   14, 151, 174, 214, 218
Wayne State University   106, 171, 201
Weber, Samuel   193
Wellek, René   14, 142, 147, 151, 153–5, 174, 212, 214, 215, 218
White, Hayden   2, 9, 16, 94, 99–123, 170–1, 175, 195, 196, 201–7
  and Auerbach   143–4, 154–7, 213, 215, 216
  "The Burden of History"   100, 102–3, 105, 201
  emplotment   106–10, 112, 115, 119–21, 167, 220
  The Fiction of Narrative   175, 201–4, 205, 207, 216, 218, 219
  Figural Realism   111, 121, 204–6, 213, 215
  figuralism   111–13, 121–2, 137, 143–5, 155, 202
  historical past   102–6
  Metahistory   16, 99–100, 106–11, 114–20, 201, 203–5, 207, 220
  practical past   9, 102–6, 116, 119
  The Practical Past   100, 103–6, 116, 119, 202–3, 205–6
  and Said   159, 163–4, 167, 217–20
  tropes, tropology   106–11, 118–19, 201, 203, 204
  Tropics of Discourse   113, 201, 202, 204
  "What is a Historical System?"   100, 102–3, 105, 201
Wilde, Oscar   87
Wills, David   196
Wiseman, Boris   176

Yale University   13, 174, 199
Young, Iris Marion   23–4, 177
Young, Julian   73–4, 194

Zabala, Santiago   194, 203
Zionism   120–1
Zlomislić, Marko   62, 191
Zola, Émile   146–7

www.ingramcontent.com/pod-product-compliance
Lightning Source LLC
Chambersburg PA
CBHW050138240426
43673CB00043B/1711